PRAISE FOR

How to Travel the World on $50 a Day

"Whether you're a savvy backpacker or just dreaming of getting a passport and going overseas, Matt's collection of easy-to-employ money-saving strategies will open your eyes to the near-infinite ways of seeing the world without busting your budget."

—Matt Gross, former *New York Times* Frugal Traveler

"If you've longed to travel the world but figured it was just an unattainable pipe dream, take that pipe out of your mouth and read this book. Matt Kepnes does the math and shows you how to make this dream a reality, from how to save for an extended trip, which credit card to get, and how to handle banking on the road to a breakdown of how to save on accommodations, transportation, food, and activities. Matt proves that for most Americans, traveling is cheaper than staying home."

—Marilyn Terrell, *National Geographic Traveler*

"A celeb in the travel blogging world, Matt is your go-to guy for all things budget backpacker. This book is an awesome resource for any traveler looking to maximize their adventures without maxing out their credit cards."

—Julia Dimon, travel writer, Outside Television

"There are very few people in the world who have gathered as much first-hand knowledge about long-term world travel as Nomadic Matt. This book will guide you from the first exclamation of 'I'm going traveling!' through the planning, takeoff, and navigation. Filled with insider strategies and resources, it's a valuable primer for your upcoming adventures."

—Tim Leffel, author of *The World's Cheapest Destinations*

How to Travel the World on $50 a Day

TRAVEL CHEAPER, LONGER, SMARTER

Revised, Updated, and Expanded

Matt Kepnes

A Perigee Book

A PERIGEE BOOK
Published by the Penguin Group
Penguin Group (USA) LLC
375 Hudson Street, New York, New York 10014

USA • Canada • UK • Ireland • Australia • New Zealand • India • South Africa • China

penguin.com

A Penguin Random House Company

Copyright © 2013, 2015 by Matthew Kepnes

Revised Perigee edition ISBN: 978-0-399-17328-8

The Library of Congress has cataloged the first Perigee edition as follows:

Kepnes, Matt.
How to travel the world on $50 a day : travel cheaper, longer, smarter / Matt Kepnes.
p. cm.
ISBN 978-0-399-15967-1
1. Tourism.   I. Title.   II. Title: How to travel the world on fifty dollars a day.
G155 .A1K44   2013
910.2'02—dc23   2012039979

PUBLISHING HISTORY
First Perigee trade paperback edition / February 2013
Revised Perigee trade paperback edition / January 2015

PRINTED IN THE UNITED STATES OF AMERICA

10 9 8 7 6 5 4

Text design by Kristin del Rosario

To all the people I've met on the road—
you changed my life in ways you'll never know.

CONTENTS

INTRODUCTION

We are told travel is too expensive to do long term. Fancy tours, hotels, five-star meals, and budget-blowing flights are supposedly what travel is all about. The travel industry keeps this image alive with advertisements in magazines, on TV, and on the Internet. These advertisements always have the uncanny knack of showing a luxurious holiday in some far-off destination where we can go to get away from the stress of our day-to-day life . . . if only we pony up the money.

At least, that's what big corporate travel tells us. But they are lying by omission. They are hiding the fact that travel is affordable because you can't run a big magazine or media company by selling hostels, discount transportation, or cheap tours. You need big ad revenue and luxury travel companies have that money.

So the media promote a style of travel that is more upscale and thus more lucrative. Even when I read budget travel magazines, they often list "budget" accommodation at $150 USD as if anyone could afford that! That is probably out of the reach of most of us, and seeing those kind of prices keeps most of us at home.

Yet everyone I know wants to travel more. Many of the people I encounter in life dream of wasting their days in paradise sitting on a beach as a breeze cools their face and a beer quenches their thirst. But when most people travel, they always seem to head out on a short vacation. Even if they had the time, most think it's too expensive to travel longer. We internalize what those magazines and ads tell us, we never consider the possibility that travel could be affordable.

Experience has shown me the opposite is true. It has shown me that travel can be done cheaply without sacrificing comfort. *Actually* traveling showed me that everything I knew about traveling was wrong.

But that realization didn't happen overnight.

Back in 2003, I was planning my first trip overseas. I had just graduated from college and was working as a hospital administrator. I was putting in forty-plus-hour weeks and looking forward to my precious two weeks per year vacation. I booked a trip to Costa Rica and spent two weeks falling in love with travel. I loved the sense of adventure. I loved how every day held something new. I loved the feeling of endless possibility each day brought, which was in stark contrast to my well-planned-out days in the office. The next year, I used my limited vacation days in January simply because I couldn't wait to get somewhere else again. Costa Rica had given me the travel bug, and when 2004 rolled around, I left right away.

And that's when my life changed.

In January 2004, my friend Scott and I ventured to Thailand. While we were in the northern Thai city of Chiang Mai, I left him for a day to visit a temple outside the city. I shared a tuk tuk (the name for inexpensive shared taxis in Asia) with five non-American backpackers. On the ride we began discussing vacation time, and they were amazed that as an American, I only got two weeks of vacation per year. They all received at least a month in their home countries.

I was extremely jealous. I wanted that much time off to explore the world. Our whole conversation made me rethink my life. It was heading down a road that I realized I wasn't ready for—marriage, house, kids, 401(k)s, playdates, and college funds. While those things aren't bad, at twenty-three, those weren't the things I wanted right now. I wanted to travel.

A few days later, while lying on a beach in southern Thailand, I turned to my friend Scott and said, "I'm going to quit my job and travel the world." I knew the second I told Scott that I was making the right decision. I didn't want to go back to working sixty hours a week at twenty-three. I had my whole life to do that.

I came home, quit my job, finished my MBA, and, in July 2006, hugged my parents good-bye and left for the open road. I used the money I had saved and invested from working in my hospital job to fund my initial trip. I had $20,000 to last me for a year.

It was supposed to be a one-year trip. It turned into eighteen months, and then eighteen months suddenly became six years.

There was a lot I didn't know back then. I made rookie mistakes I look back and laugh at now. But the more I traveled, the more I found ways to save money without sacrificing comfort. I'm here to share that knowledge with you because what I have learned over the years is that the greatest lie ever told is that travel is expensive.

I'm writing this book to dispel the myth that travel is expensive. I'll show you how to travel the world for $50 USD a day or less. I'm here to tell you that you don't need to tap a trust fund, have your parents pay for you, or win the lottery to travel. Anyone can travel cheaply and comfortably if that person knows the secrets to saving money on the road.

When I returned home in 2008, I started my blog, Nomadic Matt (nomadicmatt.com), and began spreading the word that travel could be affordable. Within months of going home, I was back out on the road (and I'm still on the move!).

But blogging has its limits. You can't write a sixty-thousand-word blog post. This book allows me to go deeper into the subject of travel and create a planning guide that can't be done on my blog.

Nothing I tell you in this book is a secret to those who have traveled. I didn't need to join a special club to learn these things. I didn't take a course. Experience on the road showed me what most travel companies don't want you to see. I saw behind the machine. I saw that travel is really affordable because a host of budget options exist for tours, accommodations, food, and flights. They just aren't advertised.

If you are told a lie frequently enough, you begin to believe it, and we as a whole believe the myth that travel is expensive.

I know I did when I started traveling.

But actual traveling taught me that everything I learned from those magazines and ads was wrong. There *are* many ways to travel cheaply; they just weren't advertised. It took the *experience* of traveling to learn about the tricks and tips, and the goal of this book is to share my knowledge with you, so you know travel *is* within your reach, even if you don't have a lot of money (I didn't either).

This book is about using your money wisely and knowing the tricks to save money. You don't need to be rich to travel—you just need to travel smart. I don't go to Italy to avoid nice meals. I don't go to Bordeaux to avoid a wine tour. I didn't save money at home so I could cook cheap dinners in hostels. I don't go to Australia because I dream about the outback only to turn around and say, "No, that trip is a bit out of my budget. Maybe another time."

You should note that it's not possible to travel on $50 a day at every destination in the world. You'll be hard-pressed to live on $50 USD a day in Australia, New Zealand, and Europe. Southeast Asia, China, India, Central America can all be easily done for much less than $50 per day. But between all these destinations, you'll average $50 USD per day on your total trip, which is why this book is titled *How to Travel the World on $50 a Day*.

The more deals and tricks you know, the more you can stretch your budget. And "cheap" doesn't mean traveling like a pauper. It's about traveling (as the cliché goes) like a local because when you are home, you don't spend a lot of money per day and neither do the locals where you are visiting. If you know just a few general tips and some location-specific advice, you can always have a first-class experience without paying a first-class price.

This book is structured to take you from the planning stages to the time you get to your destination. Before I left, as much as I was excited about traveling, I had so many questions. I had no clue how to travel. Would I meet people on the road? Is it safe to travel alone? What kind of bag do I bring? Will I find a job when I get back? What if the news is right and everyone does hate Americans? I answer all those questions and more.

Part One offers specific, actionable ways to lower your expenses before you even set foot on a plane. From setting up bank accounts that earn you money, to getting tons of free airline miles for free flights, to what gear to get, and what to do with your stuff, you'll learn how to save money from day one.

In Part Two, you'll find ways to save money on the road that can be applied to destinations throughout the world. These are general travel tips.

In Part Three, I get into specific world destinations. This part is structured by location so you can jump right to the information you need. Each chapter includes typical costs, ways to save money, things to do, and area-specific resources. I've picked the most visited and popular destinations in the world for travelers.

I firmly believe you can travel well without paying a lot of money, and this book will help you travel better, cheaper, and longer. Travel has given me so many wonderful opportunities in my life. I've met countless friends who despite distance remain close. I've scuba dived in Fiji, hiked the Grand Canyon, cruised the Galápagos Islands, and lived in foreign countries.

As you read through this book, you'll find a lot of advice geared toward people taking multi-month long-term trips. After all, this book is about traveling the world, right? But not everyone is going to jump overseas for months on end. Some people just want to save money on their two-week holiday.

Don't worry if you only go away for a week or two—this book is still for you. My tips are not just for those who want to quit their job and travel the world. They can be used for a trip of any length. Whether you are going to Paris for two weeks or two months, you'll still need to know how to get a cheap flight, good insurance, and how to find cheap food in the city.

In writing this book, I strove to make the majority of tips applicable to people going on a trip of any length of time. Whether you are looking for a credit card to travel with or trying to figure out how to get a cheap flight, this book will help you.

So grab a coffee and a map while you sit back, relax, and learn to save.

SINCERELY,
"NOMADIC" MATT KEPNES

Planning Your Trip

Getting Over Your Fears

THE most difficult part about traveling the world isn't the logistics of a trip—it's finding the motivation to go in the first place. It takes a lot of courage to leave your life and journey into the unknown. It's the step that most people never get past. For me, it took a trip to Thailand to get me to make the leap. For others, it's a lot more difficult. Instead of the nudge I required, some people require a full-on shove.

While most of this book will talk about the practical, financial side of travel, the first thing I wanted to tell you is that you don't need to be afraid of traveling the world. It's only natural to second-guess yourself when making a big life change.

And this is a big change.

One of the most common emails I receive asks me whether or not someone should travel the world. Do they quit their job and go for it? Are they in the right stage of life? Will everything be OK if they leave? Will they get a job when they return? These emails are peppered with nervous excitement over travel's endless possibilities, but there is also always one underlying message in the emails: "Matt, I want to go, but I'm also afraid. I need someone to tell me it will be all right."

In my meetings with strangers, they ask me questions about my adventures. People are curious about my travels, experience, and how I got started doing this. They dream of traveling the world. "It must be such the adventure," they tell me. "I wish I could do it." And when I ask them what stops them, they come up with a book full of excuses as to why they can't:

I can't afford my trip.

I have too many responsibilities at home.

I won't be able to make friends on the road.

I don't want to be alone.

I have too many bills to pay.

I'm not sure I could do it.

I'm simply too scared.

With all that fear and doubt, it's easier for someone to stay home in his or her comfort zone than to break out and travel the world. As the saying goes, "People go with the devil they know over the devil they don't." Home is our safe zone. We know it. We understand it. We may not always like it, but we get it, and that is a powerful force. In the end, held back by their own fears, most people stay home, dreaming of that "one perfect day" when they will finally travel.

But you know what? That day never comes. It will never be perfect.

Tomorrow, you'll still have bills.

Tomorrow, you still won't have just the right amount of money.

Tomorrow, there will still be someone's wedding to attend or a birthday party to go to.

Tomorrow, you will still second-guess yourself.

Tomorrow, you'll find another excuse as to why you can't go.

Tomorrow, people you know will still feed the seeds of doubt in your head.

Tomorrow will come and you'll say, "Today isn't the right day. Let's go tomorrow."

Dropping everything to travel takes a lot of courage, and while many people claim "real-world responsibilities" are the reason for not traveling, I think fear of the unknown is really what holds people back.

If you bought this book, you are probably already on the right track. Taking a long-term trip is already on your mind. Maybe you are already committed or still on the fence about it. But no matter what side of the coin you fall on, know that even the most experienced travelers had doubts when they began.

I want to reassure you that you are doing the right thing.

Right here. Right now.

You Aren't the First Person to Travel Abroad

One of the things that comforted me when I began traveling was knowing that lots of other people traveled the world before me and ended up just fine. While long-term travel might not be popular in the United States, it is a rite of passage for a lot of people around the world. People as young as high school graduates head overseas in droves for long-term trips. As you read this paragraph right now, millions of people are trekking around the world and discovering foreign lands. And if millions of eighteen-year-olds on a round-the-world trip came home in one piece, I realized there was no reason I wouldn't either. There's nothing I can't do that anyone else can do. And the same goes for you.

You won't be the first person to leave home and explore the jungles of Asia. There is a well-worn travel trail around the world where you'll be able to find support and comfort from other travelers. Columbus had reason to be afraid. He had no idea where he was going and he was the first person to go that way. He blazed a trail. You're going on a trail that has already been blazed. That realization helped take away some of my fear because I knew there would be other travelers on the road to comfort me.

You Are Just as Capable as Everyone Else

I'm smart, I'm capable, and I have common sense. If other people could travel the world, why couldn't I? I realized there was no reason I wouldn't be capable of making my way around the world. I'm just as good as everyone else. And so are you. Early in my travels, I managed to turn up in Bangkok without knowing one person and live and thrive there for close to a year. I made friends, I found a girlfriend, I had an apartment, and I even learned Thai. It was sink or swim, and I swam. I recently navigated my way through Ukraine, a country where few people speak English and even fewer signs are in the Roman alphabet, as they use the Cyrillic script there. Then there are little things like figuring out a local subway, using a map to navigate unknown streets, and making yourself understood without learning the local language. I once went "choo choo" to a taxi driver to make it understood I needed to go to the train station. It worked. Nobody steps out into the world knowing it all. They pick it up along the way. Don't doubt yourself. You get by in your regular life just fine. The same will be true when you travel.

The World Isn't as Dangerous as the Media Says

CNN, FOX News, and other major media outlets often make the world outside our borders look like a pretty scary place, where you'd be crazy to leave the safety of the United States. They paint a picture of a world filled with violence, anti-Americanism, rampant natural disasters, and lots of crime. But in all my years of traveling, I have never encountered any problem or suffered from any anti-Americanism. One of the main reasons why the world seems so dangerous is because we have instant communication now. Whenever anything happens, we can know about it right away through twenty-four-hour news, Twitter, or Facebook. Earthquakes have always happened, but we could never find out about them instantaneously through online media before.

My mother constantly tells me when I go anywhere in the world to "be careful," as if the world is a big scary place. She'll tell me how nervous she is if I end up in a country that she once heard about in the news . . . in 1975. I try to tell her that the world is not that scary and I could get mugged just as easily in New York, Miami, or Houston as I could in London, Beijing, or Brazil and sometimes she'll agree, stating "I guess you have a point." Many of my old coworkers do the same. My friend was going to join me in Thailand, and when she told her coworkers that, they replied, "Why would you want to go there? Hawaii has beaches and do they *even* have electricity in Thailand?"

We believe what we hear on TV so easily because we don't hear otherwise. I remember watching *The Tonight Show with Jay Leno*, and he often did a sketch called "Jay Walking" in which he would ask Americans questions about foreign leaders or countries, and most people were stumped. According to the Pew Research Center's *State of the Media 2010*, only 10.5 percent of news coverage is related to international affairs. That is shockingly low. It's no surprise to me that so many people know so little about the world, when they are exposed to such little information.

However, realize that everyone around the world wants the same things that you want. They all have jobs, families, and things to do. They want their kids to be safe, earn money, and be allowed to live life. They want to be left alone. They aren't looking for trouble. Travelers from all corners of the world are crossing paths every day without any problems. In any city in the world, use your street smarts to avoid dodgy situations, and you will be fine. Parts of New York City can be just as unsafe as other parts of the world.

As a whole, the world is no more or less safe than any part of the United States. Using common sense, you will not encounter any problems you can't find in an American city.

You Will Make Friends

People always ask me how to make friends on the road. They tell me they're not very social and that it's hard for them to meet and talk to strangers. After all, not everyone can walk up to a stranger and say hello. You might spend the first few days traveling by yourself, afraid of making the first contact. I was really shy when I hit the road. I could talk my friends' ears off, but when meeting a stranger, I grew silent. Now I have no problems talking to people, and I can thank travel for learning that skill.

The good news is that when you travel, you are never alone. There are many solo travelers making their way across the world who are in the same boat as you. They want companionship. They want friends. You'll find people who will come up and talk to you out of the blue. When people see me sitting alone in a hostel, they walk up to me and ask if I'd like to join them. I was recently having a beer in Bangkok, and another guest at my hostel came up to me and we struck up a conversation. Two of my best friends were met because I said hello in a guesthouse in Vietnam. I have attended the weddings of friends I met while asking to join their Frisbee game on the beach. After a while, it becomes normal to strike up a conversation with a complete stranger.

Travelers are friendly people who want to make friends. And one of those friends is you.

You Are Never Too Old

Budget travel, backpacking, round-the-world trips—these trips aren't just for the young. While I was in Poland, I met a sixty-five-year-old American in my hostel. He was traveling around Europe before heading to India. And people were talking to him. He was sharing stories from his youth and drinking a few beers with the younger backpackers. He was never an outcast. My friend once saw a man in his seventies making a big trip around the world because, as he said, he didn't have much time left and wanted to see the world. It was now or never. And he had a number of ailments and carried many prescriptions, but he still went.

I've seen families with their children on buses in Southeast Asia and retirees camping in Australia. The point is that you are never too old to go. Some of my favorite encounters on the road have been with older travelers, as they always have the best stories. Like they say, you are only as old as you feel.

You Can Always Come Back

If you make it three months into your trip and decide that long-term travel isn't for you, it's perfectly OK to return home. I've met a few travelers who, months into their trip, realized that they really liked being at home and missed it terribly. They missed their friends, family, and significant others. So they cut their trip short and went home.

There's no shame in doing that. There's no such thing as failure in the world of travel. Your trip is your own. You went away for yourself, not for other people. And, in the end, you only need worry about yourself. Getting up and going is more than most people do, and if traveling isn't for you, at least you tried it. That in itself is a major accomplishment. Whether you are gone for one day, one month, or one year, you still will have learned and grown from your adventure.

If there is anything I've learned over the years, it's that these fears, like all fears, are unfounded, because in the end, life works out. Your bills disappear when you cancel your cable, phone, and Internet.

Walking away was easy for me, but I understand that not everyone can just cut loose as quickly as I did. Some of us have mortgages, parents to take care of, or children. But that doesn't mean it's impossible to travel.

People think that once they have children, they can't travel. But every year, families set off to travel the world. Having children didn't stop the James family. Craig and Dani James of thewidewideworld .com took their two children on a yearlong trip around the world in 2008. As Dani (the mom) puts it, the James children "would soon be on their way to adulthood. We were rapidly approaching our last chance to do something really special together as a family—to do something that would impact the way we thought of ourselves, individually and as a family."

The Jameses saw an opportunity to travel as a family. They wanted it and went for it, but it wasn't always easy. Taking your kids out of school can be a real concern too. To which the Jameses said, "You can minimize any disruption to schooling with some careful planning. Conor was missing sixth grade and Caroline, ninth. Conor's middle school was excited about his adventure and confident he could handle seventh grade when we returned. For Caroline, it was slightly more complicated because there are state requirements for high school graduation. We needed, at a minimum, to get Caroline through English 9 while we traveled, to keep her on grade level. To keep Caroline on track we enrolled her in an online homeschool program accredited by Montgomery County. This way, she had a professional teacher available via Internet and we would get a transcript, making reentry into the school system easier. We had no trouble getting either kid enrolled with their peers in the fall. I had worried a lot about the high school credits being easily accepted. It turned out not to be a problem."

Having a family doesn't need to be a barrier to world travel. The James family did what thousands of other families had done before them and have done since. Don't believe having a family means ending your travels.

Moreover, owning a house doesn't need to be a hindrance to your travels. Sean and Dawn Lynch of wanderingwhy.com had a house before they went away. As Dawn put it, "Being a homeowner is only an excuse if you make it one. Sure, it was something we had to figure out how to handle while we were gone, but it is really not all that difficult. Decide if you are selling or renting, take action, and go—you'll have no regrets."

Having a home creates many questions, such as what do you do with your home and your stuff? As Sean said, "Look into a reputable property management company to watch after your home while you're away. For 5 to 10 percent of the rent, they should run a complete background check on any potential tenants and have the means to handle the property maintenance while you are away. The objective was not to turn a profit on our home, but to hit the pause button while we were away."

The James family also had to do something with their house. Dani recounts, "A friend of ours needed to rent a house near Washington, DC, for a year, so our house in the Maryland suburbs was a great fit. It was a fortunate circumstance—our friend needed a furnished house, so we didn't have to put any furniture in storage. We had no worries about our house or our belongings—we knew they were in good hands."

For every excuse, there is a solution.

As people in your life offer both praise and criticism of your trip, you may be nervous and wonder if you are doing the right thing. It's normal to have these fears. Just remember the above tips, calm your nerves, and ease your fears.

Your future may hold mouthwatering meals in foreign countries, tropical beaches you only thought existed in a postcard, winding alleyways in European cities that throw you back into the Middle Ages, or jungles so dense and teeming with wildlife you'll feel like you are living in an issue of *National Geographic* magazine.

Is Travel Really Too Expensive?

L ET'S put the "travel is too expensive" myth to death right now, beginning with a short exercise.

Get out a sheet of paper and write down all your set expenses. Write down your rent (or mortgage), your car payments, cable bill, cell phone, and the like. Tally them up.

Then write down all your discretionary spending. This is food, movie nights, drinks, shopping, that daily coffee from Starbucks, cigarettes, and the like. If you don't know what you spend money on, track your expenses for a two-week period and see what you spend.

Total up all your expenses to get a monthly and then yearly figure.

Now, take that number and think about the title of this book— $50 USD per day. That's $1,500 USD per month or $18,250 USD per year. When you add up all your monthly spending and costs, it's more than $1,500 USD, isn't it?

If your rent is $900 USD per month, that's $30 per day, which is 60 percent of the daily budget set out in this book. Add in food costs, gas, insurance, and cable and your set expenses are mostly higher than the number you need for a year abroad. And that's before you've done anything else with your life.

You might look at the cover of this book and think, "I spend way less than $50 USD per day." That's because we often don't consider our fixed costs, like housing, insurance, and debt payments, when we think of our spending. We may not go to the ATM every day, but we are constantly spending money without even thinking about it.

Now, imagine if all your living expenses were less than $50 USD per day. Everything. Your house, food, transportation, travel, nights out at the movies, or drinks at a bar. How wonderful would that be? How wonderful would it be to live on $18,250 or less per year? Pretty wonderful, huh?

For that much money, instead of being at home, you could be out traveling the world. And even if you can't save that much money, travel *is* within your reach.

I recently met a girl while in Bangkok. Sarah was an American who lived in New York City working a job that barely paid her enough to live. She had to cut a lot of corners, but after two years of saving, she'd scraped together enough money to travel the world. She didn't have a lot of money, so she went to Southeast Asia, one of the cheapest areas of the world. As Sarah put it, "It's true that I didn't have much in savings, but if I waited until the perfect time to travel, I'd be waiting a long time. Of course I was nervous about leaving a steady job and the life I had created in New York. I worried about going broke in the first two months and having to turn around and live in my mother's basement until I found another job. I'm doing this on a tight budget while still paying student loans, and I'm happy to be doing it now rather than waiting an eternity until retirement. You definitely don't have to be wealthy to pick up and travel."

And if the money does run out, there are plenty of ways to work overseas. It doesn't need to all be about savings. Travelers around the world work in hostels, teach English, work on farms, pick fruit, live on kibbutzes, or get service jobs. When I decided to travel longer, I stopped in Thailand and taught English in order to earn more money. And if that doesn't appeal to you, just come home. It's better to have six months traveling the world than no months traveling the world. As the saying goes, "Don't put off to tomorrow what you can do today."

How to Save for Your Trip

I remember when I began saving for my first trip around the world. I had a rough estimate of how much money I would need ($16,000 USD) and thought, "Whoa. How will I ever save that much?" It seemed like an impossible number to reach. But after writing out all my expenses and seeing where I spent money, I realized that if I made a few changes to my lifestyle, I could save that much. I still had a job, so all I needed to do was cut my expenses and watch my savings grow.

The first thing I did was draw up a list of all my expenses—from rent to car payments to the movies I saw on a weekly basis. After all, you can't know what you need to cut if you don't know where you are spending money. You'll be surprised at how many little things drain your money slowly without you ever noticing it.

At the start of this chapter, you wrote down all your set expenses and all your discretionary spending. Take another look. You can't cut down expenses without knowing what you spend money on. Here are some proven methods for reducing your expenses and increasing your travel fund:

Eat In: Eating out is one of your biggest expenses and the easiest of low-hanging fruit to pick. Instead of having $10 USD lunches and $20 USD dinners, brown-bag it to work and cook dinner at night. When I saved for my trip, I spent $70 USD per week on groceries. I cooked once for dinner and had leftovers the next day. Sure, cooking can be intimidating, as not all of us are Julia Child in the kitchen. However, I found learning cooking was an invaluable skill, not only because it saved me money before my trip, but because it's also one of the easiest ways to cut down your expenses when you travel.

Cut the Coffee: Love your Starbucks? Well, Starbucks loves your money. Coffee is the little thing that quietly drains your bank account without you ever noticing. That daily coffee costs you $60 per month ($2 for a coffee). At $720 USD per year, that's a lot of money. What's more important—your daily cup of joe or getting to spend an extra month on the beaches of Thailand or exploring the jungles of Borneo in Malaysia? Give up the coffee or switch from the cappuccino to a standard brew, move to tea, or brew your own cup. Folger's might not taste as delicious as a Venti triple mocha latte with whipped cream from Starbucks, but it's a lot cheaper.

Drink Less: It may not be appealing to spend your nights indoors and not out with your friends, but spending money out can be an even bigger drain than coffee. Before I went traveling, I'd go out on the weekends with my friends to places where drinks could cost around $5 USD. I enjoyed going out with my friends, but those drinks really add up. Since I can't nurse one drink, I simply stayed home. It wasn't fun staying in while my friends were out on the weekends, but that year of semi-solitude paid off greatly, as I had more money to enjoy the food in Europe. But if you are stronger than me, go out but cut down on the drinks.

Lose the Car: Cars cost a lot of money, between insurance, repairs, and filling your tank with gas. If you can, get rid of yours. Learn to love the bus or subway, or walk. It took me longer to get to work using public transportation, but you'll find that you don't really need a car as much as you think. I understand this tip may not be feasible for everyone, especially those in smaller towns that don't have a good public transportation system. A good alternative is to sell your car and buy a cheap used car. You will only need a car to last you until you go away. Buying a "throwaway car" will allow you to pocket the money from your better car and put it toward your trip. Additionally, consider getting a bike as an alternative to the car altogether. No gas, no insurance, no repairs—it will not only save you money but will keep you in shape!

Move Out: Lowering your housing costs will allow you to see huge gains in your savings. Get rid of that apartment or bring in some roommates. If you can, try to move in with Mom and Dad. Six months before I went abroad, I moved in with my parents. It wasn't that fun being twenty-five and living with my parents, but I saved more than $3,000 USD in rent. If this is not an option for you, bring in a roommate. Turn that living room into a spare room and get a housemate. In New York City, people turn living rooms into bedrooms and studio apartments into two bedrooms by adding a folding screen through the middle of the room. It's not the most ideal living situation, but it does save money. If you're spending hundreds of dollars per month on rent, cutting that figure in half or reducing it to zero will give you the biggest whole number jump in your bank account.

Get a New Credit Card: While I will go into more depth about credit cards in Chapter 4, a travel credit card can give you free money, free rooms, and free flights. You can accrue miles and reward points on your card and redeem them for free travel on your trip. And that trip doesn't need to be long—you can use those points on a trip that is two weeks or two months. A free flight is a free flight. After all, the best way to save money is to avoid spending it. You'll see the most benefit from this by starting early. As soon as you decide to travel the world, get a travel-related credit card and begin earning free points on your daily purchases.

Get Rid of Cable: In the age of Hulu (hulu.com) and free (and legal) streaming TV, there's no reason to be spending $50 USD per month on cable television. Get rid of it and just watch everything online for free.

Open a Savings Account: While you are saving money, you can have it grow a little bit more by putting it in a high-yield online savings account so that it can earn interest. This is what I did while preparing to go away, and I netted a few hundred dollars extra. You can refer to Chapter 3 on how to set this up.

Earn Extra on the Side: The rise of sharing websites has made it easier to earn extra money on the side. The website TaskRabbit (taskrabbit.com) lets you do tasks (many are online) that people don't have time to do—from cleaning to moving, doing research, or helping with errands. Another similar website is Elance (elance.com), which is geared toward more professional tasks. Finally, the website Zilok (zilok.com) allows you to rent out your unused stuff for money. These sites can provide an easy way to earn money on the side. Be sure to check them out as a way to earn extra money for your upcoming trip.

Frugality is the watchword of great travelers. While it sometimes made me feel like an old grandmother, I clipped food coupons to save money on food. I saw matinees if I went to the movies. I did my shopping when there was a sale. If it was nice out, I walked. None of it was "convenient," but when I went abroad with more money than I needed, it was all worth it.

Doing a few little things each day can keep you motivated and help you toward your goal. As David Lee of www.gobackpacking .com recounts, "I set an overall goal to pay off my credit cards and save $30,000. This was the figure I felt was necessary to justify quitting my job and uprooting my life. From there, I worked backward to set smaller, monthly goals. I taped these goals to my bathroom mirror, where I was reminded of them every day. I established a habit of saving money from every paycheck. At first it was just $25, but over the years that grew to $500. And as a short-term investment, I participated in my company's stock purchase plan."

At the end of the day, the more you save, the longer you can be on the road, the more comfortable you can be, and the more activities you can do. You sacrifice now because of the rewards later. Because when you are on safari in Africa or sailing the Galápagos Islands, you won't even be thinking about those missed nights out or fancy dinners.

Banking Overseas

YOUR trip will go a lot smoother if you budget and organize your money before you leave. That starts with the right bank account. You'll be accessing your money multiple times a week from locations around the world, so it's important to have a good bank that is easy to work with and has few fees.

In the previous chapter, we discussed how you can save for your trip and lower your day-to-day living expenses. Now I'm here to tell you in a few easy steps how to make those hard-earned dollars stretch even further so you can have some extra money on the road. The biggest mistake most travelers make is that they don't make their money *work for them* while they are away.

Setting Up a Checking Account

The first thing you want to do is set up a checking account at a major, global bank. While we may hate the major banks for their involvement in the economic crisis and the subsequent bailouts they got, unfortunately smaller banks don't always have the leverage to get better currency exchange rates or keep operations and ATMs around the world. Most of the world's major banks have partnership agreements where they waive their out-of-network ATM service charge.

Below is a list of the banks linked through the Global ATM alliance, the principal international banking network. All the major banks listed here have agreements with one another wherein if you belong to one bank, you can use the ATMs of all the other banks without being charged a fee:

ABSA (South Africa): absa.co.za/Absacoza

Bank of America (United States): bankofamerica.com

Barclays (England, Wales, Spain, Portugal, Gibraltar, and certain countries in Africa): barclays.co.uk

BNP Paribas (France, Ukraine): bnpparibas.com/en/home

China Construction Bank (China): ccb.com/en/home/index.html

Deutsche Bank (Germany, Poland, Czech Republic, Spain, Portugal, and Italy): db.com/us

Santander Serfin (Mexico): santander.com.mx/Nueva Version/index.html

Scotiabank (Canada, Caribbean, Peru, Chile, and Mexico): scotiabank.com

Westpac (Australia, New Zealand, Fiji, Vanuatu, Cook Islands, Samoa, Tonga, Papua New Guinea, and Solomon Islands): west pac.com.au

UkrSibbank (Ukraine): ukrsibbank.com/en/pid921/home.html

Note: Bank of America charges a 3 percent transaction fee on all currency withdrawals, even for banks within the alliance.

However, there are many alternatives to these banks that allow you to avoid ATM and transaction fees all the time. In my opinion, the best U.S. bank to use is Charles Schwab (schwab.com). While Charles Schwab doesn't have deals with any banks overseas like those mentioned above, it is one of the few banks that reimburses all your ATM fees at the end of each month. You will need to open a high-yield checking account (schwab.com/public/schwab/banking _lending/checking_account) in order to qualify, but there is no minimum deposit required and no monthly service fee. Charles Schwab not only reimburses its fees but also the fees of the other bank you used. You'll never pay a fee with this bank. Their ATM card can be used in any bank machine around the world. If there isn't a Charles Schwab branch near you, you can open this account online by going to their website.

I also use HSBC (hsbc.com). They aren't very widely located in the United States. At the time of writing they only have branches in New York State, Florida, California, Delaware, Pennsylvania, Oregon, Washington State, and Washington, DC. However, you can open an account online no matter where in the United States you live. I like HSBC because they have ATMs all over the world, so you can avoid fees by simply using HSBC ATMs. If you do end up using a non-HSBC ATM machine, as of May 2014, the fee is only $2.50 USD, which is cheaper than major banks in the United States, like Bank of America or Chase, where the fee is typically $5 USD.

I also recommend Capital One's money market account, which has an ATM card (capitalone.com/directbanking/online-savings -accounts/high-yield-money-market-account). Capital One doesn't have a fee when you use non–Capital One ATMs, but you still might be charged a fee by the owner of the ATM machine.

Note: If you bank with a small, community bank, check with them regarding their overseas fees. They might also waive overseas usage fees. There are thousands of banks, and policies are always different. Before you switch banks, be sure to double-check what's available with your current bank.

Before we move on, I want to emphasize one very, very important point: You *must* get an account at two separate banks. If your ATM card gets lost or stolen, it is important to have a backup so you can still have access to money. While visiting Bangkok a few years ago, my HSBC ATM card stopped working, and at the time it was my primary bank card. When I called to inquire, I was told that HSBC had found fraudulent charges on the card, from Moscow. (I've never been to Russia.) Someone had duplicated my ATM card, and my account had to be closed. A new ATM card was sent to me—in the United States, which didn't help because I was in Thailand. However, since I had a backup bank account, I still had a way to access my money.

This also happened to my friend Sarah, the girl from Bangkok I mentioned earlier, but she didn't have a backup card. As she says, "I came abroad with an ATM and a credit card, both tied to the same account. I didn't realize how silly this was until I got an email from my bank asking me to approve some suspicious charges. I had just arrived in Malaysia and assumed that my ATM withdrawal had been flagged in the system. When I learned that someone in Bulgaria had withdrawn $900 from my account, I quickly realized how naive I had been to travel without any backup. The bank closed my account, and I didn't have access to money for a month of traveling. I borrowed from friends until my new card arrived."

Her story is an example of why you *always* should travel with a backup bank account. You never think it will happen to you, but when it does, you'll be thankful you were prepared.

I also put spending caps on my accounts by simply calling the bank before I go overseas and asking them to limit my withdrawal amount. This limits the damage thieves can do if my card does get stolen. Additionally, I put a second user on all my accounts (a parent or trusted friend) so that if there is a problem with one of my accounts, there is someone who can call up and help troubleshoot any issues in case I'm not able to.

ATM fees can really add up. If you're traveling for a year, you will probably take out money from an ATM twice a week. Fees vary around the world, though on average you end up paying $5 USD per withdrawal. That is $10 USD per week, $40 USD per month, or $520 USD per year. Even if you only use the ATM half that time, that's still $260 USD per year. Most travelers I know go to the ATM even *more* than twice a week, which only increases the amount of fees they pay. Why give banks money you need for travel? You did a lot of work saving up your money; don't waste it by giving it to a bank.

Opening an Online Savings Account

The second thing you want to do before you go away is open an on-line money market savings account in order to earn interest. Before leaving for your trip, you saved a pile of cash, which you will slowly drain as you go around the world. What do you do with all that money you saved up?

Even though you might not be working, you can still earn money by having your savings earn interest. According to the finance website Bankrate.com, most traditional "brick and mortar" banks (think Bank of America or your local credit union) pay less than 0.30 percent interest. At that rate of interest, you'll be home long before you even notice any uptick in your bank balance. Online money market accounts offer much higher interest rates because they lack many of the overhead costs traditional banks have. Though rates are really low right now because of the ongoing economic crisis, the average rate online as of September 2012 is 0.75 percent interest. That's not very much, but it's better than earning 0.30 percent.

Let's say you saved $18,250 USD for your trip (that breaks down to $50 USD per day for a year if anyone is still counting). If you put your extra money into an online money market account at 1 percent interest, you will be *gaining* $182.50 USD per year. Now, since you will be taking money out on a regular basis, I'd say a more realistic number is $120–130 USD.

In order to maximize the interest I earn, I keep only two weeks' worth of living expenses in my checking account at a time. When I need more money, I transfer it from my savings. That way my money has more time to earn interest for me instead of sitting in a checking account earning nothing.

It might not seem like $120 USD would make a big difference in traveling, but in some areas of the world, especially in developing countries, you only need about $25–30 USD per day to survive. You are looking at close to an extra week of travel you wouldn't have had otherwise, which makes $120 USD in free money sound a lot more appealing.

The following online banks offer high-interest online savings accounts:

Ally Bank: ally.com/bank/money-market-account; interest rate: 0.90 percent, no fees or minimums

Bank of the Internet (USA): bankofinternet.com/bofi; interest rate: 0.80 percent, no fees or minimums

Discover Bank: discoverbank.com; interest rate: 0.80 percent, no fees, $2,500 USD opening deposit

Ever Bank: everbank.com; interest rate: 1.01 percent, minimum balance to avoid fees $5,000 USD, $1,500 opening deposit

HSBC: us.hsbc.com; interest rate: 0.80 percent, minimum balance $1 USD

ING Direct: home.ingdirect.com; interest rate: 0.85 percent, no fees or minimums

Virtual Bank: virtualbank.com; interest rate: 0.70 percent, no fees or monthly minimums, $100 USD opening deposit

All of these banks are insured by the FDIC (Federal Deposit Insurance Corporation). Interest rates change frequently, so be sure to check the bank's website for the most up-to-date rates. I use Bankrate

(bankrate.com), which monitors interest rates from around the country. While I like the banks above, interest rates always change, so it's best to look up the current rates online.

The third and final thing you need to do is interlink all your accounts. You'll have two checking accounts (with an ATM card) and one online savings account. Link both checking accounts to your online savings account so you can use that online account to shift money to whatever ATM account you want to use. When my HSBC card got stolen, I shifted money from HSBC via my Emigrant Direct account into my Bank of America account.

Minimizing Conversion Fees and Penalties

Next we want to minimize the conversion penalties and fees you pay for using your card overseas. Every time you use your card in a foreign country, your bank converts the foreign currency you were charged into your local currency for billing purposes. And they charge you a small percentage (typically 3 percent) for doing so.

Since banks take a little off the top of each transaction, you'll never be able to get the listed official exchange rate you find online through currency rate sites like XE (xe.com). It's impossible unless you become your own bank. However, there are seven things you can do to get a rate close to the official rate:

Use a Credit Card: Credit card companies offer the best exchange rates and convert your money closest to the official exchange rate. Whenever possible, I always use my credit card for purchases overseas so I know that I am getting the best exchange rate possible. I hardly ever use cash. I'll discuss this more in the next section, about which cards are the best to travel with as well as which ones can help you avoid a fee for using them overseas.

Use an ATM Card: ATM machines offer the best exchange rate after credit cards. They aren't as good as credit cards, since commercial banks take a little more off the top, but it's much better than exchanging cash.

Withdraw a Lot: If the exchange rate has moved in your favor (for example, country X's currency just fell against your country's currency and you get ten times more money), withdraw more than you need. That way when the exchange rate changes back, you'll have scored yourself some extra money with no added work. While I was living in Thailand in 2007, the Australian dollar collapsed to around 20 baht to the dollar. I ran to the bank and exchanged a lot of my Thai baht for $1,000 AUD, since I was going to Australia the following month. A week later, the Australian dollar recovered to 28 baht. In acting fast, I saved myself 8,000 baht, which is more than $250 USD, giving me more money for my trip. You don't need to be a financial expert, but watch the currency rates when you travel. Looking at a simple graph can tell you if the rate is getting better or worse. I had no idea if the exchange rate would get better or worse, but I knew that drop in Aussie dollars was a big deal and it was worth taking advantage of, even if the rate went down more. You'll need to be comfortable carrying cash, though, and stay in a place where you can lock up your extra cash in the hostel or hotel safe in order to ensure that it's not lost or stolen.

I use the website xe.com to check exchange rates. If you have a smartphone, like an iPhone, BlackBerry, or Droid, the free Currency app is also a good way to monitor rates. You can get the app from currencyapp.com.

Don't Change Unneeded Cash: Changing cash, especially at the airport, is the worst thing you can do. Unless I am stuck with cash I need to get rid of or the exchange rate suddenly changes a lot, like in the example above, I never change money. Most exchange bureaus are so far down the financial food chain they don't have the clout to offer good exchange rates. Moreover, nonbanks charge especially high commission and fees for exchanging money, and if they don't, they make their money by giving you an even lower exchange rate. Simply put, unless you have to, never exchange cash—whether that is at an airport or in the middle of town. Just withdraw money from the ATM.

Don't Use ATMs in Weird Locations: Using those ATMs you find in hotels, hostels, local 7-Elevens, or some other random place is a bad idea. They may be convenient, but you'll pay for that convenience. They often charge high ATM fees and offer horrible exchange rates. Even if you get the ATM fee waived, the exchange rate will be worse than a major bank. Avoid these ATMs.

Don't Change Money at Airports: Most airport exchange bureaus don't offer good exchange rates. It is sometimes shocking to see how bad the exchange rates are. Never, ever use an exchange bureau. I'm not a fan of exchanging cash in the first place but if you must, skip these and use a bank. Moreover, avoid using the company Travelex at all costs; they have the worst rates and fees I've ever seen, and I always avoid them and their ATMs.

Always Pick the Local Currency: When you use your credit card abroad, you are often given the option of being charged in your home currency (for example, instead of being charged in euros, they will charge you in U.S. dollars). Never say yes to this option. The preset rate at which they are converting the currency is always worse than the rate your bank will give you. Pick the local currency and let your credit card company make the conversion. You'll get a better rate.

A quick note on traveler's checks: Don't use them. Many banks won't even exchange them, and they are too easily lost or stolen. There's nothing they can do that a piece of plastic can't do better. I used them once back in 2004 and realized that with an ATM offering a better exchange rate, I was silly for getting them. They are outdated, and I would never advise someone to get them.

It's important to be proactive when it comes to banking and currency exchange. I see too many travelers who hit the ATM without paying attention to the latest exchange rates or considering the fees they are paying. Be smart and bank smart so you give the banks less and have more for your trip.

Getting the Right Credit Card

TRAVEL credit cards are crucial to reducing your travel costs and making life easier. These credit cards can get you free stuff and cheap flights, help you save on exchange rates, avoid fees, and make you money. There are many travel credit cards out there that offer different kinds of rewards, from general points programs to branded hotel and airline cards. I think they are great if you use them right (and pay off your balance at the end of each month). They are better than cash, especially when you can get so many rewards and freebies from them.

No matter how long your trip is, you should have a special credit card for when you travel. Travel credit cards offer too many benefits to pass up. With bonuses, I've accumulated probably over a million points. Here are just *some* of the goodies I've earned:

More than 400,000 American Airlines miles

More than 120,000 United Airlines miles

More than 100,000 British Airways miles

More than 50,000 Virgin Atlantic miles

Four free nights at the Marriott

Citibank points for two free flights to Europe and $300 USD cash

Hilton Honors Gold membership and 60,000 Hilton Honors points

A free first-class ticket from London to Hong Kong

Dozens of free hotel rooms at the W Hotel

That's just for starters. I've been travel hacking for so long that the list of things I've earned could fill a whole book.

All these points have translated to free first-class flights, free nights at hotels, free upgrades, and free money. And it didn't take me years to accumulate them either. I received a lot of points through sign-up bonuses and special offers that allowed me to get lots of points within only a few months.

You're probably thinking that while all those points sound good, you don't want to hurt your credit rating by opening so many credit cards, or pay fees on multiple cards. So let's discuss that first.

First, all the credit cards I've ever gotten have waived the yearly fee in their introductory offer. When it comes time to renew the cards and pay the fee, I simply cancel the credit card to avoid the fee. Additionally, if you call up the card issuer and let them know you are thinking of canceling, many times you can get the fee waived for a second year or get your account switched to a no-fee card.

It's true that "churning and burning"—that is, opening and closing a lot of credit cards at once—can hurt your credit score. But opening a few accounts over a longer period of time won't kill your credit score. I've been opening and closing accounts for years, and I still have a credit score close to 800 and have never been denied a card.

As Brian Kelly from thepointsguy.com, a website that teaches people how to use credit cards to gain loyalty points, told me, "While in its own words, FICO says 'opening several credit accounts in a short period of time represents greater credit risk,' that's because you're applying for multiple lines of new credit rather than submitting several inquiries for a single new line, such as a mortgage. In general, however, the impact on your score from multiple inquiries is small—and remember that new credit counts only 10 percent toward determining your overall FICO score. So as long as you are strong in the other areas that determine your score, like payment history and amounts owed, you should be fine to apply for new cards."

Brian is constantly opening credit accounts and has had the same experience as I have. He recommends that "ideally you should space your applications several months apart." That's the key. Your credit score will slightly dip every time there is an inquiry into it, whether that is a credit card or home loan or car loan. It's how the system is set up. But so long as you space out your applications and maintain good credit, you won't do any long-term damage to your credit. Your credit rating rises over time as long as you maintain it; you aren't going to have a bank officer tell you years from now, "Sorry, because you canceled three credit cards in 2012, your loan is denied." I once canceled four credit cards in one day, and the impact on my score? Nothing.

What Makes a Good Credit Card

So now that that is out of the way, let's talk about why these cards are important for travelers and how to find the right one for you. Travel-related credit cards are good for two reasons:

First, most travel credit cards offer bonuses of at least twenty thousand points just for signing up. Don't sign up for a card that doesn't offer this, because without it, it will take a long time to exchange reward points for hotels, cash, or airfare. Starting at twenty thousand points is a lot better than starting at zero. Most of the time, the points are worth at least a free domestic airline ticket, as most U.S. carriers begin award tickets at twenty thousand points for a flight in the continental United States. The American AAdvantage card offers around twenty-five thousand miles just for joining (that's a free round-trip domestic ticket). United Airlines gives you around forty thousand miles for signing up. Delta Airlines offers the same. Starwood Hotels often has specials that give you thirty thousand points for signing up with their card. Even general-use cards, like Chase Sapphire, offer a sign-up bonus of forty thousand points. In short, by not getting a credit card, you are leaving free flights and hotel rooms on the table that could be used to lower your travel costs. Free is the best word in the English language after all!

Since offers and bonuses vary from time to time, it's important to keep track of the latest deals. The best websites for that are the following:

Flyertalk: flyertalk.com. A forum site where people post the latest flight bonuses and miles specials.

Boarding Area: boardingarea.com. A website that contains a series of blogs that discuss how to fly for free and gain airline miles and elite status quickly.

The Points Guy: thepointsguy.com. Run by Brian Kelly, this site helps people navigate credit card bonus and airline and hotel reward programs.

Second, travel credit cards offer many perks besides their sign-up bonuses. Many will give you elite loyalty status. There's nothing better than getting elite status and the perks that come with it for doing nothing. The American Express platinum card gives you Starwood Gold status, access to airport lounges, and a $200 USD travel credit. The Hilton card gives you gold status. The United card gives you priority boarding and free checked bags. The list of freebies goes on and on.

Most good credit cards also give you extra points when you shop at specific retailers, or, if it is a branded credit card, you'll get extra points with that particular brand. You're going to shop anyway, so why not earn something for doing it? These cards are meant to get people to be loyal, so they include lots of perks so you don't use a competitor. I received triple miles by buying clothes from Gap using an airline's credit card, since Gap was a preferred merchant. United gives you double points when you use their credit card for booking flights directly on their website.

If you don't want to be tied down to one company, a general rewards credit card like Capital One Venture Card (capitalone.com), Chase Sapphire and Ink cards (chase.com), or American Express (americanexpress.com) would be best. You will still get points for free flights and discounts, as well as cash back. You won't get any of the elite status benefits that a branded credit card gives, but you will have access to a wider range of brands and companies while still receiving points that can be redeemed for free travel.

When you are choosing which card to get, it is important to look for the following three things:

A Huge Sign-up Bonus: As mentioned above, most cards offer sign-up bonuses of twenty thousand points/miles. Don't get one that doesn't; otherwise it will take you ages to get a free flight. Lately, in a bid to get more people to join their card programs, many airline- and hotel-specific cards are offering bonuses between sixty and one hundred thousand points. I simply won't sign up for a card that doesn't give me at least twenty thousand points when I sign up. Most cards have an everyday sign-up bonus of around thirty thousand points.

Extra Points: Most credit cards offer one point for every dollar spent. However, the good credit cards will give you extra points when you shop at specific retailers or, if they are branded credit cards, with a particular brand. This will help you earn points a lot quicker. I don't want just one dollar to equal one point. I want the ability to get two or three points every time I spend a dollar. Therefore, look for cards that have retail partnerships so that when you go shopping, you gain more points quickly. When I used my AA credit card to sign up with Netflix, I received an extra five thousand points.

Low Spending Minimum: Unfortunately, in order to get the large bonuses these cards give, there is usually a required minimum spending amount before you'll be eligible to receive the bonus. But sometimes the spending requirement is too high. I love the Starwood Amex card, but you must spend $5,000 USD before you get the reward bonus. While all cards give you six months to reach that spending level, I'd prefer to have a lower threshold. After all, spending money just to get points is not worth it. I want to be able to get the bonus using my normal, day-to-day spending. Only sign up for cards that have a spending requirement of less than $1,000 USD.

How to Leverage Your Cards

With so many choices in credit cards, which ones do you pick? Well, the short answer is, all of them. I mean, grab as many as you can. Why put a limit on how many points you get?

But that being said, if you aren't a crazy travel hacker and are looking for only a couple of cards, don't care which ones you get, and simply want the most bang for your buck, consider the following criteria when choosing them.

WHAT IS YOUR GOAL?

The important thing to do when you begin travel hacking with credit cards is to come up with a plan. While the most ardent of travel hackers will sign up for anything and everything to gain points, for the casual or new hacker, it's best to start slowly and focus on a few key goals. The first thing you want to ask yourself is what you want: Free flights? Hotel points? Something else? Then note if you're loyal to one brand.

For example, if you are a really loyal flier with American Airlines, the best cards to start off with would be the Citi American AAdvantage card (40,000 point sign-up bonus) and the Starwood Amex (25,000 sign-up bonus plus 20 percent transfer bonus) because you can transfer points to your American Airlines account.

If you just want points to spend wherever you choose, get the Chase or American Express cards because you can use their points with a variety of companies. They each have their own rewards programs (Chase Ultimate Rewards and American Express Membership Rewards), and points can be transferred to multiple airline or hotel partners as well as be used to book travel directly via their sites.

Free hotel rooms? Sign up for the hotel cards. By focusing on what you want at first, you can maximize your short-term goals and get the hang of travel hacking. For example, I tend to avoid hotel cards because I rarely stay in hotels. I dislike Hilton and Marriott and would rather focus on getting points related to Starwood (W is my favorite hotel brand) or miles for flying. So unless there is a good sign-up bonus, I focus on what matters most to me: getting free flights.

Therefore, I concentrate my efforts on cards that get me airline miles or have good transfer bonuses to airline programs.

Below is a list of websites that monitor the latest credit card offers:

creditcards.com/airline-miles.php (US)

creditcardfinder.com.au/travel-rewards-credit-cards (Australia)

uk.creditcards.com/travel.php (UK)

rewardscanada.ca/topcc2012/index.html (Canada)

Avoiding Foreign Transaction Fees

If you don't want to be bothered with points, miles, status, and everything else involved, then you should simply get a card with no foreign transaction fee. The majority of credit cards charge a 3 percent fee when you use them overseas. Credit cards are great to use because you get a good exchange rate from them, but if you are paying a fee every time you use the card, then it doesn't work out as well.

That is why I recommend the Capital One Venture Card. You get some rewards with it (one point for every dollar spent), but the rewards structure is really, really awful. I use this card for one reason: There are no foreign transaction fees when you use it overseas. I get a good conversion rate (see Chapter 3 for the discussion on banking) and I don't pay any fees. Between this card and my Charles Schwab ATM card, I never pay any bank fees when traveling outside the United States. Note: Some Chase, Discover, and American Express cards also have no foreign transaction fees.

If you are willing to do a little work, you can use credit cards to gain tons of free miles and reward points before you go on your trip, to keep you in free flights and hotels for a long, long time. It's never too early to sign up for these cards, and I would begin signing up for as many as you feel comfortable signing up for today. After I got my free rewards, I simply stopped using the cards. There was no reason to. They served their purpose. I use the cards before I leave for my trip to gain points, and I use my Capital One card overseas to avoid transaction fees. I win twice and so can you.

Travel credit cards and the lucrative bonuses and awards they can get you are predominantly an American thing. But that doesn't make it impossible for non-Americans to use these points and loyalty systems to their advantage.

In Canada, you can find large bonuses on some cards. A link on the Points Guy site (thepointsguy.com/top-deals-3) shows the latest and greatest card deals near the bottom of the page. Additionally, the following blogs can teach you how you can best use travel credits to your advantage:

Canadian Kilometers: boardingarea.com/canadiankilometers

Rewards Canada: rewardscanada.ca

Canadian Travel Hacking: canadiantravelhacking.com

The best site in the UK is Head for Points (headforpoints.com), which keeps its thumb on the pulse of getting rewards and free flights. Australia has some deals once in a while and the website listed on page 40 can help you find them, but they are few and far between.

For everyone else in the world, I'm sorry to be the bearer of bad news, but the large credit card bonuses just don't happen in your countries, and there's nothing that can be done about that. You just have to accept this fate.

5

Airline Tickets

THE age of cheap flights is over, as oil prices rise and airlines reduce capacity, cut routes, and raise fares. It is becoming harder
to find the cheap flight deals that a few years ago let you jet off to
some exotic location on a whim for relatively cheap.

But if you are going to be traveling around the world, or even if
you just want to go to Paris for a few weeks, you are going to need to
find a way to fly cheap. The more you pay for a flight, the less you'll
have to travel with day to day, and the less likely you will be to go on
a trip. The most common reason I hear for why people don't take a
vacation? "I can't afford the plane ticket!"

Since I want you to afford that plane ticket and head off to somewhere amazing, I'm going to lay out the best ways to fly around the
world and score cheap flights.

But before we get into the particulars, let's talk about why flights
are expensive. If you've been flying for at least the past few years, you
might have noticed ticket prices, even the cheapest ones, seem to be

going as high as the planes you'll be flying. Save some flash sale or price war, consumers are paying a lot more than they used to.

Why is that? Ticket prices are high today for a number of reasons. For starters, the industry has consolidated a lot over the last few years. Thanks to bankruptcies and mergers, there are now only three major airlines in the United States. In Canada, you only have two. In Europe, Air France-KLM and Lufthansa control the bulk of the market. As airlines have partnered up, merged, or gone bankrupt, there is little incentive or need to create low fares to win your business.

Second, the price of airline fuel has increased tremendously. Back in 1996, airline fuel cost 55 cents per gallon. As of May 2014, it was $2.88 per gallon. Airlines can't absorb all that increase, so they pass some of that on to the consumer, leading to higher fares.

Additionally, airline taxes and security fees have also increased, adding hundreds of dollars onto your base fare.

Moreover, following 9/11 and the recession, demand fell; to compensate, airlines reduced both the number of routes they offered and the frequency of their flights. They did this to save money and fly fuller planes. Fuller planes mean more passenger revenue and fewer costs for the airline. It's why if you live far from a major city you've seen fares go up and the number of flights go down. Planes fly close to full now and airlines are quite happy about that.

Why Do Prices Fluctuate?

Prices go up and down for many reasons. No one can really predict when or if a price is going to go up or down. Only the airline knows that. But there are four major things that drive prices: competition, supply, demand, and oil prices.

Together, those four things all affect a lovely thing called the "load factor." Airlines want to fill their planes and maximize profits, and they do this by calculating a plane's load factor, which is essentially the percentage of seats sold on a flight.

On a U.S. domestic ticket, a flight might have ten to fifteen different price points. Airlines want to fill a plane with the people paying the highest price and get maximum revenue. So they constantly change their price to get bodies on the plane.

If the load factor and demand is low for a flight, an airline will increase the availability of cheap fares. If the load factor and demand are high for a flight, the airline will raise prices.

Airlines have developed sophisticated computer systems that constantly compare booking trends to past sales history and are always changing prices based on the load factor, time of year, and competitor behavior.

As a traveler, you have two options for flying: You can either buy a round-the-world ticket before you go or pay for your flights as you fly from point to point. Neither option is better or worse than the other. The one that is best is the one that suits your travel style and itinerary.

Round-the-World Tickets

Round-the-world (RTW) tickets can be a convenient way to fly around the world. They get you where you want to go without having to worry about booking flights along the way. You prebook all your tickets in advance, and by purchasing them in one giant bulk package, you can often save money off the total price of all the individual tickets.

HOW ROUND-THE-WORLD TICKETS WORK (AND THE RULES!)

RTW tickets are actually airline alliance passes. You buy from an airline a ticket that can be used with them and all their alliance partners. Each of these alliances offers you the ability to travel around the world on that airline's partners. For example, if you book with United Airlines (Star Alliance), your ticket is only good for airlines United partners with. If you book with American Airlines (Oneworld), you can only use their partners.

An airline alliance is a partnership in which airlines share seats on planes, passengers, and elite status benefits. For example, American Airlines can't fly everywhere in the world, and you may need to get from New York City to Nairobi, Kenya, a destination American doesn't serve. So while you may book with American Airlines for that route, you will actually fly one of its airline partners on the portions American doesn't fly.

The two largest airline alliances are Star Alliance and Oneworld. The Star Alliance (staralliance.com) includes the following airlines: Adria Airways, Aegean Airlines, Air Canada, Air China, Air New Zealand, All Nippon Airways (ANA), Asiana Airlines, Austrian Airlines, Avianca Holdings, Brussels Airlines, Copa Airlines, Croatia Airlines, EgyptAir, Ethiopian Airlines, EVA Air, LOT Polish Airlines, Lufthansa, Scandinavian Airlines, Shenzhen Airlines, Singapore Airlines, South African Airways, Swiss International Air Lines, TAP Portugal, Thai Airways, Turkish Airlines, and United Airlines.

Oneworld (oneworld.com) includes Air Berlin, American Airlines, British Airways, Cathay Pacific, Finnair, Iberia, Japan Airlines, LAN Airlines, Malaysia Airlines, Qantas, Qatar Airways, Royal Jordanian, S7 Airlines, TAM Airlines, and SriLankan Airlines.

There is a third alliance, Skyteam (skyteam.com), that includes Aeroflot, Aerolíneas Argentinas, Aeroméxico, Air Europa, Air France, Alitalia, China Airlines, China Eastern Airlines, China Southern Airlines, Czech Airlines, Delta Air Lines, Garuda Indonesia, Kenya Airways, KLM, Korean Air, Middle East Airlines, Saudia, TAROM, Vietnam Airlines, and Xiamen Airlines.

While Skyteam offers RTW tickets, their tickets don't cover as many destinations as Oneworld's or Star Alliance's. Most of the alliance members are small airlines that don't fly many long-distance routes. Skyteam is simply not the best option when choosing a RTW ticket. I would not recommend booking one with them, because of their limited options.

It's important also to remember that none of these alliances include any of the world's budget airlines. A budget airline is an airline that usually offers fewer amenities (think cattle car) and cheaper fares than the "major" airlines of the world (that is, large, international carriers that are part of an alliance). Think Southwest versus United, or Ryanair versus Air France. You will find these airlines throughout the world, and there is an especially large glut of them in Europe. Some budget airlines are Ryanair (Europe), easyJet (Europe), Southwest (US), Spirit (US), Air Asia (Asia), Tiger (Asia/Australia), Jetstar (Australia), and Transvaia (Europe). We'll talk about them in more detail in the next section, on getting cheap point-to-point flights.

These airlines have much cheaper fares than major, international airlines (think Delta, American, British Airways, or United), but since they only fly regionally and don't partner with anyone, you can't use them on your round-the-world ticket.

Each airline alliance has its own rules for how its round-the-world tickets work:

Star Alliance

Star Alliance passes are based on how many miles you travel, and they offer passes in 29,000-, 34,000-, or 39,000-mile increments. To put that in some context, 29,000 miles will get you roughly three continents (outside of the United States), 34,000 miles will get you four continents, and 39,000 will get you five or six continents. The more miles you get, the more destinations you can see and vice versa.

Each pass is allowed up to fifteen stopovers (a stopover is considered twenty-four hours in one destination), and you can get the ticket in first, business, or economy class. There is also a special Starlite economy-only fare for 26,000 miles, but this is limited to a maximum of five stops. The more miles you want on your ticket, the more places you can visit—but also the more money you will pay.

Star Alliance also requires passengers to start and end in the same country, though not necessarily in the same city. Also, you can backtrack over continents but not over oceans. This means you can fly from Australia to New York and then New York to Los Angeles, but you can't go from Los Angeles back to Australia. When you cross an ocean, you have to keep moving in your original direction. It should also be noted that backtracking, surface sectors (what they call the parts of your trip you take overland and not with an airplane), and transits and connections all count against the mileage total.

For example, if you fly from LA to London and then from Athens to Bangkok, the mileage from London to Athens is counted against your trip even though you might be doing it overland on a train or flying with a cheap budget airline like Ryanair.

Oneworld

Oneworld offers two different kinds of passes: one that is segment-based and another that is mileage-based. Global Explorer is Oneworld's more conventional, mileage-based round-the-world ticket. There are three levels—26,000, 29,000, or 39,000 miles—in economy class as well as a 34,000-mile ticket in business and first class. Just as with the Star Alliance mileage-based RTWs, all miles are counted, including overland segments. This pass follows the same rules as above.

Oneworld's other pass is much better and in my opinion the best RTW pass you can buy. The Oneworld Explorer is based on the number of continents visited (from three to six) and has no maximum mileage limit, and up to sixteen segments can be included in your ticket. A flight segment counts as one flight, so a ticket with sixteen segments would have sixteen flights. That includes any connections. If you want to go from London to Hong Kong but the ticket includes a stop in Dubai, that counts as two segments. With the Oneworld Explorer, there are no overland penalties or mileage limits. You simply get sixteen flights.

I like this pass the best for many reasons. Unlike with other tickets, overland segments don't count against you and there are no mileage requirements. One of the benefits of the segment system is that every segment is counted the same, so out-of-the-way destinations like Easter Island or the island of Tahiti, which are far from any main airport, count the same as a two-hour flight. All flights are equal.

TERMS AND CONDITIONS

Round-the-world tickets come with a number of terms and conditions. Generally speaking, with all alliances, a round-the-world ticket is valid for one year from the start date and requires you to end in the same country you start in. You don't need to end in the same city, but you need to end in the same country.

Moreover, all round-the-world tickets require you to travel in one direction as well as to cross the Atlantic and Pacific oceans only once. What that means is you can't fly from New York to London and then back across the Atlantic to Brazil and then continue on to Asia then back to Europe and finally home to New York. That's not one-way travel, that's backtracking, and tickets don't allow backtracking between continents.

Additionally, tickets require a set number of stopovers, each of which is defined as a stay of more than twenty-four hours. Tickets require you to have a minimum of three stops and a maximum of fifteen. Oneworld has a two-stopover maximum permitted in the continent of origin.

Travelers can change the dates and times on their ticket at no extra charge so long as they don't change the destinations. If you have a Tokyo–to–Los Angeles flight you want to change, you can change the date and time without a fee. However, if you decide to fly from Tokyo to San Francisco instead, then you have to pay a fee of $125 USD. Any changes in the destinations on your ticket incur a fee.

RTW Alliance Alternatives

While you can book RTW tickets directly with the airlines by calling the reservations line listed on their website, sometimes you can find a better deal by booking through a third party such as Airtreks (airtreks.com). Airtreks operates differently than the airline alliances. Instead of creating a round-the-world ticket, Airtreks pieces together individual airline tickets based on the lowest available fares they find. They don't just deal with one alliance—they mix and match from all available airlines (excluding budget airlines) to find the lowest price. Because of this, the rules pertaining to alliance tickets don't apply here. You can fly anywhere and in any direction you want, and the overland mileage doesn't count against your flight, because there is no mileage limit.

Airtreks' fees range anywhere between $50 and $250, depending on what airline you're traveling on. Unlike with airline alliance tickets, you will be charged for changing your date and travel times. Since Airtreks books regular airline tickets, those tickets are subject to regular airline ticket rules. So, while fares are cheaper, because Airtreks has to abide by normal airline rules, the change fees are higher.

In that sense, booking with a third-party booking site like Airtreks is a much better option because of the increased flexibility, but as nothing is ever 100 percent in travel, it's important to price out your ticket using all the options.

HOW MUCH DO RTW TICKETS COST?

RTW ticket prices generally average $2,700–10,000 USD, depending on your mileage, route, and number of stops. However, a simple two- or three-stop RTW ticket might cost as little as $1,500 USD. Here are some sample round-the-world ticket prices, including taxes and fees, based on a search in February 2012:

New York–London–Athens–Johannesburg–Bangkok–Sydney–Los Angeles

Star Alliance: $6,600 USD

Oneworld: $7,700 USD

Airtreks: $4,051 USD

As you can see, booking directly with the alliances costs a lot more than booking through a third-party agent. Simply put: Use Airtreks or another similar agent, like STA Travel (statravel.com) or Flight Centre (flightcentre.com), instead of booking directly with the airline. If you do purchase a RTW ticket via the airlines directly, do so using the miles gained through credit card bonuses and methods discussed in the next section. That will cut the cost from thousands to a few hundred dollars.

As we saw above, RTW tickets can cost a lot of money. Spending $7,000 to fly around the world is simply not a realistic figure for most people, and it's certainly not going to allow you to travel for $50 USD per day. If you do decide to purchase a RTW ticket, do so on miles if at all possible. As discussed in Chapter 4, there are plenty of ways to jump-start your frequent-flier-mile balance right away. In the upcoming section on point-to-point flights, we'll discuss non-credit-card-related ways to increase your balance even more.

SHOULD YOU BUY A RTW TICKET?

RTW tickets are perfect for people with a set schedule. If you know your travel dates and destinations and don't plan on changing your trip very much, a RTW ticket will save you a lot of time and a bit of money. As Steve Kamb puts it, "I knew I was going to continue traveling, as I had some obligations to return home for later in the year, so I knew that one way or the other I'd be returning. If I had plans on just traveling nonstop without having anything to return home for, booking a one-way ticket and figuring things out as I went might have been a better option. However, for me the RTW made perfect sense."

But these tickets are rigid, and that is why I don't use them. Your dates are already set, and they can be a problem to change sometimes, as you are subject to limited availability. If you decided to change your dates and times, you might find they don't have a flight for you. And while date and time changes (so long as the destination remains the same) are free, other changes are not. If you decide to change the route of your flight, you will have to pay a fee of around $125 USD.

Since RTW tickets are valid for only one year and you need to finish where you started, if you decide to go away for longer, you're essentially throwing away the last leg of your trip. Once the year has passed, any flights not used become invalid and you just wasted a lot of money.

When I first went around the world in 2006, I didn't buy a RTW ticket. Instead, I spent $3,100 USD to fly from Boston to Boston. My first journey around the world in 2006–2007 broke down this way:

Boston, Massachusetts, to Oslo, Norway: free with miles earned on my Citi Thank You points card

Oslo, Norway, to Athens, Greece: $600 USD on flights, buses, and trains I used to get around Europe for three months

Athens, Greece, to Bangkok, Thailand: $500 USD on Thai Airways (major airline)

Bangkok, Thailand, to Perth, Australia: $200 USD on Tiger Airways (budget airline)

Perth, Australia, to Sydney, Australia: $800 USD in buses

Sydney, Australia, to Los Angeles, California: $800 USD on Qantas (major airline)

Los Angeles, California, to Boston, Massachusetts: $200 USD on American Airlines (major airline)

TOTAL: $3,100 USD

Looking back at the prices listed earlier for round-the-world tickets, you can see my cost was much lower than the cost of a RTW ticket of equal destinations because I used airline miles for free flights and used budget airlines to get cheap flight deals.

Unlike Steve, I didn't know what my plans were or where I was going, and getting a RTW ticket would have reduced my flexibility. Since I never know exactly what I am going to be doing when I travel, having such a rigid schedule is not for me.

I don't think RTW tickets are bad. They are perfect for people who have a set route and set time frame. But I don't think people with a really flexible itinerary or fluid travel plans should buy a RTW ticket. If you're such a person, you'll likely be able to price out a cheaper ticket by using budget airlines, applying frequent-flier points, and waiting for fare sales.

With so many ways to get free and cheap flights (see the next section), anyone with even a little flexibility should consider avoiding a round-the-world ticket.

How to Find Cheap Point-to-Point Flights

If you decide a RTW ticket might not suit your needs, you'll need to find another way to fly around the world. One way is buying single point-to-point tickets. This is the method I use when I travel. I find I can save more money flying point to point for three reasons:

For starters, I never know my plans until the last minute and I am notoriously fickle. I'll change plans a hundred times before I finally decide on a destination. I once bought a flight from Moldova to Ukraine only to wake up and decide to head to Romania instead. I canceled a ticket to Singapore so I could go to Malaysia. I can never make up my mind. That doesn't always work out well with a RTW ticket because changing your route costs $125 USD each time.

And, as you read earlier, I get a lot of free flights by using the frequent-flier points from travel credit cards. In fact, the reason I strong-arm people into getting travel credit cards is because after the sign-up bonus and some normal spending, you'll earn enough for a free flight (or more), and that's the best way to fly—for free. (In this section, I'll talk about ways you can increase your frequent-flier points besides just using credit cards.)

Lastly, I fly a lot of budget airlines. When these airlines have fares half the cost of major international airlines, they are hard to pass up. If the flight isn't that long, I don't care that I am squashed like a pack of sardines on the plane. I just want to get from point A to point B as cheaply as I can.

A lot of people don't like budget airlines because of the fees they charge. In order to keep their fares extremely low (sometimes just $1 USD), the airlines make their money by adding fees that come with stringent rules they hope you'll break so they can charge you.

Some require you to bring copies of your boarding pass or you'll have to pay a fee. You might need to check in online, or if your bag is over the weight limit, you'll pay more—the list goes on. These fees suck. Charging a "convenience fee" for paying with a credit card is not convenient.

But I still use these airlines, because if you follow their rules and get their low fares, the tickets cost less than a ticket from a major carrier. Ryanair has flights around Europe as low as $30 USD, which is about a third less than the major airlines. I flew Air Asia from Hong Kong to Bangkok for $170 USD, which was more than $200 USD cheaper than the major carriers Thai Airways and Cathay Pacific.

I find point-to-point tickets to be more convenient for my schedule. Over the years I've accumulated a number of methods for getting those flights cheap (besides flying my beloved budget airlines):

BE FLEXIBLE WITH YOUR TRAVEL

Ticket prices vary greatly depending on the day, time of day, time of year, and upcoming holidays. If the kids are on school break, expect higher fares. If it's a holiday, the fare goes up. Anytime more people want to fly, fares go up. Want to go to Europe in the summer or Hawaii during Christmas or Disney when the kids are on break? So does everyone else. So airline tickets are priced at their highest during those times because the demand is so great. Be a contrarian traveler and save.

Being flexible with your dates and times is one of the most important ways to save money. The difference of a day can mean the difference of hundreds of dollars. You want to fly when no one else is flying.

It's cheaper to fly midweek than on a weekend because most people travel on the weekends and airlines raise prices for those flights. If you fly right after a major holiday, prices tend to be a bit cheaper. Think about Thanksgiving, which is on a Thursday. Everyone flies home that Tuesday and Wednesday so fares are higher on those days. Since people return on Sunday or Monday, fares are high those days, too. But because most people want to stay with their families and shop on that Friday, returns are low on that day.

Moreover, early morning and late night flights tend to be cheaper. Few people want to be up at 5 a.m. for a flight or to fly overnight. Most business travelers leave on Monday and come back on Friday and families tend to travel over the week, thus midweek fares tend to be less expensive.

If you aren't flexible in the dates and times you want to fly, you will never be able to find a cheap flight.

BE FLEXIBLE WITH YOUR DESTINATIONS

Instead of going to a place with an expensive flight, go where the flight is the cheapest. Kayak offers an "Explore" tool that allows you to put in your airport and see route prices all around the world. Just look to see what destination is the cheapest! Google Flights (google .com/flights) has a similar (and better) feature, that I use often. If you are flexible with where you want to go (as in anywhere but home), this is a great way to start researching your next trip.

I always enter in my departing airport and search for "anywhere." Whatever comes up the cheapest in an area I want to explore is often where I go!

Fly Budget Airlines

In America, there are only a handful of budget airlines. In Europe, there are dozens and competition has kept prices there very low. In Asia, Air Asia has led to a huge drop in fares and is a great budget airline to fly. Often these low-cost airlines offer no-fare tickets; you pay just the taxes. Flying the budget airlines is a good alternative to flying the majors whenever possible. You get fewer perks, but you can save a bundle in ticket costs. But be sure to check out how far the airports are from the city center; sometimes transportation from the airport to the city can actually make a budget airline more expensive.

More and more budget carriers are doing long-haul, cross-continent flights (for example, Norwegian to the United States or Air Asia to Australia or South Korea), and these airlines represent a big savings opportunity. Be sure to fly them. Momondo (momondo.com) and Skyscanner (skyscanner.com) have the best listings of budget carriers.

Find Alternative Routes

Not only is it important to be flexible with your dates, but try being flexible with the route you take. There are so many budget carriers around the world that taking advantage of a good deal to another city and then hopping on a budget flight to your destination is sometimes the best way to go. I had to go to Paris once. The flight was $900 USD but I could fly to Dublin for $600 and get a $60 flight to Paris. It meant more flying time, but the $240 I saved was worth it. I use Google Flights to look for a cheap major airport to fly into and then Skyscanner or Momondo for a budget flight to my final destination.

By working various airlines and special offers, you can save a lot. This method is more work as you have to figure out lots of different routes and check different airlines, but it will often shave money off your flight, giving you more to spend at your destination.

CHECK MULTIPLE SEARCH SITES

Whenever most Americans do a web search for airline tickets, they search the big three: Expedia, Travelocity, or Orbitz. People make a big mistake by only doing that. You need to search as many flight search websites as you can to ensure you are leaving no stone unturned. Many sites don't list budget carriers because those airlines don't want to pay a booking commission.

It's important to check multiple booking sites because all websites have their weaknesses and do not include every airline. You aren't going to find Air Asia, Ryanair, or most other budget airlines on large US-based sites. All booking sites have blind spots since they don't cover every region of the world and every airline equally. Check multiple sites. I search the following websites when I look for a plane ticket:

Skyscanner: skyscanner.com

Momondo: momondo.com

Google Flights: google.com/flights

Hipmunk: hipmunk.com

Kayak: kayak.com

ITA Matrix: matrix.itasoftware.com

Vayama: vayama.com

Although it's not 100 percent proven that booking sites and airlines track your cookies and change prices, there's enough circumstantial evidence for me to say that if you're going to be checking prices over multiple days, clear your cookies each time. It's better to be safe than sorry.

TAKE ADVANTAGE OF STUDENT DISCOUNTS

If you are a student, there are many, many discounts available to you. Check out STA Travel (statravel.com) and their search engine. You can find flexible student tickets on their website and at agency stores. I used them for a $400 ticket from Athens to Bangkok. That wasn't even the cheapest flight, either, just the cheapest direct flight. There are many student codes out there, and many of the tourist agencies in backpacker areas can help find you a cheap ticket.

USE FREQUENT FLIER MILES

Airline rewards programs are a great way to get free flights, free upgrades, and free companion tickets. No matter how often you fly, you should be signed up for the airline's reward program. I stick to US-based airlines because they are involved in all the major alliances and you can earn miles on their partner flights. For example, if I fly Singapore Airlines, I can earn United Airlines miles because they are partners. I get Delta miles on Air France flights and vice versa. Or American Airlines and Cathay Pacific. You should always be earning miles when you fly. If you aren't from the States, simply use the airline you fly most and bank miles to them.

Moreover, there are a lot of other ways to earn miles if you aren't jet-setting around the world all the time:

Shop the Airline Portals: All airlines have special point offers for large retailers. Shopping at those stores will earn you two to four miles per dollar spent (sometimes more). All you have to do is shop online via the links on an airline's website, and you'll get the extra points added to your account. It's a lot better than earning one point per dollar spent by going to the store directly. The products don't cost any extra. I do all my shopping through these portals simply for the extra miles.

Watch for Special Offers: I sign up for newsletters because they often feature offers not found on an airline's website. This could be triple miles on a selected route, taking a survey, participating in a Facebook contest, or simply installing an airline shopping toolbar in your web browser. These bonuses aren't high but they take minimal effort and add up over time.

Be a Crazy Flyer: On forums like FlyerTalk, where people hunt out the latest chances for miles, you often find people doing mileage runs. This means that an airline will offer triple miles or double elite qualifying miles (these miles, unlike normal miles, count toward your elite flyer status and can be earned only by flying) if you fly a certain route. When airlines get into price wars or offer new routes, they often launch ridiculous double or triple mile offers. Many people then fly these routes just for the miles. They will fly from California to New York and back again if they find a dirt cheap fare in order to gain miles. Mileage runs are very common and, while not free, can be a useful method to gain a lot of miles on a cheap fare.

Put Everything on the Card: I pay nothing in cash. I put everything on my travel credit card—from Starbucks to phone bills. My total monthly spending, including my business expenses, is about $3,000 per month. That's 36,000 miles just for doing nothing special. That's a free one-way flight to Europe right there.

In the movie *Up in the Air*, George Clooney's character said, "I don't do anything if it doesn't benefit my miles account." Think like that. By following the tips in this chapter and using the websites listed in the credit card section for finding bonus offers, you'll be able to accumulate a lot of flight miles.

DON'T MISS OUT ON SALES

No one likes to clutter up their inbox, but by signing up for mailing lists from airlines and search engines, you'll be able to get updates about last-minute deals or mistake fares (like a recent $130 USD New York to Tokyo flight on Priceline). Many times, ticket sales are available for only 24 hours, and if you aren't always checking the web, you miss out. I would have missed out on a round trip ticket to Japan for $700 USD (normally $1,500) if I hadn't been on the American Airlines mailing list. Mailing lists are essential, and I subscribe to a ton.

The websites Airfarewatchdog, Holiday Pirates (Europe based), and The Flight Deal are great sites that will keep you alert of last-minute specials or deals.

Stay on Top of Twitter Feeds

Twitter can be an excellent place to find cheap airfares. Many airlines offer specials that can't be found anywhere other than Twitter. You don't need to have a Twitter account to be eligible for these fares or even to be able to see them, as Twitter feeds are open to the public. For example, Jetblue (twitter.com/jetblue) is famous for their Tuesday Twitter fare sales.

You can find a good list of all the airline Twitter handles at twitter.com/johnnyjet/lists/airlines.

Buy at the Right Time

The best time to book a ticket is six to eight weeks before your flight, or twelve to sixteen weeks ahead if booking during peak season. During this time period, airlines know if a flight is going to sell or not and will begin to either lower or increase fares based on demand. Don't wait until the last second because airlines realize if you are booking close to departure, you probably need the flight. On the flip side, don't book too far in advance because airlines are going to wait as long as possible to release the cheaper fares.

Know Your Price

People always try to get the lowest price, wait too long, and then pay too much. We all know airline prices bounce up and down, yet most of us miss the lowest price by holding out a bit too long. Therefore, it's important to know what you want to pay, not what you hope to pay. What's the lowest price for *you*? What do you feel comfortable paying? Don't wait for the perfect price; wait for *your* price.

Be realistic too. If the lowest available price is $1,000 for a flight but the average is $1,500, don't try to wait for $800; that's probably not going to happen. Given that flights are best bought around eight to twelve weeks out, I'll begin to look for tickets around three months in advance and slowly see how the price is. If it starts moving to the high end of my comfort zone, I'll look at available seats on the flight I want. If there aren't many left, I'll book the flight because normally this indicates prices aren't going to go down (a mostly sold-out plane means airlines have no incentive to lower the price). Sometimes I don't find a price I'm comfortable with and I look for a new place to go.

The prices of airline tickets aren't going to get any cheaper anytime soon. While tickets are historically cheap when compared to inflation, it certainly doesn't feel that way when the ticket we bought last year is twice the price this year. We can't go back to the time of cheap tickets, we can only hope to avoid paying the highest price for the flight we want, and with the tips in this chapter you'll be able to do just that.

CHECK AN AIRPORT'S CARRIERS

One thing I often do is visit an airport's website to see what airlines fly into it. Sometimes you find small airlines that are not listed on flight search aggregators like Kayak, Expedia, Momondo, or Skyscanner. This is to make sure I checked all possible airlines and turned over every rock for potential deals. After all, I don't want to find out later that there was an airline that offered a cheap flight that wasn't listed on a booking site.

When I was flying from Tallinn, Estonia, to Aarhus, Denmark, I couldn't find any flights listed on the flight booking websites. Checking the Tallinn airport website, I found Estonian Airlines listed, and checking their website I found that they flew to Aarhus via their partner SAS. This didn't show up on any booking results. I ended up finding the flight I needed simply because I took the time to check which airlines fly in and out of the airport and to go to their websites directly.

I use point-to-point tickets between all destinations I travel to. This is better if you travel like me and are unpredictable. If you are part of a frequent-flier program, you can use reward miles to pay for tickets as you go, or you can simply wait for cheap flights and use discount carriers.

For the best flight savings, I recommend combining the point-to-point method with using frequent-flier miles for a free flight. If you managed to get one travel credit card with a large sign-up bonus, you can use those miles to get a free flight. Then using budget airlines and the tips above, you can reduce your flight costs even further.

6

Buying a Backpack

THE most important gear you are going to carry on your trip is the bag that holds all your belongings. For most round-the-world travelers, this is the backpack. Most travelers use a backpack over a rolling suitcase because it is easier to travel with. It just slings on your back and you don't need to lug it over streets, across cobblestones, or up stairs.

Suitcase or Backpack?

I hate suitcases. Despise them. On the road, traveling around the world, it is much easier to move around carrying a backpack. Your luggage is going to get thrown about and piled high on buses in random countries. It will get used and abused, and it's simply hard to walk up hills and stairs with your suitcase bump, bump, bumping everywhere. Suitcases are a pain in the butt. Backpacks are simply more versatile. They're easy to carry up stairs and pack into tight places, and overall, they just make life simpler. I don't need to pick one up on the escalator. I can just walk. Simple. Easy.

Even if you are only going on a two-week trip, I still suggest ditching that oversized, heavy suitcase. Suitcases are great for weekends away or if you'll be staying in one place for a long time. But if you are moving around a lot, it is far better to have a backpack. Backpacks just make more sense, which is why this chapter is devoted to them and not suitcases.

If you have back problems and can't use a backpack, a smaller suitcase with wheels and a long handle can be a good substitute. It will still be difficult carrying it up and down stairs, and annoying as you roll it across uneven sidewalks, but there are many companies (those listed at the end of this section) that make fairly good and lightweight travel cases.

CHOOSING THE RIGHT BACKPACK

Picking the right backpack is one of the most important things you'll do before you leave on your trip. If you pick one that is too big, you'll be carrying around too much extra weight. If your backpack is too small, you won't be able to fit everything you want inside. If you pick the wrong material, your stuff will get soaked when it rains.

There are many backpacks in the world and many, many places where you can purchase one. No matter where or what you purchase, know that the best backpacks—those that last the longest—have all the following characteristics that make them durable, protective, and long-lasting:

Material

While it does not need to be 100 percent waterproof, make sure your bag is made of a semi-waterproof material so everything doesn't get wet in a drizzle (many packs come with tarps you can put over them in case of a severe downpour). Moreover, make sure the material won't stay wet long and thereby get musty. I look for material that is a little thick but somewhat lightweight. I should be able to pour a cup of water over it without the insides getting wet. I'm not traveling a lot during torrential downpours or monsoons, but I have been caught in small rainstorms before, and because my backpack is made out of a good waterproof material, I've never opened my bag to find wet clothes.

Lockable Zippers

Make sure each compartment has two zippers so you can lock them together. While I am not really worried about people breaking into my bag and stealing my dirty clothes in a hostel or hotel, I like locking up my zippers when I am traveling. I'm always paranoid that someone is going to put something in my bag or a grabby baggage handler is going to take my stuff. When purchasing locks, make sure the package says they are TSA-friendly locks. These locks have a special release valve that allows the TSA to open and check your bag. That way when the TSA checks your bag for security, they don't have to break your locks. You can purchase TSA locks at any large retail store, such as Target or Walmart.

If your pack doesn't have two zippers, you can always get Pacsafe (pacsafe.com), which wraps a lockable metal mesh around your whole bag and can be tied to a large object. It means that not only is no one breaking into your stuff, no one is walking away with it either.

Pacsafe is a good form of protection for your bag, especially if you are going to be somewhere where your bag will be unattended for a long time. One thing to remember about Pacsafe is that this metal mesh also adds a lot of weight to your bag and it can be burdensome to carry around. Most people I know who use Pacsafe are photographers who carry a lot of expensive equipment around.

Multiple Compartments

I like a bag to have multiple compartments. This way, I can break up my belongings into smaller sections so it's easier to find and access the stuff I need. My clothes are in the main compartment of my bag, my umbrella and flip-flops in the top, and my shoes in the separated side compartment (that way they don't get anything dirty). It saves time I'd spend having to dig around my bag. You want convenience, and multiple compartments help give you that.

Internal Frame

The majority of backpacks today are internal-frame packs, meaning the support rods and frame are built into the backpack and hidden from view. However, there are still some external-frame backpacks out there, where the rods are separate from the actual pack and stick out. Think backpacks you see in old hiking movies or movies about people backpacking Europe in the 1970s. A big clunky metal frame. Don't get one of those. An internal-frame backpack not only looks better, but the rods won't get caught on anything and your bag will be slimmer, making moving around easier. Additionally, internal-frame packs tend to be lighter, as the frame is composed of a lighter alloy.

Padded Hip Belt

Most of the weight you carry around will be pushing down on your hips, so you'll want a padded belt to make supporting the weight more comfortable. The belt will help provide support and distribute the weight load more evenly on your back, causing less strain and fewer problems. The hip belt should also be adjustable so you can tighten it for extra support.

Padded Shoulder Straps

These make carrying your load more comfortable, as the weight of your pack will be pushing downward on your shoulders. The pads will put less pressure on your shoulders and also help take pressure off your lower back. Make sure the padding is very thick and made up of a single piece, as it will be less likely to split and thin out. After seven years, the padding on my backpack is slightly worn but still comfortable.

Chest Strap

A backpack with an adjustable chest strap helps move the weight of the backpack forward on your back and distributes the weight evenly across your upper body, making that walk up the hill to the hostel much, much easier. It also takes a lot of the pressure off your shoulders and helps avoid shoulder and back problems.

Contoured/Padded Back

A lumbar-shaped pack makes carrying it more comfortable, as it helps distribute weight more evenly. The same principle applies that is used in contoured chairs. It allows for a more natural arch, to ensure no back pain. Moreover, this type of pack creates a small space between your back and the bag, allowing air to move through and help keep you slightly cool. Lugging your bag around can build up a sweat!

SIZE DOESN'T MATTER

One of the most frequently asked questions I get about backpacks is about size. Everyone wants to know what the perfect size is. Well, there is no perfect size. Backpacks come in a number of sizes. The smallest backpacks are usually 43 liters, and they can go up to as large as 110 liters. There are also a number of torso and hip sizes available to ensure that everyone—no matter how big or small—can find a pack that fits him or her. No one backpack size is better than another. What matters is that your backpack should be both proportional to your body and comfortable. If your backpack is too big or too small, the weight won't be balanced properly and will cause back pain or maybe even make you topple over. You don't want a skyscraper rising up from your back, but you also don't want a pack that is clearly too small and overflowing with stuff. When you are at the store (and any good camping/outdoors store will do this), they should be able to stuff your backpack with the equivalent of thirty pounds (fifteen kilograms) so you can see how that much weight feels on your back.

You want a backpack that is big enough to hold just a bit more than the stuff you are bringing and not more than that. If a backpack fits everything you want, has a bit of extra room, and feels comfortable, then you have found the perfect backpack size. Manufacturers also have suggested torso and waist sizes for each model they produce, but I've found that the best way to know if a backpack feels right is to simply try it on.

It's important to remember that the bigger your backpack is, the less likely it is that you'll be able to carry it on the airplane. You won't face any baggage fees from the major airlines for checking your bag when flying internationally. The only inconvenience will be having to wait at baggage claim for your bag. Budget airlines charge a fee for checking a bag based on weight, so the more your bag weighs, the more you will have to pay to check it at the gate. Additionally, since you can no longer bring liquids in containers larger than three ounces on airplanes, you'll be *forced* to check the bag if you have soap and liquids in it.

PRICING OUT A BACKPACK

Most backpacks cost between $99 USD for a small model and as much as $300 USD for a large backpack from a brand name. The medium-sized store-brand names generally cost around $199 USD. Backpack prices depend a lot on size, fabric, and brand. Store brands are cheaper than big name brands like North Face, Osprey, and Gregory.

I don't believe any backpack is worth $300 USD, no matter how nice it is. These expensive backpacks tend to be large and have more bells and whistles, special padding, and material than you really need. I think any backpack under $200 USD (not including tax) is fine. That's the most I'd be willing to pay for something I was going to use for a long trip and could use for years to come. The difference in quality between a $200 USD backpack and a $300 USD backpack isn't that much. Everything a $300 USD backpack can do on the road, a $200 USD backpack can do just as well.

One way to get backpacks cheaper than the listed price is to buy last year's models at a discounted price at an outlet store. An outlet store sells all of last year's products that brands got rid of to make room for the new models. REI has a good outlet store (rei.com/outlet), and others include Backcountry (backcountry.com), Sierra Trading Post (sierratradingpost.com), and Campmor (campmor.com). All these companies sell gear for about 30–50 percent less than the current model's price.

To find the perfect backpack, I recommend visiting any of the stores listed below to try one on. Stores will allow you to try them on and will help fit you for the perfect backpack. I tried on more than ten backpacks before I finally settled on the one I currently use.

Additionally, you'll find that most travel backpacks are hiking backpacks. Hiking backpacks are packs meant for camping and multiday treks in the woods. Buying a backpack that was meant to be used in the Rockies instead of the streets of New Zealand doesn't matter—backpacks are pretty interchangeable these days, and getting a backpack meant for the outdoors simply means you'll have a stronger and more durable pack.

So what's on my back? I use an REI Mars pack. REI (Recreational Equipment Incorporated, rei.com) is a sporting and outdoors company in America that sells a wide variety of sporting, outdoors, and travel gear. I've had this backpack since 2004, and it works, looks, and feels just as good as the day I bought it. You know those advertisements where they try to destroy products in order to prove how good they are? Well, my life is that ad. I have put this backpack through the wringer. It's been crushed, thrown around, dropped, squeezed into tiny places, dragged, and kicked around. Most people think it's a brand-new backpack and are shocked to find out I've been carrying it around since 2004.

Besides selling their own gear, REI sells gear from other quality manufacturers, like North Face, Eagle Creek, and Osprey. They are an excellent company, with locations around the United States that offer very good prices on backpacks and other travel gear. I find their customer service superb and their sales staff to be very helpful and knowledgeable.

But they aren't the only game in town! Another option is EMS (Eastern Mountain Sports, ems.com), another U.S. company, similar to REI. They usually have backpacks $10–20 USD cheaper than REI, though REI allows you to buy a membership that saves you 20 percent off your purchase. The company MEC (Mountain Equipment Co-Op, mec.ca) is the Canadian equivalent of these two companies. Moreover, any large sporting goods store will have a good selection of backpacks to choose from.

In the end, you have to try on a variety of backpacks to see which one is the perfect fit for you and which matches the size needs of your trip. Just go with what feels right. After trying out a lot of packs and even road testing a few, I found the best backpacks meet a lot of the above criteria.

7

Travel Insurance

I'**VE** been a scuba diver ever since a fellow travel writer told me if I didn't stop being afraid of going, he would make fun of me to all the other travel writers out there. In the face of potential public embarrassment, I gave in and I *loved* it. I was a fool for waiting so long. Recently, while in Thailand, I sought to share my joy of diving with friends. On the last day of their dive course, I joined them, and unable to equalize the pressure in my ears properly, I popped my left eardrum. It was a minor injury (I can still hear), but the hospital bills and medicines ended up costing me a couple of hundred dollars. However, because I had purchased travel insurance, I was fully reimbursed.

You never know what accident or illness could happen while you are traveling, and most regular health insurance plans don't cover you overseas. Purchasing insurance in case you get sick is a smart move—you don't want to take risks with your health.

Before you purchase travel insurance, be sure to check if your current medical coverage extends to overseas travelers. Generally, it doesn't, which is why the travel insurance industry is so big. I've yet to find a general health plan that covers people overseas unless they buy a separate policy, but with so many different insurers and policies around the country, it's simply smart to double-check.

Additionally, check your credit card to see if you have insurance coverage for goods you buy. Many credit cards, especially travel rewards cards, provide you with trip cancellation insurance in case something goes wrong. Be sure to check what is and is not covered by your plan. Forgoing normal travel insurance might leave you exposed if your credit card doesn't cover everything.

After you have checked to see what is and is not covered by your existing companies, start shopping around for travel insurance to make up the difference. As you can imagine, there are many options to choose from. This is a multibillion-dollar industry and there are a lot of names out there.

While many people think "I'm healthy, I don't need travel insurance. I won't get sick," travel insurance is much more than just medical protection. It covers you when your camera breaks, your flight is canceled, a family member dies and you have to come home, or if something is stolen. It is much more than just health insurance, and for the little money it costs per day, you're foolish not to get it.

Travel insurance is something you need on the road. You never know what could happen, and most health plans won't cover you overseas. I never thought I would pop my eardrum while I was scuba diving or break my camera in Italy. My friend never thought he would break his leg hiking or that another friend's father would die and she would have to fly back home.

Travel insurance was there when all those things happened. It is something you hope you never have to use, and with plans costing just a few dollars per day, in my view, it's foolish to not get it. I would rather hedge my bets and not be stuck with a giant hospital bill.

Travel insurance is one of the most complex and confusing aspects of trip planning. With the myriad available plans and companies, people can easily get confused about what they should get and why.

The most important part of travel insurance is medical coverage. If your current health plan doesn't cover you overseas, travel insurance is a must. It's the only way you will be able to get care on the road without paying a large hospital bill. Medical evacuations can cost hundreds of thousands of dollars.

I've had to fix my eardrum on the road. My friend Matt broke his leg so badly while hiking in New Zealand that he was hospitalized for a week. I've known people who needed medicine while traveling when their prescription ran out. Even though many countries have socialized medicine, doctors still cost money, and as a foreigner you aren't often able to receive the free or subsidized treatment locals get.

In order to ensure I am covered for any accident and receive the care I need, when I purchase travel insurance, I make sure my policy has two important medically related features:

First, make sure they have a high coverage limit on your medical expenses. Most good travel insurance companies provide up to $100,000 USD in coverage care, though more expensive policies will cover you for higher amounts. The maximum coverage limits you can find are around $1,000,000 USD. High coverage limits are important because if you get really sick or injured and need serious attention or long-term treatment, you want to make sure your high hospital bills are covered. The worst thing you can do is go cheap and get a policy with a $20,000 USD coverage limit, break a leg, and use that limit up in a surgery. Don't be cheap with your health.

Also make sure your medical coverage includes your hospital stay and will cover any preexisting conditions you might have (travel insurance usually does, but with insurance companies, you never want to assume anything).

Second, make sure your insurance policy covers emergency evacuation. For example, if you are hiking out in the woods and break your leg, your travel insurance should cover your evacuation to a hospital. If a natural disaster happens and you need to be evacuated to somewhere else, your insurance should also cover you. This protection usually covers an expense of up to $300,000 USD.

Emergency evacuation also means evacuation from the hospital to your home country. Standard emergency evacuation usually includes this provision, but it's important you double-check that your insurance company will cover the cost of your flight back home if needed.

Beyond covering medical emergencies (which is really the main reason to get insurance), travel insurance offers other benefits. It can cover lost or stolen property, provide other emergency services, and offer trip cancellation protection. Here are additional criteria to look for when choosing your insurance provider:

Coverage for travel to most countries in the world. Make sure the insurance provider covers all the countries you are visiting.

Insurance companies will have a list of the countries excluded from their policy (usually war zones and countries listed by the government as "not safe"). If you are traveling to those countries, your policy will not cover you while you are there. Read the list of covered countries.

Twenty-four-hour emergency services and assistance. After all, you don't want to get sick and find out you need to "call back during normal business hours" for help.

Coverage for lost, damaged, or stolen possessions. If your backpack full of clothes gets stolen or falls off the back of a bus in Brazil, it's important to know that your travel insurance will give you money to buy new supplies so you aren't stuck with just the clothes on your back.

Cancellation protection. For things such as hotel bookings as well as flights and other transportation bookings.

Family emergency coverage. If your mother or another family member suddenly gets ill or dies and you need to go home, you'll want to know that there is coverage available so the flight home will be paid for. As Dawn from wanderingwhy.com states, "While we were in Thailand, my father passed away unexpectedly. I called my insurance carrier, World Nomads, before I bought my ticket home to the States. They told me to go ahead and buy the ticket, and we would sort out the details when I got home. Once things settled down at home, I called them and filled out a form online, and although it did take numerous phone calls, I did receive a check for my plane fare prior to my return to Thailand."

Personal accident coverage.

Coverage for legal expenses if incurred.

Financial protection. If the tour company or airline you're using goes bust (and this happens a lot, especially with airlines), ensure you're covered up to $10,000 USD. This is a relatively new addition to some policies, so you might have to shop around to find it.

On the subject of electronics, most travel insurance companies only cover a small amount, usually up to $500 USD as part of their basic coverage. You can often buy supplemental insurance for a higher amount. For instance, Clements Insurance (clements.com) offers special coverage for your electronics. Prices vary depending on the country you visit (between $145 USD and $195 USD per plan), but they don't offer insurance for the whole world. You have to get coverage for your specific country. World Nomads Insurance, one of the most popular companies in the world, only covers up to $500 USD, but you can purchase a supplemental plan to cover more expensive electronics, and they cover a trip around the world.

Many regular insurance companies and home insurance companies such as State Farm offer plans that can help you cover your electronics. If you already have homeowner's insurance, there is a possibility some of your gear is covered if it is already specified in your existing policy. If your travel insurance doesn't have a high coverage amount for electronics and you aren't covered via your homeowner's insurance, consider buying supplemental insurance.

It's also important to know what is not covered by your plan.

Travel insurance policies do not cover accidents sustained while participating in extreme adventure activities, such as hang gliding, paragliding, or bungee jumping, unless you pay extra. The vast majority of insurance companies won't cover you if you injure someone on the road (called third-party liability).

If you are drunk and fall out of a window, most travel insurance companies won't cover you because you were drunk and that would be considered recklessness. As would being under the influence of drugs. All policies may become void if you are under the influence. If you book a trip somewhere but then decide to cancel it because of conflict, unless there has been a State Department warning that advises travelers to stay away, your trip cancellation insurance won't cover you. You decided not to go not because your destination was officially declared dangerous. Knowing these exclusions will become very important when you decide to make a claim.

Every insurance company is different, and you should look around to see what companies offer and which are best for your trip. For that, I highly recommend the website Insure My Trip (insuremytrip.com). They compare insurance policies for more than twenty insurance providers, and because they let you compare plans in a grid layout, it's easy to see exactly what each company covers. You'll be able to compare medical coverage limits, emergency evacuation coverage, trip cancellation coverage, dental coverage, disaster coverage, and everything else under the sun.

Some of the most popular travel insurance companies include STA Travel Insurance (statravel.com), World Nomads (worldnomads .com), MedEx (medexassist.com), MedjetAssist (medjetassist.com), and IMG (imglobal.com).

Generally, insurance will run you between $600 USD and $1,000 USD per year for a single person. Your policy will begin the day you specify when you purchase the insurance.

Canadians will find a plethora of companies available to them. Most banks offer their own travel insurance, and there are many province-specific companies. Some good ones are April International, BMO (Bank of Montreal), GMS (Group Medical Services), International SOS, TIC Travel Insurance, Travel CUTS Bon Voyage, and World Escapade. Check out the insurance comparison site Kanetix before you buy.

In the UK, some of the best companies include 1 Stop Travel Insurance, Cheap Travel Insurance, Columbus Direct, Direct Line, and World First.

Making a Claim

If you make a claim, remember that any travel insurance company, no matter how good, is there to make money and will try to avoid paying out as much as they can. In order to ensure that you do get paid for your claim, make sure you have all your receipts and necessary forms. Be sure to keep a receipt for all the money you paid, so you can have proper documentation. Receipts, police reports, and official letters—all of this will help make your claim go by a lot quicker.

When thinking about her claims process, Dawn recommends this: "Keep a running journal of the dates/times, who you talked to, outcomes of all phone calls, emails sent, and legwork you do on the ground. I found writing everything down was the biggest lifesaver in keeping track of what happened during this time. When you are making a claim, something bad is happening, and your memory will be skewed. Keep track as it is happening."

Remember that travel insurance is not meant to be a health insurance plan. It's not meant to cover you for regular doctor visits, checkups, or replace a normal insurance policy. It's simply meant to help travelers out during emergencies.

I don't think there is one perfect travel insurance company. My personal favorite is World Nomads (worldnomads.com). Based out of Australia, they are a global insurance brand and cover people from around the world. While their insurance policy is similar to those of many of the other companies listed in this section, I enjoy World Nomads for the following reasons: I can purchase and renew my insurance policy online in a matter of minutes; they have a very friendly and responsive staff who answer questions and help solve problems via social media; and they have very positive customer feedback. Moreover, Lonely Planet guidebooks and *National Geographic* also recommend them. I've been using them since I first went away in 2006.

They tend to be more expensive than the other companies (most policies cost around $1,000 USD), but dealing with insurance companies is a hassle. At the end of the day, if all the policies are equal in every way except cost, I am going to choose the company with the best customer service and the one most likely to reimburse me. In my opinion, that's World Nomads.

Picking your travel insurance is going to take some time, and in the end, you should go with the company you feel most comfortable with and the one that gives you the coverage that meets the needs of your specific situation.

Get a Travel Discount Card

TRAVEL discount cards will save you money on hostels, airfare, transportation, and tours. While some are only for students or those younger than twenty-six, there are still quite a few available for anyone, no matter what profession or age. These special discount cards should not be confused with destination tourism cards such as the London Pass, iAmsterdam card, or VisitOslo card, which give you discounts for a specific destination. I'll discuss these cards in far more detail in Part Two. The cards listed in this chapter are more general and can be used around the world for a variety of reasons.

The most widely accepted and best discount cards are in this chapter. Sadly, these cards skew a lot toward students, Australasia, and Europe and are not usable globally. As a general rule, the cheaper the country, the less likely you'll be able to use one of the cards.

ISIC (International Student Identity Card): This student-only card provides discounts on tours, hostels, and transportation.

It can be purchased through their website (isic.org) or through travel agencies like STA Travel. The card costs $22 USD. There is no upper age limit on the card, so you can get one as long as you are a full-time student; it doesn't matter if you are twenty-one or fifty-one. Part-time students aren't allowed to get this card.

There are a total of forty thousand discounts offered with this card, ranging from discounts in museums, reduced booking fees for accommodation sites, free tours, reduced transportation costs, and tour deals. Many airlines offer exclusive student/youth fares to ISIC cardholders. This is truly a great card to have and will definitely help you save money, especially on accommodations and attractions. I have found this card particularly useful in Europe, where museums give you a 50 percent discount with the card. ISIC also offers discounts on magazine subscriptions, Skype credit, and online booking fees from sites like Hostelworld.

If you're not a student, there is also a version of this card for teachers and people under twenty-six (IYC). These cards have the same features and benefits as the ISIC card and are available at STA Travel and isic.org. These cards also cost $22 USD. They are all issued by the same company.

The ISIC card can be used worldwide and is available online. You can also find a local issuer at isic.org/student-card/apply-for -a-card.html.

YHA (Youth Hostel Association): This hostel discount card is good for Hostelling International or Youth Hostels Association members. (Actually it's the same organization that uses two different names depending on where you are in the world!) It provides a 10 percent discount on prices at this worldwide chain of hostels.

This card can be purchased when you check into any YHA member hostel. Prices vary depending on the country in which you purchase the card, and it is always priced in the local currency. Getting your membership in the USA costs $28 USD, while it costs $42 USD to get the same membership in Australia. Since membership is open to everyone, it's best to get your membership in the United States before you travel so you can avoid paying more money for it in other countries. Your membership will be valid worldwide.

The YHA card gives you access to more than four thousand Hostelling International Youth Hostels in more than eighty countries around the world. The card also provides discounts on train passes and bus tours, and members receive basic travel insurance. (Don't get too excited! They only cover $1,400 in medical bills and $1,250 in trip interruption.) Depending on the country you are in, you also receive discounts at local attractions. You'll find a full list available at hiusa.org/member ship/member_benefits.

But the main reason to get the card is for the 10 percent discount on accommodations. You can check out their main international website for more information at hihostels.com.

VIP (General Purpose Discount Card Primarily Used in Australia and New Zealand): This card provides discounts on global tours, travel, and accommodations, but it is mostly used in Australia and New Zealand. You can purchase it at hostels and tour operators throughout Australia and New Zealand or online at vipbackpackers.com.

It has a steep cost at $43 USD, but this card can pay for itself very quickly, and since it is good for multiple countries, you have plenty of chances to recoup your costs. You can generally save $3–4 on accommodations, get free bus tickets, up to 20 percent off tour providers, and much, much more. The VIP membership card also doubles as a rechargeable phone card to make international calls. Since the card is widely accepted among hostels, using it for only eleven nights' accommodation will allow you to recover your costs. Add in 10 percent off tours, which in Australia (see prices in the next section) cost at least $300, and just two tours pay for the card and then some.

BBH Card (Budget Backpacker Hostels): This is a New Zealand hostel card that saves you $2.50 USD when you book at participating hostels. The card costs $37 USD per person, and membership is valid for one year. You can purchase this card online at bbh.co.nz, at New Zealand visitor centers, or at any of the participating hostels in New Zealand.

Most independent hostels and guesthouses in New Zealand are members of this organization, so if you are staying awhile, you will find that it will quickly pay off as you move from place to place. Members also get special discounts at around one hundred tour and activity operators in the country. You can find the latest discount offers on their website at bbh.co.nz/bbh_Club CardDeals.aspx.

Nomad Card: The Nomad MAD Card offers discounts at hostels and on activities and restaurants and is used primarily in

Australia, Fiji, and New Zealand. It is offered through the No-mads Hostel chain and is similar to the VIP card. It costs $37 USD and can be purchased at nomadshostels.com/Buy-your-MAD-card or at any Nomads Hostel in the region.

The card gets between $1 and $3 USD off every night you stay, or stay for six nights and get the seventh night for free. You can also use your card for discounted Internet at the Global Gossip chain in the region, and receive party vouchers worth up to $1,200 USD that include free meals, free drinks, and free club entry. Unlike the VIP, this card is much more focused on Nomads Hostels and their partners.

I strongly recommend getting travel discount cards. The ISIC card and its youth and teacher counterparts will get you many discounts around the world. When I was eligible for them, I loved getting 50 percent off museums, tours, and public transportation. These cards will also get you discounts throughout the world. In Australia and New Zealand, those discount cards saved me hundreds of dollars because I used them for all the tours and activities I took part in, which, as you'll see soon enough in their respective sections, are not cheap (on average $300 USD or more).

These cards allow travelers to get discounts at a wide variety of places and should not be overlooked. Saving every penny counts.

9

What to Do with Your Stuff

BEFORE you go, you'll find yourself walking through your house looking at all your possessions, wondering what you are going to do with them all. You can't take it with you. If you are going on a long trip, you can store your things in a public storage locker, but that costs money. I've found the best solution is simply to sell everything you own. While I know that seems like a huge undertaking, you'll see in this chapter that there are many ways to get rid of your stuff and lighten your load. It simply takes time. When you come back, you'll find you have a new appreciation for simplicity, and you'll be amazed at how much stuff you had that you didn't really need—so sell everything. I used to have so much stuff. Now, when I do go home, I find myself needing less stuff than I did before. You just learn to live without. That might not be good for everyone, but at the very least, selling your stuff provides you with money for your trip.

There are many websites out there that can help you sell your stuff. In the United States, the best and most famous site is probably Craigslist (craigslist.com). You can buy and sell anything there, and I used it to get rid of my stuff before I traveled. In the UK and Australia, the equivalent site is Gumtree (gumtree.com), while in New Zealand their Craigslist equivalent is trademe.co.nz. Moreover, you can always sell things on eBay (ebay.com) or have a garage sale.

If you do want to keep your stuff and can't store it at someone else's home or keep it in your own home while you rent it out, you can rent a public storage locker, though again, this costs money. Storage companies like Public Storage (publicstorage.com) start at $35 USD per month. That's money you could be spending on your trip.

Whatever your choice, try to minimize as much as possible. This not only reduces the amount of stuff you have to store but it frees your mind. No one wants to be worrying about a TV or computer or paying that storage bill while hiking through the mountains of Nepal.

What to Do with Bills and Mail

Sometimes we can't get rid of all our bills. When we go on the road long-term, we ideally lose lots of bills—car payments, insurance, rent, phone bills, and cable. However, there might be loans or debt you have to pay off that you just can't get away from. I am still paying off my student loans, albeit slowly and with small payments. Even if we can't get rid of our bills, we can still make our life easier and give ourselves fewer headaches. Most people use automatic bill pay these days. I use it for everything. My student loan is automatically deducted from my bank account each month. I don't worry about cutting a check.

Moreover, I only use one credit card on the road. I used to use a few, but I found I was always missing deadlines. By tying everything to one card, you'll make it much easier to remember to pay your bill while on the beaches of Thailand than if you try to remember to pay all sorts of different bills when all you really want to do is lie on a beach.

Even if you have a home and mortgage that needs to be paid, you can still set up automatic bill payment. As Sean Lynch from wanderingwhy.com told me, "There are some programs that allow you to pay your mortgage using your credit card. We didn't go with this option. Most online banking today includes a 'bill-pay' service of some sort. We were able to plan our budget for the time we were gone, set the money aside, and set up automatic payments for the bills each month. Occasionally we would log on from the road and make sure things were still humming along."

This is something the James family, who were mentioned in Chapter 2, also dealt with before their round-the-world trip: "Our mortgage—and our other regular bills—were on autopay. We left deposit slips for our renter to deposit rent checks directly into our account. Craig's brother helped manage other bills—our renter would forward any bills to him and he would email us to let us know about them."

With the prevalence of electronic banking these days, you'd be hard-pressed to find a company that wouldn't let you set up automatic payments.

As for your mail, well, chances are you won't get much. After you automate all your bills, sign up for paperless statements. This will send all bills to your email instead of piling up at your parents' house or a forwarding address. I find now the only time I ever get mail sent to my parents' home (which is my legal mailing address) is when I sign up for a new credit card, or I am getting junk mail I never asked for. It makes my life a lot easier and far less complicated. If you do find you are getting mail about important things that need to be taken care of, ask a trusted friend or family member to help. I've made my parents users on my credit cards to troubleshoot any problems. If you have a friend or relative you trust, you can make that person an official user on all your important accounts to help.

If you really do need your mail, you can sign up for the service Earth Class Mail (earthclassmail.com). Earth Class Mail scans your mail and lets you decide what you want to do with it. In the email they have a scanned image of the envelope and a link to your account. From there, you can decide what you want to do with the mail: scan (they open and scan all pages), ship (they send it to wherever you want), recycle (they put it in the recycling bin, unopened), or shred. The basic service starts at just $9.95 USD per month.

Bills and mail should be the least of your problems when planning your trip. In our modern electronic era, it is very easy to automate your bills and get rid of your mail.

PART TWO

On-the-Road Expenses

The Savings Mind-Set

S AVING money on the road requires breaking away from the conventional mind-set that travel is expensive and that we need to stay in hotels, eat at world-class restaurants, and go on package tours to have a good time.

When we are home, we live within our means. If life was as expensive as we think travel is, it would be just as hard to get by at home as it would be while on the road. We couldn't afford it. We spend less money than we earn because we know the consequences of not doing so. So why shouldn't we do the same when we travel? People in the destinations you visit live a day-to-day lifestyle similar to yours back home. Folks in Paris aren't staying in hotels or eating five-star gourmet meals every night. They cook and shop at markets just like you. You don't need to splurge every day in order to "experience the culture." In fact, if you want to truly experience life in a particular region, you do the exact opposite—live frugally, just like the locals.

Under the logic of the travel industry, if you spend a lot of money, you will have a wonderful time, and if you don't, you'll have a crappy time. A cheap holiday is a horrible holiday. But that's not true. That same line of thought would imply that if we don't spend lots of money at home, we can't be happy. We know that isn't true either.

We need to look for value when we travel. It's about not taking the first offer you see. It's about doing research and planning. It may be more work than just jet-setting off to some exotic destination, but it will help you save and stop wasting money on the road.

Part Two of this book teaches you the tricks and tips needed to get into the savings mind-set. Once you know a few basic tricks, you can easily spot the deals, and finding them becomes second nature to you.

Why You Need to Budget If You Don't Want to Go Home Early

Once you're on the road, you're going to have a lot of opportunities to spend money. If you aren't careful, you'll quickly find that you've busted your budget. Travel is filled with temptation. There's always some activity to enjoy, a new restaurant to try, or people looking to drag you to the nearest bar. Travel can suck your money out of your wallet like a vacuum cleaner.

Making your money last is as much about knowing how you spend as it is about knowing how to find good travel deals. The way to do that is to be smart and realistic about how you spend money— because it all starts with the budget.

When I travel, I don't budget a lot of money for accommodations, tours, or even transportation. I find the cheapest accommodation or

I use services that let me stay with locals for free. I don't take a lot of tours and I walk almost everywhere. I budget a lot of money for food and drinks because that's what I want to enjoy the most. I didn't spend every night at home so I could fly to Australia and not go out or head to France to make meals in my hostel. No, not me. I came to live. I came to eat and drink in the culture. I have no problem sleeping on someone's floor if it means I can have a nice meal.

I know what I like, what I want, and how I spend. Because of that, I can set realistic spending goals relating to my trip.

Sure, there will always be something you didn't predict. I didn't predict having to buy a new camera after falling into the ocean with mine or taking a last-minute flight to Fiji from New Zealand to meet friends. I didn't expect to learn how to scuba dive in Fiji. Stuff happens on the road. That's just the way it is.

But you can anticipate a lot of your costs if you know what you want to spend money on. I too often hear: "Wow! That tour is so expensive. I blew my budget." Or "I didn't expect to drink so much!" Or "This place is more expensive than I thought." My response to these statements is "Why? What did you expect to do on the road?" If you do your research well, you will know exactly how much things cost and you can plan your budget accordingly. And if you know yourself well, you will know how you will spend your money.

I write down in a journal everything I spend money on. This way you can keep track of what you are spending so you know when you are going over your budget and when you need to cut back. The people who have to go home early are always the ones who have no idea how much money they are spending on the road.

In the following chapters, I will lay out some general travel tips that can be applied to a trip of any length and to any destination.

These tips will help you stay on the budget you just created. While a lot of this book is about taking an extended break around the world, the tips in the upcoming chapters are universal—it doesn't matter if you are taking a two-week trip to Madrid or a two-month trip through South America.

Because once you are in the savings mind-set, you can find deals for every type of vacation.

11

Tips for Saving Money on Accommodations

ACCOMMODATIONS are one of the biggest day-to-day expenses you'll have. Cutting that cost down can have the greatest impact on your budget. You can always spend a night on the train, follow the rule that the more beds in a room, the cheaper it is, or try to stay with your grandmother's friend's cousin to save money. But if those don't appeal to you, here are some other ways to save money:

Hospitality Exchange

The best way to save on accommodations is to not have to pay for accommodations—and a hospitality exchange does exactly that. Hospitality exchange services connect travelers with locals who offer a free place to stay—no strings attached. Sometimes it's a bed, sometimes it's a couch, and sometimes it's literally just space on the ground.

These sites work by having users sign up, create profiles, and connect with one another with the expectation that one day, those who will be hosted will pay it forward and host someone else. You don't necessarily have to host anyone in the future, but most people find the experience of being hosted rewarding and do want to host someone else in return.

There are four major hospitality exchange organizations:

Couchsurfing (couchsurfing.com): Founded January 2004, this is the largest exchange, with more than 3 million members in seventy thousand cities. Membership is free and you create a comprehensive user profile about yourself (like Facebook, except public). Other users can leave public reviews and recommendations on your profile. The majority of users on this site are in their twenties and thirties.

Servas (joomla.servas.org): This is the oldest hospitality exchange in the world. Servas was created in 1949 and is actually recognized by the United Nations. Unlike Couchsurfing, participation in Servas requires two letters of reference, a membership fee, and a personal interview with a local Servas coordinator. After the interview, the traveler gets a "letter of introduction" that's good for one year of travel, and a list of hosts in the country the traveler is visiting. There are about thirteen thousand members in Servas, who are primarily baby boomers and senior travelers.

Hospitality Club (hospitalityclub.org): Founded in 2000, Hospitality Club is the second-biggest hospitality exchange, with around 450,000 members. Membership is free, but to register, a member must provide his or her full name and address, which gets verified by a team of volunteers to ensure you aren't a crazy psycho killer. As with Couchsurfing, you can leave reviews that are visible to the public.

Global Freeloaders (globalfreeloaders.com): Started in 2005, this website has about thirty thousand users and has a particularly strong user base in Australia. Membership is free, but you are required to host someone within six months of being hosted.

Camp in My Garden (campinmygarden.com): This UK-based community started in April 2011 and features home campsites around the world. Its simple premise: Connect campers to people who will let them camp in their backyards for free or a small fee. You have to bring your own camping gear but most properties will let you use their facilities (no peeing behind a bush!). Locations are found predominantly in the UK and Europe but the site is gaining traction around the world.

While all the sites market the same service, I use Couchsurfing over all the others. It has the largest membership base, the most active members, the best user interface, strong levels of verification, and the biggest range of nationalities. While I love the fact that I can get free accommodations, what draws me to the site over and over again is that I get to experience the local side of a city. I get taken to local parties, gatherings, restaurants, and sites that aren't in any guidebook. I get to learn about Australian politics while in Australia, experience a Danish family's Sunday dinner in Copenhagen, and be taken to a German rock show in Munich because of the people I meet through Couchsurfing.

People are often scared to use these services because they are concerned about safety. I understand that concern. There you are, in a new city, with all your stuff—in a stranger's home. What if they try to murder you in your sleep? What if they steal your stuff? What if they are rude or smell? However, I've found that people who are willing to open their homes to strangers tend to be very open-minded and friendly people and are also usually former travelers themselves. They know what you are going through. They want to help. They want to show you their city and what makes it special. And, anyway, you never really know who has the key to your room in a hotel or hostel. You are always trusting a stranger. I figure, why not trust a stranger who thinks the way I do?

Couchsurfing is also aware of this security concern and takes many steps to provide safety. It offers its own verification system where you confirm your identity with a credit card and a letter (which you have to return) to your listed address. Moreover, users can leave comments on people's profiles talking about their experience and friendship with those people. If someone is a creep, liar, or weirdo, you are going to be able to find out. Benny Lewis of Fluentin3months.com, who has hosted more than two thousand couch-surfers, says references are very important: "If a person on the site has at least three references, then you know you can trust them."

When I am looking for a Couchsurfing host, I use the following criteria to ensure that my host is a legitimate person:

- There has to be a picture with the profile so I can see that this is a real person who is interested in showing his or her face.

- The profile has to be filled out completely, as it shows the person is interested and involved. Most people aren't going to spend the time to fill this out if they aren't going to be comfortable with strangers in their home. If someone hasn't bothered to fill out a profile, that person probably doesn't use the site often.

- There should be reviews from other users. If other people have stayed with or have at least traveled with the host and had a good experience, you and your stuff will probably be fine. You might not get along with the host, but at least you know the person isn't a creep. The more positive reviews, the better.

- Though not necessary, I do like it when people have gotten verified by Couchsurfing. Knowing that a person has been verified reduces the likelihood that they are going to be a crazy psycho killer. However, if someone hasn't gone through the verification process but has a lot of positive reviews, that's OK with me.

After I've found a host, I send an email letting the host know information about me, why I think we would have a good time together, and the dates I would be in the city. I also tell the host I'm a good cook and in return will cook a meal. That wins a lot of people over. (Side note: I am actually a good cook!) When I do this, I tend to email five to ten potential hosts to compensate for the fact that some people just might not respond and others might be busy and say no.

You can also find a host at the last minute, but it's better to ask in advance so hosts have a chance to plan for your arrival. Try to ask at least a week in advance of your arrival if not more. There are groups on these websites for emergency situations if you need a couch last-minute, but unless it's a big city with a lot of hosts, I've rarely found success with them.

All the rules above apply to all the hospitality sites, not just Couchsurfing.

No matter what, you need to use your own judgment when picking a host from a hospitality exchange. You can talk with hosts over email to get a feel for them and their expectations. If it doesn't seem right, don't do it! But once you use a hospitality exchange for the first time, you'll see that there was really nothing to fear after all.

Farm Work

World Wide Opportunities on Organic Farms (wwoof.org) or WWOOFing, is a service that matches people looking for work on farms with farmers who are looking for labor. It's more a loose affiliation of like-minded groups using the same name than one large international organization. In order to become a WWOOFer, you will need to sign up for the national organization in the country you want. There is no international WWOOF membership, so you'll have to buy a membership from each WWOOFing country's organization. Annual membership usually costs around $30 USD per country.

There are currently ninety-nine countries that participate in the WWOOFing program worldwide. There is no central database on the number of farms, as each country maintains its own list. By visiting the website of the umbrella organization, you can get access to the national chapter you need.

You don't need any previous experience in farming to do this—just a desire to work. Bethany Salvon from beersandbeans.com spent time WWOOFing in Serbia and Italy and says: "We did not have any experience on farms or as WWOOF volunteers before our first farm in Italy. Most WWOOFers we have met have no experience at all—

they are simply interested in learning more about organic farming and they have a desire to help out local farmers."

Moreover, you don't just get your hands dirty on the farm. You do a number of chores. As Nora Dunn of theprofessionalhobo.com describes her experience, "Although the WWOOF acronym implies work on organic farms, the opportunities and responsibilities vary well beyond gardening at many places. Where I volunteered for over six months, I did everything from cooking for large groups of people, to cleaning lodges, to promotional work, and only occasionally did I get my hands dirty in the garden or tend to the expansive nature trails."

If you don't want to join WWOOFing but still want to work on a farm, the best way around membership is to simply show up in an area you want to work in, find a hostel, and ask about nearby farms that take volunteers. Since most WWOOFers are travelers, hostels in regions popular with WWOOFing keep track of which farms take volunteers. Ask them where you should go. This method was used by Nora Dunn successfully in New Zealand, when she didn't want to pay the membership fee but still wanted to work on a farm.

Once you sign up for the program in the country you want, you will receive a booklet of all the authorized WWOOFing farms in that country with information about the farms and ways to contact them. All you have to do is contact the farms that interest you, discuss with the host, and make arrangements for your arrival and duration of stay. There is no formal contract involved and you are free to leave anytime you want. You will simply be required to work for around five hours per day for five days a week (you get weekends off!). The whole process is relatively straightforward.

Name Your Own Hotel Price

There are a number of websites that give you last-minute deals on rooms or let you name your own price, saving you up to 60 percent off the normal rate. These websites include LateRooms (late rooms.com), Last Minute (lastminute.com), Hotel Tonight (hotel tonight.com), Priceline (priceline.com), and Hotwire (hotwire.com).

I find Priceline and Hotwire to be the best, as they have the largest inventories and the lowest prices. My searches on the other websites don't yield as many results. A search on Priceline for New York City came up with 398 results while on LateRooms it was 164 and Last Minute came back with 177 results.

Hotwire and Priceline have two booking sections: one that lets you bid on hotel rooms like an auction and another for discounted hotels. In the auction side of the websites, you choose your city, the location within the city you want to stay in (you can choose), the class of service you want (one-star, two-star, three-star, etc.), and the price you want to bid.

For example, say you want a three-star hotel in Chicago for $100 USD. You place your bid, and if Priceline finds a match, they book you into a hotel of that class, and after the money is received they will tell you the name (you can't find out beforehand—it's a blind auction). If the site doesn't find a match, it will let you search again with a different bid, up to three times. After that, you'll have to search again in different areas or try again in twenty-four hours.

Hotwire uses a different but similar system. Instead of letting you bid on a hotel, its "Hotwire Hot Deals" gives you a price for a hotel in a location of the city you desire. So instead of seeing "Hilton New York City" you would see under Hotwire Hot Deals "5 star hotel in Midtown East Manhattan for $150." You don't know where in Midtown East the hotel is or what the name is. Hotwire will tell you a list of some hotels in that class they have, but in general, it's a crapshoot. You don't know exactly what you are going to get until you book.

Despite the risks associated with booking an unknown hotel, I've never had a problem such as getting stuck with a bedbug-ridden flea trap, and I quite like the fact that you can get hotels up to 60 percent off their listed price.

If you are going to bid, I also recommend the website Better Bidding (betterbidding.com). Better Bidding has a forum in which people post their most recent successful bids and the current hotel deals each site has. This lets you know the going rate so you don't overbid and end up paying double what the guy next door to you paid. Using Better Bidding to find hotel prices in New York City, I got a room in Times Square during the Christmas season for $90 USD per night. You don't need to be a member of the forums in order to see the bids other people placed, but you do need to be a member to post on the forum. There are two other sites that do the same, Bidding on Travel (biddingtraveler.com) and Bid on Travel (bidontravel.com), but they focus exclusively on Priceline.

The second side of Priceline and Hotwire allows you to book discounted hotels as on any other hotel booking website. You won't get the substantial savings you get by bidding, but you will get to know where you are staying. The rates on Priceline and Hotwire are comparable to the other booking sites mentioned, as well as the widely known Hotels.com (hotels.com).

Like the airline websites discussed in Part One, every hotel search engine is different. While both Priceline and Hotwire have a large inventory and good prices, LateRooms and Last Minute have really good inventory in Europe. Just like you need to check many airline websites, it's good to just double-check prices on at least three sites before making your purchase.

House-Sitting

House-sitting is exactly like it sounds—while someone else is on holiday, you watch their house and take care of any pets they have while they are gone. The biggest house-sitting websites are:

House Carers (housecarers.com): One of the largest of these sites on the Internet, with a strong inventory in Australia and New Zealand. They've been around for more than ten years. Membership fee is $50 USD.

Mind My House (mindmyhouse.com): A smaller site with a better user interface and lower membership fee ($20 USD), this site has a strong inventory in Europe, the United States, and Australia.

The Caretaker Gazette (caretaker.org): Founded in 1983, this is an online and print newsletter that publishes a classified-style listing of jobs. It is the oldest and largest house-sitting organization. Membership begins at $29 USD per year.

House-sitters pay a $20–50 USD registration fee on the sites that list houses and create a profile and fill in security information. You're then able to search for houses in your destination and contact the owners. After you and an owner have come to an agreement, you sign a legal form with the terms and conditions you both agree to. (This form protects all parties in case something goes wrong. After all, you don't want someone to say you stole something when you didn't or have the homeowner be unable to get back damages because you broke a window.) Additionally, you should ask to be connected with any previous house-sitter so you know what you can expect from the home and homeowner. In many ways, house-sitting is like a job, and you want your employer to be pleasant and not a jerk.

House-sitting commitments tend to be long-term (that is, a month or more) and are suited for travelers who want to stay a longer time in one specific place. Nora Dunn from theprofessionalhobo .com uses house-sitting regularly to save money: "One of my specialties is house-sitting around the world, and I have done it in six countries on three continents—and counting. In exchange for free accommodation you are charged with keeping an eye on the house in the homeowners' absence, and sometimes caring for pets, gardens, farm animals, or performing other chores."

If you are going to house-sit, it is important to make sure you do your research to ensure the home is in the location you want and that your responsibilities are spelled out. Nora advises you to "be sure to determine exactly what your responsibilities will be before you agree. In one case I was charged with the care of three big dogs and a large house and garden, and although I loved the position, it was a lot of work; in retrospect, I should have been paid a stipend, given my daily time commitment and the money the homeowners were saving by not having to put their dogs into a kennel and hire a gardener." That is why the legal contract is so important—it spells out your responsibility.

Of her experience, Nora says, "House-sitting is a fabulous way to experience the comforts of 'home' on the road, often for extended periods of time."

Hostels

Hostels are one of the cheapest forms of paid accommodation in the world. Hostels are places that offer shared (and sometimes private) rooms for travelers looking for cheap rooms. For the most part these rooms are dormitories that have between four and twenty beds in them. The more beds, the cheaper the room.

Hostel prices are about a third less than a hotel room. A cheap hotel in New York City is $100 USD while a hostel room is $30 USD. In Thailand, where a hotel is $30 USD or more, you can get a cheap hostel room for $5 USD. In Australia, a hostel room is $25 USD versus $110 for a hotel.

Hostels have a bad reputation in America. We think of them as being filled with dirty, stinky dorm rooms with bad beds and no security. Or we view them as places from movies like *Hostel* where we are going to get kidnapped and end up in some sick twisted medical experiment.

One of my favorite travel movies is *A Map for Saturday.* When the star and director, Brook Silva Braga, reaches Europe, his friends come to visit. In an interview, one of his friends asks, "Why would you want to stay at hostels? You have to worry about your stuff all the time." Brook responds that hostels have lockers, and his friend admits he didn't know that. I think that is emblematic of people's perception of hostels. In America we just don't know a lot about hostels. We don't have a big backpacking culture, and instead of cheap hostels, we have Motel 6. Thus, what we think about hostels comes from what our parents told us when they traveled in the 1960s and what we see in movies.

It's true that hostels are composed of dorm rooms, but the popular American assumptions end there. The beds can be quite comfortable, there is wi-fi in most hostels, free breakfast, hot showers, bars, individual lockers for your stuff (don't have a lock? you can rent one from the hostel!), and bed lights to read at night. The vast majority of hostels have common rooms with pool tables and kitchens. It is a growing rarity that hostels don't have some sort of communal space these days. They also help you book and organize tours.

Sure, there are still dirty hostels out there, just like there are dirty hotels. You get what you pay for after all. But so long as you are staying at a highly rated hostel (and you can see hostel ratings on the booking sites listed in Appendix A), you'll be staying in a clean and comfortable place.

Hostels are the best way to save money on accommodation if you are going to pay for it. Dorm rooms are cheaper than any hotel, and while hostels aren't free like Couchsurfing or house-sitting, if you are one person in a big city, a hostel in somewhere like Paris is going to be markedly less expensive than a hotel.

You can book hostels via the two largest booking sites: Hostelworld (hostelworld.com) and Hostelbookers (hostelbookers.com). I prefer Hostelworld, as they have a larger inventory of hostels and a better booking interface.

Apartment Rentals

One option for group travelers, or even people traveling alone but not interested in hostels, is apartment rentals. Such rentals are apartments owned, furnished, and taken care of by someone else and that you rent like a hotel room. People list an extra room, couch, or property they own and want to make money from. It's like Couchsurfing, except you pay for it and get your own space. There are many companies in the world that will help you find these apartments, such as:

9flats (9flats.com): With about thirty thousand listings, 9flats has a good inventory that is particularly strong in Europe but weaker worldwide.

Airbnb (airbnb.com): The largest apartment website out there, with a strong inventory throughout the world. It is the most popular and has the largest variety of room offerings.

Homeaway (homeaway.com): One of the oldest and largest rental companies, with a strong global presence and a focus more on renting whole apartments and houses than single rooms.

Roomorama (roomorama.com): An emerging company with a strong presence in Europe, the United States, and Canada, with listings in more than three thousand cities.

Wimdu (wimdu.com): Airbnb's largest competitor, with listings in more than one hundred countries, they have the second-largest inventory in the world and have a strong focus on small apartments, bed-and-breakfasts, and single rooms.

Apartment rental prices depend on a number of factors: distance from the city center, competition on the site (lots of choices equals better prices), size, and amenities. Prices can be as little as $20 USD per night or as high as $200 USD per night. Generally, a single room, near a train station, in a city center will cost around $50 USD per night. Larger rooms for groups of three or more will cost from $100.

In order to book an apartment, after searching for and finding a place you like on one of the above websites, you create an account (many of these sites use Facebook Connect and you can sign in with your Facebook account), add your personal information, and book a place. The companies verify your identity and credit card, then connect you with the apartment's owner, who either approves or disapproves you. If the owner approves, your booking is confirmed.

Scams have happened in the past, and companies are now doing a lot of work to ensure that people don't end up robbed, in places that don't look as advertised, or that owners don't end up with renters who steal everything. Safety and security have become chief concerns over the years.

To ensure that your money is safe, payment is always made via the company website and never directly to the property owner. The website holds the money for twenty-four hours after check-in, in case there is a problem, the host doesn't show up, or something is not as advertised. If there is a problem and you leave, the host does not get paid and you get a refund.

To ensure you are safe, these websites require property owners to have complete profiles, photos, and verified addresses and to use their real name, provide telephone numbers, and have a credit card on file. Additionally, they allow users to leave reviews of their stay and rate the property. Homeowners can get verified by the companies with site visits. Just as with the hospitality and home exchange websites, these sites go to great lengths to ensure that everything is aboveboard.

I think these apartment rentals are good for anyone who is spending a long time in a place, and can't afford a week at the Hilton, but doesn't want to spend a week in a hostel either. A rental will be a lot quieter and more relaxing than a hostel. You'll also be able to cook your own food, helping keep costs down on your long trip.

Before you book with one of these sites, make sure you compare the prices from each of the websites, as every one has a different inventory. The inventory on these sites consists of what people decide to put up. One person may list an apartment on Airbnb but not 9flats, so there is no real uniformity among these services like the uniformity often found among hotel booking websites.

12

Tips for Saving Money on Food and Beverages

AFTER accommodations, food is going to be your next largest expense. After all, people need to eat. You can eat cheap canned beans throughout the world if you really want, but if you're looking to actually enjoy the local cuisine, try these methods instead:

Cook Your Meals

A week's worth of groceries is cheaper than a week's worth of restaurants. I generally find that when traveling, I spend about $50–60 USD per week on groceries, as opposed to $20-plus per day at restaurants. That's a reduction of 70 percent in food expenses. Even if you are simply going away for a two-week vacation, consider cooking some of your meals. Food costs add up quick—a snack here and a dinner there and you'll be wasting a lot of money on food. The majority of hostels, guesthouses, and shared apartments have full kitchens where you can cook your meals. (They provide the pots, pans, and utensils too!) Even if you are staying at a hotel without a kitchen, you can still prepare your own food by making sandwiches. However, I recommend trying to stay in a place with kitchen facilities so you can cook some of your meals and reduce your expenses still further.

While we all love to travel to try new food, you don't always need to do so by eating at a restaurant. Supermarkets are a good place to learn about the food of a culture. How people eat, what they eat, and what they don't eat tells much about how they view food, life, and health. In America, our emphasis on big, quick, and easy shows that we aren't foodies as a culture. Food isn't as important as speed. We eat a lot of fast food, prepared meals, and on-the-go food.

Going to the supermarket tells us a lot about the place we visit. What kind of food do people like? What are the local delicacies? You see a lot of fish in Scandinavia, lots of different meats in Austria, packed shelves of wine in France, and a wide vegetable and cured meat section in Italy. In Bangkok, you see a lot of prepared meals with rice. In Australia, it's skewers ready to be thrown on the BBQ. All around the world, the emphasis on food is different.

Lunch Specials

In many parts of the world, especially in Europe, you can dine on dinner menus at lunch-special prices. The "plate of the day" is the best bargain in the world. For example, while I was in Barcelona, I went to eat at the seafood restaurants near the beach. However, dinner was around $50 USD. Yet coming back the next day for the lunch special allowed me to get the same meal for only $20 USD. Another destination that is great for this is Singapore. Singapore is a very expensive place by Asian standards—food here can cost as much as it does in the United States. Yet restaurants here have fixed menus for lunch that cost between $10 USD and $15 USD as opposed to $25 USD for dinner. In England, pubs provide set meals for as low as $10 USD.

Sadly, there is no one website where you can find all the restaurants in the world that offer lunch specials. They vary from city to city and region to region. What you can do other than wander aimlessly around the city in hopes of finding a place (though I have done that) is to ask the tourist office or the staff at your hostel/hotel if they know where to find lunch specials. They are usually very aware of food deals.

Refill Your Water Bottle

You need to stay hydrated when traveling, and buying water every day costs money. Even if a bottle of water only costs $1 USD, assume that you'll buy two per day and suddenly that becomes $60 USD per month for something you can get from the tap for free. Get a metal water bottle or reuse your plastic water bottle a few times to save money. I usually use a plastic water bottle for about four days, more if I can find a place to clean it. Instead of buying three bottles a day, I usually buy two per week. I may only be saving a small amount of money each time, but over the course of a long trip that can really add up. Moreover, it reduces the amount of plastic I use, which is also good for the environment. It's win-win.

Everyone always wonders "Is the tap water safe to drink?" The answer is usually yes. The water in every Western/modern country is safe for consumption. From Singapore to Australia to Japan to

Greece, the water is safe to drink. Heck, you can even drink the water in Costa Rica. The United States doesn't have a monopoly on safe tap water. If you are in doubt, you should always double-check to make sure.

If the tap water in your part of the world is not drinkable, you can use Steripen (steripen.com) to purify your water, save money, and reduce your use of plastic bottles and waste. These products use ultraviolet light to purify water and are small enough to be carried in your pocket. Prices begin at $99 USD. If you are traveling to parts of the world with a lot of unsafe drinking water, I advise getting one of these devices.

Eat with Locals

Just like with hospitality networks, the Internet has allowed people to open their homes for people looking for a culinary delight. Many websites have sprouted up that connect travelers with locals looking to host a dinner party. Eatwith (eatwith.com) lets locals post listings for dinner parties and specialty meals that people can sign up for. There is a fee (each host sets his or her own price), and you can pick from a variety of cuisines (depending on what the host wants to cook). EatWithaLOCAL (eatwithalocal.socialgo.com), Meal Sharing (mealsharing.com), and COlunching (colunching.com) are similar networks worth investigating. The Ghetto Gourmet (theghet.com) is an older version in which locals organize free dinner parties. It's not as widespread, but it's the free option.

Never Eat in a Tourist Area

This is a simple enough tip, but one often forgotten, since we tend to be in these areas because they are where the attractions are. Prices in tourist areas tend to be 20 to 50 percent higher because tourists are often willing to spend more money, since they are away for a short time and unfamiliar with local prices.

Walk away, go explore some side streets, and find a place where you don't hear a lot of English. It's more challenging and more work, but the food is a lot better and you'll be paying the local price instead of the tourist price. While in Barcelona, my friends and I wandered the city away from the touristy La Rambla and found a tapas restaurant. We filled our stomachs for $12 USD each with what would have cost double that on the tourist street La Rambla, where a single dish can be $20 USD.

If you are unsure of where to eat, try smartphone food apps like Yelp (yelp.com) or Urbanspoon (urbanspoon.com). I use them often to find recommendations for food in the cities and towns I visit. If you don't have a smartphone, ask the tourist office or the staff at your hostel/hotel or taxi drivers, who tend to eat at cheaper ethnic stalls. They will have good recommendations. After all, the local staff isn't going to eat in the tourist area.

More important, be sure to ask, "Where do you eat?" not "Where should I eat?" Most people will think to send you to the popular restaurants tourists go to, so by asking where they eat, you will get recommendations for more local restaurants. Small word change, big results.

Tips for Saving Money
on Transportation

EACH region around the world will have its own way to save money on transportation, and the methods vary a lot, but the tips below can be applied to everywhere. For specific destinations, see Part Three.

Take Local Transportation

Forget the private coaches, taxis, and tourist buses—do what the locals do and take buses or trains. It may be easier to get in that tourist bus, as companies will pick you up from your hotel or hostel and take care of any logistics for you, but it's more fun to figure out the local transportation system, and you'll save lots of money by doing so. Even in hyper-expensive countries like Norway or Sweden, the city train is never more than $4 USD. It may take some time to figure out the map and where you need to go, but learning the way is half the fun of traveling, right?

Hostels and hotels have maps and timetables for public transportation. When you arrive at the airport, the information booth will also have timetables for you.

And even if you don't speak the local language, the signs and timetables at the bus stop usually have a price listed. If the price isn't listed, I've never found a bus driver who didn't understand "how much?" or at least a confused look on my face and holding a bill out in front of me!

Get Train Passes

Train passes are offered in many regions of the world and can represent a 50 percent decrease off the price of train tickets. These passes will either allow you a set number of train rides or unlimited rides for the duration of the pass. This option is of particular widespread use in Europe, as discussed in Chapter 13. Rail passes in Australia save close to 70 percent! If you plan on using the train system often, strongly consider a rail pass. Country- and region-specific passes are discussed in Part Three.

Buy Metro Fare Cards

City metro cards provide a considerable discount off buying point-to-point tickets. Even if you are simply going to be in a city for a few days, you can usually buy a set number of tickets for a cheaper price. For example, in Paris you can buy a *carnet* (card) for $16 USD, which is $6 USD less than paying for trips individually. In Bangkok, you can purchase day passes for the subway for $4 USD, for unlimited travel at the cost of four trips individually. In New York City, the metro is

$2.50 USD per ride but a seven-day unlimited-ride pass is only $29 USD.

If I plan to be in a city for more than two days, I ask at the subway station, tourist information, or hostel if fare cards are offered, and if they are, I purchase them. These tickets aren't advertised in tourism offices, as they usually want you to buy their local tourist card instead. I just go into the closest metro station and ask what options are available and select the pass that meets my needs. Never assume just because you aren't in a city long that you can't get one of these cards. They aren't just for commuters!

Share a Ride

Need a ride? Get one with a local! The rise of the sharing economy has made it easier for locals to offer to drive visitors around their city as well as post ride share opportunities. If you are going from Sydney to Melbourne or London to Manchester and want to either share the cost of fuel or ride with someone instead of taking the bus or train, there are websites to help facilitate that:

Liftshare (liftshare.com/uk): UK based

Mitfahrgelegenheit (mitfahrgelegenheit.de): in German

Gumtree (gumtree.com): in the UK, Australia, and New Zealand

Kangaride (kangaride.com): in Canada

BlaBlaCar (blablacar.com): in Europe

In the United States, check out Lyft (lyft.com), Sidecar (side.cr), or Uber (uber.com) and get locals to pick you up and drop you off where you need to go. They are often 30 percent cheaper than a taxi, though rates are "suggested" donations and the companies take a commission. While still predominantly U.S. and Canada based, Uber and Lyft are slowly expanding overseas.

14

Tips for Saving Money on Activities

N0 one wants to spend twenty bucks every time they enter a museum or pay full price for a tour. At those prices, pretty soon all you can afford is to see the museums from the outside. Luckily, you don't have to pay full price all the time. Here's how.

Get Tourism Cards

I will never figure out why travelers don't use tourism cards more often. Local tourism offices (think London Tourism, Paris Tourism, New York Tourism, etc.) issue cards for all their attractions, tours, and restaurants. These cards (which you will have to pay a onetime fee for) give you free entry and substantial discounts on all the attractions and tours in a city, free local public transportation (a huge plus), and discounts at a few restaurants and shopping malls. The cards are typically valid for one, three, five, or seven days. The first day begins when you first use your card, whether that is at a museum or on the train.

In Oslo, Norway, the VisitOslo card offered by the city tourism board costs $60 USD. However, each museum in the city is between $12 USD and $15 USD. I saw nine museums in the city. I saved $30 USD with the pass plus got free public transportation. By buying the Paris museum pass, I saved $85 USD off the normal price.

When I was in London, I used the London Pass. This tourist card cost me $95 USD for two days of sightseeing. (Note: That's more than $50 USD for a day, you say! You're right, but as I mentioned, the $50 USD is a daily average. Some days you spend more, some days you spend less. And while this pass costs $95 USD, it saves you money off what the attractions would cost without it.) It covers more than thirty-two destinations and offers free public transportation. You can get a pass for up to six days for $150 USD. However, I didn't have much time or the desire to see all thirty-two spots. With the pass, I saw the following paid sites:

Westminster Abbey

Tower of London

St. Paul's Cathedral

Ben Franklin House

Britain at War Museum

Shakespeare's Globe Museum

London Tombs

Without this pass, these attractions would have cost me $170 USD. I saved 45 percent by using the London Pass, and I didn't even use it for everything it offers.

I have many examples of when tourism cards saved me money. They may have an up-front cost, but even if they save me just $1 USD, I buy them.

Most travelers never think of these passes because they aren't very well advertised or promoted. I hardly ever used them during my first trip around the world. It was only when I got into travel writing that I learned about them. In fact, I don't think I've ever met a backpacker who has gone out and gotten these. Now, if I know someone is going to see a lot of things, I shake them and say, "Save money; buy a tourist card!" They are the single best way to save money if you plan to do a lot of sightseeing.

Free Museum Days

Most museums have special discount times or free nights. Even famous museums like the Louvre and the Guggenheim offer free entrance. If I don't have a tourism card that offers free entrance into the museum I want, I look up the museum on the Internet to find out which days and times it offers free entrance.

Before you go anywhere, make sure you look on the museum website to find out if they offer free visiting hours.

Use Discount Cards

The discount cards mentioned in Chapter 8 all offer discounts at museums, attractions, and activities throughout the world. It's important to get those cards, since they can be used for a large majority of attractions. As mentioned earlier, these cards can get you 50 percent off regular admission, adding up to a substantial savings over the course of your trip.

Make sure you also visit the local tourist office. They usually have discount cards for major attractions and can let you know what deals are happening at that time. While at the tourist office, take some of those advertisement brochures that offer discounts. Most of them (especially the maps) contain ads for discounted tours and meals.

Local tourist offices can be found at airports, the main train stations, or usually around the city center, where the main tourist attractions are found. When arriving in a new city, head to the information booth at the transportation hub you arrived at and ask where the tourism office is—they will know.

Get a Personal Tour Guide

Connect with local guides and hire them for unique experiences through Vayable (vayable.com). A rating system for the guides allows you to know in advance if the guide/tour is worth your time. I enjoy and like this site because it allows me to experience niche, offbeat, and interesting tours that bigger tour companies might not run (like a street art tour in Los Angeles). Plus the groups tend to be very small, making for a more intimate experience.

* * *

One thing I can't stress enough is that you should always visit the local tourism office. They are going to have up-to-date information on what is going on in a city: free events, festivals, and concerts, for example. That's their job. If you are ever in need of free or cheap activities, be sure to go to the local office and just ask. I always wander into the local tourism office before I start exploring a new city.

PART THREE

Breaking It Down by Region

While there are general travel tips and rules that can apply to every region in the world, there are many tips and tricks that are specific to individual destinations. And while the Internet provides a great resource for finding deals, sometimes tips and tricks only come from experience. You learn them from mistakes and being on the ground.

It is important to keep in mind that each person has a different style of travel, and therefore traveling will not cost the same for everyone. Though some might not prefer the life of a budget traveler, long-term travel requires us to always save money where we can. The costs, the savings, the tips are not set in stone. Some may not apply to you. You may end up spending more money than I list because of how you travel. Some people can travel on a few dollars a day and some need hundreds. The tips and tricks in the sections here represent a framework to start with. The exact dollars you spend in each destination will depend on you.

Secondly, the destinations listed are the ones that most travelers in the world visit and the ones I have visited. I've never been to Central Asia. I have no idea what it is like there. But most travelers don't go there either. Most travelers don't visit much of Africa or spend time in Oman. The destinations and regions of the world were picked because it would be hard to have a book featuring information on the 193 countries in the world.

Appendix A has a complete list of booking websites and tour companies for everything mentioned in the following chapters. If you want to book a hostel in New Zealand or a tour in Thailand or a bed-and-breakfast in Chile, all that information is easily accessible in the appendix.

15

Europe

EUROPE is not a monolithic place, and prices vary greatly depending how far north, east, south, or west you travel. You could spend $70 USD per day in one place and then switch countries and spend $30 the next. While not all of Europe is as expensive as most people believe, it isn't the easiest destination to live on $50 USD a day either. But it isn't impossible. It just takes more work. By balancing expensive countries like France and England with cheaper destinations like Poland, Romania, and Greece, you can keep your daily average low. I spent more than $100 USD per day while visiting friends in Sweden (mostly because they kept taking me to restaurants and clubs), but while exploring Eastern Europe, my daily average was closer to $30 USD per day.

When talking about Europe, I think it is best to break it up into three zones: Western Europe, which consists of mostly Eurozone countries and Great Britain; Eastern Europe (countries of the old

Soviet bloc); and Scandinavia. The countries that are included in each zone tend to be similar in price and in ways to save money.

Western Europe
Eurozone countries, Switzerland, England, Scotland

Western Europe is expensive. High taxes, prices, and high-valued currencies (euro, Swiss franc, British pound) are a deadly combination. You have to be creative to do Western Europe cheaply. While I've had friends get by on as little as $50 USD per day, they had a very tight budget that consisted of not eating out and limited sightseeing.

ACCOMMODATIONS

Hostels
The most popular form of budget accommodation is hostels. Hostels in Europe contain a wide range of amenities—free breakfast, wi-fi, kitchens, common rooms, bars, dorms with their own bathrooms, and tours, just to name a few things. In my opinion, European hostels are some of the best in the world; they foster a great sense of community and go out of their way to organize activities.

Hostel dormitory rooms cost between $26 USD and $39 USD per night, depending on the room's size and the popularity of the hostel. You can find dorm rooms as low as $15 USD per night in Greece, Spain, Portugal, and some parts of Germany. I stayed in a six-bed dorm in Berlin for $16 USD, while the same one would have cost me around $30 USD in Paris. Information about popularity, size, and proximity to the city center can be found on the hostel booking sites mentioned in Chapter 11.

If the idea of a dorm bed isn't appealing to you, the majority of hostels have private rooms, either single rooms for solo travelers or double rooms for couples or travelers who simply want a big bed. These rooms are quite expensive when compared to dorm rooms. For example, a room in Paris is around $83 USD, while in Amsterdam it's roughly $85 USD, Madrid averages $50 USD, and London is about $100 USD. While these rooms are cheaper than staying at a large hotel like the Marriott, I don't recommend using them, as most budget hotels offer better rooms at cheaper prices.

Budget Hotels

Moving up from hostels you'll find "pensións," as they call them in Europe, which are small family-owned budget hotels. They are those indeterminate places you see as you walk around the streets of Europe, the ones that make you think, "I wonder how good that place is."

Rooms typically come with a double bed, a private shower, heat/air-conditioning, and maybe a TV. They are no-frills establishments, and you aren't going to find twenty-four-hour room service. But they will provide a good bed for you to sleep in, privacy, and usually a small breakfast. Rooms typically cost $40–70 USD per night, depending on your location. A room in Paris will cost at the higher end and a room in cheaper Athens will cost at the lower end. While in Rome, I found a lovely place right by the main train station for $40 USD per night, while the hostel nearby had rooms starting at $80 USD. Pensións offer good value and a warm environment.

You can find a lot of these establishments on TripAdvisor

(tripadvisor.com) or via the local tourist office. Because of the fees associated with hotel booking websites, many of these small budget hotels are not on them.

My favorite website for finding hotels in Europe is Eurocheapo (eurocheapo.com). It is an independent review website that goes around and finds small, local guesthouses and budget hotels. I love their selection and include them in all my searches. You should too.

Apartment Rentals

If you are looking for the comforts of home, apartment rentals (furnished apartments) like those found on Airbnb are very common throughout this region of Europe. Apartments usually cost between $30 USD and $100 USD, depending on how many people you have, the size, and its location (the closer to the city center, the more expensive). For example, in London an apartment at the edge of the city can cost around $30 USD for one room. I stayed close to the city center for about $60 USD per night. I had a kitchen where I could prepare my meals, helping to lower my food costs. At a hostel, the cheapest private room was $90 USD.

While apartment rental prices are often on par with hotels and because you can fit a lot of people in an apartment, they work out great for groups on a per-person cost. If you are traveling in a large group, consider renting an apartment over a hotel room or getting a lot of hostel beds.

Camping

Camping is a very popular option in this region, where there are many campgrounds accessible for pitching your tent. You can find campgrounds and RV parks dotting the edges of cities throughout

Europe. Campsites cost between $10 and $15 USD per night per person for a tented space. For example, a campsite on the outskirts of Rome costs about $10 USD per night. In Paris, it is often $15 USD. In London, you'll find prices around $12 USD. If you are traveling by RV or car, expect to pay double that per night. These sites provide toilets, showers, kitchen facilities, and places for your tent (or RV). Some even provide Internet access. You can rent tents at most campsite parks for around $5 USD per night.

If you don't have a tent or don't want to camp, many campsites have dorm rooms and lodges on their grounds. Dorm rooms tend to cost around $15 USD per night, which is still cheaper than a dorm in the city center.

One thing to remember about these campsites is that they are often far from the city center, so if you want to see the city sights, you'll have to pay for transportation to and from the city each day. Make sure these campsites are near a bus or train route so you can conveniently get into the cities you are trying to see. Moreover, be aware, during the winter months, that many campsites shut down because of the weather.

You can find campsites in Western Europe listed on hotel and hostel booking websites like Hostelworld (hostelworld.com), where you can find prices, amenities, and proximity to the city center.

A very good camping service specific to Europe is Camp in My Garden (campinmygarden.com), which allows you to pitch a tent in someone's backyard for free or a nominal fee (around $5). This is a new service that started in 2010, but more and more people are signing up for it each day. All of the garden owners have profiles that tell you what services and facilities they offer. As with home and hospitality exchanges, users and owners create profiles, have photos, and leave reviews on the campsites. You'll need to have your own camping gear for this site.

Hospitality Exchange

Europe is one of the most offered regions for hospitality exchanges such as Couchsurfing. Every popular tourist destination in Europe has countless hosts to choose from. During the summer months and around the time of festivals, hosts get inundated with thousands of requests because of the influx of travelers to Europe. Hosts don't respond to the vast majority of inquiries. In order to be successful, put in your requests far before you need the accommodations, giving the potential host enough time to plan for your visit. Don't be afraid to follow up either.

Servas and Hospitality Club also have a big user base in Western Europe.

Western Europe, especially the United Kingdom, has a lot of opportunities available for people who are interested in house-sitting. Blogger Nora Dunn (theprofessionalhobo.com) had no problem finding a house-sitting opportunity in England: "For three weeks, I house-sat and dog-minded in Hampshire, England. The homeowners added me to the insurance for their car and said I could use it as I liked. It was a beautiful country house, and in their absence I enjoyed all the accoutrements of 'home'—somebody else's home, that is!" she said to me.

WWOOF

WWOOFing (see Chapter 11) is popular in many parts of Europe, such as large agriculture areas in Germany, Italy, France, and Spain. If you are looking to WWOOF in Europe, make sure you put your requests in early, especially during the popular summer tourist season. Bethany Salvon, who spent months WWOOFing through Europe, offered this advice to me on finding placement: "If you want to do a popular WWOOF activity (such as making wine in Tuscany), be sure you give yourself at least a few weeks in advance to find a farm—many of the popular farms fill up quickly for seasonal activities."

All accommodation can be booked at the booking sites mentioned in Chapter 11 or listed in Appendix A. Additionally, local tourist offices can help you secure accommodation.

FOOD

Western Europe has a variety of ways to eat cheaply. Europeans don't eat out like we do in America. We are very much a grab-and-go, quick-meal culture. Europeans tend to cook more of their own meals and shop at outdoor food markets. The mega-food stores you see around America are a rarity in Europe. Buying your groceries at markets, cooking your own dinners, and making your own sandwiches are the most inexpensive ways to eat.

You can cook your own food for around $70 USD per week. (This number is, of course, variable and depends highly on your eating needs.) You'll be able to feed yourself pretty well if you grocery shop and get food at the local farmer's markets. This is my preferred method of eating in Europe. I love wandering the local markets, tasting the local food, and having the finer points of French cheese or Italian Balsamic vinaigrette explained to me by local shop owners. In fact, shopping at an outdoor market in Paris and then picnicking in front of the Eiffel Tower sounds much better to me than spending $25 USD at a restaurant.

Throughout Western Europe, you can find small shops where you can get sandwiches, slices of pizza, or sausages for between $5 USD and $7 USD. You'll find these shops most often in train stations, bus stations, and main pedestrian areas.

These small sandwich shops, as well as European eatery chains like Maoz (falafel) and Walk to Wok (noodle shop), offer cheap food alternatives that can have you eating on between $10 USD and $15 USD per day. You won't be eating fabulous main courses and drinking a lot of wine, but you'll be saving a lot of money. I personally use these places when I don't feel like cooking but don't want to spend a lot of money on a meal. Additionally, specific to Germany and Austria, you will find street vendors selling hot dogs, currywurst (sausages covered in curry powder and ketchup), and other sausages for around $2 USD. These are quite popular with locals because they are filling and cheap.

Indian, Asian, or Middle Eastern food is also cheap throughout the area. In London, lunch at an Indian restaurant can cost about $13 for a set menu and a drink. You can get an entire Turkish meal for as little as $7 USD in Berlin or noodles in Amsterdam for the same.

Restaurant meals typically cost $15–25 USD for a main dish and drink. In this price range you'll get a sit-down restaurant with a simple menu. Picture your local Italian restaurant. It's delicious, it's satisfying, but it's not going to win restaurant of the year.

In Europe, it is common for restaurants to have a plate of the day served at lunchtime. This is a set menu that includes a few dishes at a price cheaper than what you would find for dinner. You can get a large meal for $10–15 USD with a drink included, a saving substantially off what the same meal would have cost you during dinner-time. When I eat out in Europe, I do it during lunch in order to get good local meals at reasonable prices.

The city tourism cards discussed in Chapter 14 also offer discounts on food and beverages. While the restaurants that participate in tourism card discounts tend to be more expensive than grab-and-go places, the discounts given (up to 20 percent) can make them very affordable, especially if you go for lunch.

In the United Kingdom, there is also the Taste of the UK card (tastecard.co.uk), which offers up to 50 percent off and two-for-one deals at selected restaurants. You don't need to be a United Kingdom resident to get the card, and the first month's membership fee is waived, which is perfect for 99 percent of travelers. During the booking process, they ask for an address, and I simply use the address of the place I am staying at while in the country.

Western Europe has the same type of food options we have in the United States, except that due to higher labor costs, taxes, and a stronger currency, they cost a lot more. That $8 USD meal down at your local lunch store is more like $12 USD in Europe. But luckily, just as in the United States, there are plenty of ways to eat cheap so don't fret!

TRANSPORTATION

Transportation around most European cities by local tram, subway, or bus is typically between $1.30 USD and $2.60 USD for a one-way ticket. Europe has a large and well-funded public transportation system that makes getting around cities very convenient for travelers. City tourism cards, as discussed in Chapter 14, all provide free public transportation.

Trains

Intercity trains connect every major part of Europe. Trains are my favorite form of transportation because they are spacious, there is food, and you can relax, walk around, and see the countryside as you speed from city to city. Intercity train prices vary widely from country to country and depending on whether you take the slow train or a high-speed train. High-speed trains like the French TGV or German ICE cost around $100 USD or more per trip. For example, a high-speed train from Berlin to Munich costs around $160 USD, Bordeaux to Paris is about $93 USD, and Madrid to Barcelona is about $154 USD.

Non-high-speed trains and other intercity lines are a lot cheaper, with short distances (one to two hours) costing $20–30 USD and longer journeys (three to five hours) costing around $50 USD. Train prices vary a lot by distance, but generally speaking the slow, short journeys cost about 40–50 percent of the price for high-speed trains.

Additionally, booking train tickets (high-speed or regular trains) a week or more in advance can get you prices up to 50 percent off the same-day price.

In the United Kingdom, the National Rail (nationalrail.co.uk) service is always expensive, no matter how long your trip is. It's one thing citizens in this part of the world love to complain about. Bring up the National Rail with Brits and just see how long they'll carry on. A journey from London to Liverpool can cost as little as $40 USD or it can cost as much as $200 USD during peak hours (midday).

Booking your ticket with the National Rail more than a week in advance and during off-peak hours can secure you tickets for as little as $20 USD. These seats are often available in very limited numbers. The company Megabus (uk.megabus.com/default.aspx), the

UK's cheap bus service company, also does cheap train rides. A ticket search for the London-to-Liverpool route came up with about $14 USD when booking more than a week in advance, as opposed to about $28 USD when booking via the National Rail website for the same date. The United Kingdom's national rail service is grossly overpriced, and I try to avoid it as much as possible.

Moreover, be on the lookout for deals from the national rail companies. In Germany, you can get special discounted weekend passes for unlimited train travel as well as family fares. In Denmark, there are special online orange fares that are sometimes up to 50 percent off. Be sure to always check your options online before you walk into the train station to purchase a ticket.

Rail Passes

Eurail passes are one of the most popular travel products in the world. Few travelers making their way across Europe go without one. These train passes give you a set number of stops in a set time period. You can get continent-wide passes, country-specific passes, or regional passes. Just as there are trains that go everywhere in Europe, there is a pass for everyone. Passes come in two varieties: first class for those over the age of twenty-six (you can't get a second-class rail pass) and second-class tickets for those under twenty-six (though those under twenty-six can buy first-class tickets).

Rail passes are sold via Rail Europe (raileurope.com), which is a United States–based seller. You can also find passes on the main Eurail website (eurail.com). There's no difference between the two— Eurail is the pass issuer and Rail Europe is the reseller, but often Rail Europe has cheaper prices, since they have sales while Eurail doesn't. Europeans need to use the site InterRail.

Most travelers use the popular Global Flexi Pass. A two-month fifteen-day (that is, fifteen trips) second-class ticket costs about $721 USD (a value of $48 USD per trip). A first-class adult ticket costs about $1,100 USD (a value of $73 USD per trip). A "flexi" pass allows you to use your days anytime during the two-month period, unlike consecutive day passes, which have to be used day after day. Consecutive day passes can be bought for up to three months. These passes cost up to $2,000 USD for a three-month pass and are not worth the price, because every day you don't use the pass, your money is wasted.

You buy your pass before you go, and it becomes valid from the first time you use it. You don't need to buy a ticket ahead of time, you can simply show up on the train, present the conductor with your pass, and keep going on with your journey. Some countries require you to book a seat ahead of time. When you receive your rail pass, you'll get a small book that lets you know the specific reservation rules for each country the pass covers.

Take, for example, my trip around Europe with the first-class Global Pass ($1,100 USD) on a journey that took me to Spain, France, Holland, Sweden, Denmark, and Germany. The cost of my travels was $1,294 USD for the reservation fees and the pass. The cost without the Eurail pass would have been $1,767 USD. For a second-class ticket, assuming the same reservation fees, I would have spent $878 USD, whereas the trip would have cost $1,157 USD without the pass. No matter what class I was in, I would have saved money.

Eurail passes work if you get the right pass and plan your trip well. Last-minute trains cost a lot of money, and rail passes really help in those sorts of situations. However, as we can see, short trips actually cost more with a Eurail pass. With the Global Flexi Pass, each trip is worth $73 USD, but the price of my short train trips (that is, rides less than three hours) was typically around $65 USD. However, where I saved money was on the longer journeys. My trip from Berlin to Munich would have cost me about $192 USD without the pass, so I saved $120 USD in that instance.

If, however, you like to plan in advance and are willing to buy your tickets early, you will be able to find cheap train tickets without a Eurail pass. Advance bookings of two weeks or more can get train tickets for up to 50 percent less than the cost of buying tickets the day before or the day of. If you are OK with accepting that rigidity into your trip, then a Eurail pass is not something you should get, as booking in advance will get you cheaper tickets than Eurail.

I like to go with the flow, and hardly ever know my travel plans well enough in advance to book a discount ticket. There have been many times I've said or heard other people say, "I'm going to Paris tomorrow," only to then leave three days later. Eurail passes are much better than buying the tickets the day of and they retain that same "today, I'm going here" flexibility.

The key to saving money with a rail pass is to do your homework before your trip. Most travelers' complaints are due to the fact that people either didn't get the right pass or they failed to read the fine print.

Getting the wrong pass will definitely lead to spending more than what you would spend buying individual tickets. If you buy yourself a Global Pass and then visit one to three countries close to one another, you're going to lose money. A large multi-country pass only works when you travel to many countries and over vast distances. If you are only visiting a few countries, you need to get a more regional pass.

You also need to read the fine print. For instance, some countries require you to pay reservation fees to secure your seat, while others do not. France and Italy, for example, charge reservation fees of $3–6 USD. But you don't need a reservation in Germany, Austria, or Holland. Know the rules.

A major criticism of the Eurail pass is that you have to make reservations for overnight trains and pay a reservation fee (roughly $30 USD) in addition to what you paid for your pass. But this stipulation is right there on the website, as well as in the book they send you with train times and fees. You can't just get on an overnight train in any country, find a bunk, and go to sleep. You have to reserve your bed, and if you don't book ahead, you can end up stuck in the expensive sleeper car, which can cost as much as $100 USD. Rail passes reduce the cost of sleeper trains, but unlike for day trains, they don't eliminate it.

So are Eurail passes worth purchasing? Maybe.

Rail passes are all about money. If it doesn't save you a dollar, it's not worth getting. That means you have to do a lot of math to figure out if a pass is right or not. It can be a time-consuming process but is certainly worth it in the end.

Just like the airlines, prices are now variable and no longer fixed. Depending on when you book, your ticket cost will fluctuate. If you are willing to prebook months in advance, you'll easily find some unbeatable bargain deals such as Paris to Amsterdam from $46 USD, Rome to Venice for $38 USD, and Amsterdam to Berlin for $78 USD. As I mentioned, Denmark offers orange tickets that are 50 percent off the normal price. Because rail passes cost roughly $79 USD per trip, you can't beat booking individual tickets far in advance.

But who prebooks a multimonth trip to Europe?

If you are planning on a two-week trip months from now and you already know your dates, it's not going to be a good idea to get a rail pass. Even though those early-bird tickets are nonrefundable, they are still pretty cheap, and you probably won't be changing too many of your dates.

But if you are traveling around Europe with no fixed plans, rail passes can work out to be a better value than buying same-day point-to-point tickets. To me, the pass is about flexibility and being able to hop on and hop off trains when I want. If you are traveling long term, you aren't going to schedule ahead months of travel. You are going to want the ability to go with the flow, which using a pass will give you.

I think one of the best ways to use the passes is to mix and match, using the rail pass for the expensive trains while paying for cheap tickets individually so you can maximize value. For example, for eleven days of train travel in Europe, it's cheaper to buy a ten-day Eurail Global pass plus one point-to-point ticket for the cheapest train. Additionally, I place a value on flexibility. If the math is roughly the same, I'll buy a pass because saving $3 isn't worth trading the flexibility a pass gives.

How to Pick the Option That Is Best for You

Rail passes are all about math. The only way to know for sure whether a rail pass or point-to-point ticket would be cheaper is to work out the point-to-point prices for most of the trips you're planning using the various European train operator websites.

After you have a general idea of where you want to go, visit the national railway websites and work out two sets of prices: one for tomorrow (that is, a last-minute fare) and one for two months from now (an early bird fare). Add up the prices in each category.

Next, head to Rail Europe, find your rail pass, and divide the rail pass price by the number of days you'll be traveling by train to figure out the cost of each journey on the pass.

See which is cheaper and take that option, bearing in mind that your journey may change or you may take more high-speed rails. If I know I'll be in a lot of countries that don't charge reservation fees and the prices for booking early versus using a pass are close, I'll probably go with the pass as there is value in flexibility (I change my mind a lot).

In the end, a train pass isn't right for all trips but for most people who will be spending a long time in Europe and traveling vast distances, having a pass will save them money. While the reservation fees stink, the basic principles of the pass still hold: if you are traveling long distances, using a lot of high-speed trains, and booking last minute, a rail pass is going to save you money.

Buses

In the UK, the cheapest way to travel around is via the Megabus (uk.megabus.com), where fares can cost as little as $1.50 USD. You'll need to book at least a month in advance on popular routes to get the special fare. However, even if you don't get the cheap fare, you can find fares for around $25 USD, which is still considerably lower than day-of buses on National Express Coach (coach.national express.com), which cost around $37 USD. However, for me, Megabus is the only way to go. Moreover, they now serve the cities of Paris, Amsterdam, and Brussels for around $20 USD for a one-way ticket.

The main bus service in Europe is called Eurolines (eurolines
.com), and it reaches throughout the continent. Eurolines is the continental umbrella organization for international bus travel. Every
country has its own national bus service, but for international long
distances, there is Eurolines.

Buses are cheaper than trains. Taking Eurolines from Berlin to
Paris works out to be about $100 USD, while the last-minute booking
on the train is as high as $248 USD (booking in advance will get the
price down to around $143 USD). The downside to bus travel is that
instead of being spread out like on a train, you are cramped on a tiny
bus. What you save in money, you lose in comfort.

Eurolines also offers continent-wide bus passes where you can
enjoy unlimited bus travel between its forty-three major destinations. Prices for the fifteen-day pass are $237 USD to $388 USD, depending on the season, and they're $330 USD to $370 USD for the
thirty-day pass. If you are going to travel every four or five days, this
ticket is worth it because you'll use the pass enough to make up for
its cost. However, if you are in cities for a week or more and only
traveling short, inexpensive distances, this pass is not worth buying.
You simply won't use the pass enough to justify the cost. You can find
out more at eurolines.com/eurolines-pass.

There is also Busabout (busabout.com), which is a bus service for
travelers. This company has set routes throughout Europe and lets
travelers buy bus passes that allow riders to hop on and hop off the
bus anytime they want along any one of the routes they paid for. You
can spend as little or as long as you want in a destination and then
just catch the next bus to your next stop. The passes also include
activities in many of the cities and provide help finding accommodations. Passes range from $470 USD to $1,200 USD for an adult (stu-

dent passes are 10 percent cheaper), depending on the route and number of days you travel. These buses only stop at the major cities in Europe, so if you are deviating from the route they have, you'll need to buy extra tickets. However, if you are a single traveler or someone without a lot of experience or nervous about your ability to travel alone, Busabout would be a good "get your feet wet" option, and the guides do a great job of making sure everyone gets to know one another.

Flying

The rise of the budget airlines discussed in Chapter 5 has made flying around Europe quite cheap. When I am pressed for time or just not in the mood for an overnight train ride, I fly. There are so many cheap deals that flying is often the most inexpensive way to get around. Generally, airline tickets in Europe are about 50 percent less than the cost of a train ticket. However, if you book a flight at the very last minute (within two to three days of departure), prices are equal to high-speed train prices. That being said, European budget airlines often have deals where fares are 1 euro, 1 pound, or no fare at all, you simply pay the taxes and fees. The most popular budget airlines in Europe are Ryanair, easyJet, German Wings, and Transavia. If I need to get somewhere in a hurry or far away, I'll fly because fares are cheap. You can refer back to Chapter 5 for further information on how to find cheap flights.

ATTRACTIONS AND ACTIVITIES

One thing I love about Western Europe is the uniformity of activity costs. Museums, day trips, attractions, guided tours, pub crawls—

there's not a lot of variation in prices. It makes budgeting much easier. The Louvre in Paris is $16 USD, the Prado in Spain is $16 USD, the Acropolis in Athens is $16 USD, and the Van Gogh Museum in Amsterdam is $18 USD. See? All relatively the same price. In general, prices are about $16 USD for the large, ultra-famous, everyone's-heard-of-them museums. Smaller, not so well-known museums typically cost a few dollars less. In the United Kingdom, all public museums are free.

Full-day tours vary in price depending on the type of tour you are taking and what you wish to do. For example, a wine tour in Tuscany is around $140 USD for a full day leaving from Florence, while one in Bordeaux is around $70 USD when booked via the tourist office. A tour of the canals of Amsterdam costs around $20 USD, while skiing in Switzerland will often cost about $70 for a lift ticket.

Local tourism offices, hostels, or hotels have information on tour operators and current prices. Appendix A has a list of some of my favorite operators in the region.

Pub crawls, if that is your thing, can be found in every large and touristy city in Europe and are run by either the local hostels or a major company like Ultimate Party (joinultimateparty.com) in Amsterdam, or 1 Big Night Out in London (1bignightout.com). They cost between $15 USD and $25 USD and include entrance into the pubs, free beer, and free shots.

The two best ways to save money on activities in Western Europe are by taking free tours and by getting city tourism cards. In the vast majority of Western European cities, you can find free walking tours. I take them all the time, and it is usually the first thing I do when visiting a new city. They are a perfect way to familiarize yourself with city attractions, learn some history, and get your bearings in a new environment so when you walk around alone, you know where you are. They typically last two to three hours.

The biggest walking tour company is New Europe (new europetours.eu), which organizes walking tours throughout most major cities in Europe. If you are interested in taking a walking tour and this company doesn't offer one in your city, the local tourism office and your hostel should have a list of companies that offer free walking tours.

The second-best way to save money is to get a city tourist card. Cities in Europe that are frequented by tourists have their own tourist cards that offer the benefits I listed in Chapter 8. Since most travelers tend to go to Europe to do a lot of sightseeing, these cards have their most financial impact here. After all, Europe has thousands of museums, tours, castles, and activities to do. As I mentioned in Chapter 8, the Paris museum card saved me about $85 USD. I can't recommend getting these tourist cards enough if you plan to see a lot of attractions.

Another thing I always do before I visit a city is check the local tourism board for deals. They post information about current events, specials, and tourism deals happening in the city. They are an invaluable resource. You can find the local tourist office near train stations, airports, and major attractions. If it is not listed on the map, you can ask at your hostel/hotel registration desk for directions.

Eastern Europe
Balkans, Baltics, Ukraine, Romania, Bulgaria, Moldova, Poland, Hungary, Slovakia, Slovenia, Czech Republic

When most Americans go to Europe, they envision Paris and Rome and London. They tend to skip over the east. While economic growth and integration with the European Union has made these countries more expensive over the last decade, this bloc can still be a bargain.

Regardless of where I go when visiting Eastern Europe, I always spend a fraction of what I spend in Western Europe. When I was in Romania, I spent $36 USD per day, in Hungary $30 USD, in Poland $40 USD, and in Estonia $40 USD. I always got old-world charm, but without the old-world prices.

Most of Central and Eastern Europe is overlooked by travelers; they hit Prague, Krakow, Warsaw, or Budapest and call it a day. To me, the region (and a big region, I know) offers some of the best value travel in Europe and should not be overlooked. Get out there, get off the beaten path, visit lesser-known destinations! You'll save money, see fewer tourists, and get unique experiences.

ACCOMMODATIONS

Hostels
Hostels in Eastern Europe are a bit more basic than their counterparts in Western Europe. The farther east you go, the less likely you are to get free breakfast. The majority of hostels in the east offer free Internet, have common rooms, kitchens, and can help with tours.

For hostel dorm rooms, you'll pay between $5 USD and $15 USD per night, depending on the size of the dorm room and the popularity of the hostel. The farther east you go, the cheaper it gets. In popular destinations like Budapest or Prague, rooms are a bit more expensive, with dorm rooms going as high as $20 USD. However, if you go all the way east to Ukraine, dorms can cost around $6 USD per night.

A private room in a hostel will cost you $30–60 USD per night for a double bed with a shared bathroom. When getting private rooms, the same cost rule applies—the farther east you go (or the more toward the Balkans), the cheaper the room is. I don't often get private rooms when I travel in Western Europe, because they are so expensive, but when I travel in the east I frequently do, especially if I am traveling with a friend who can split the cost. I get all the benefits of a hostel—wi-fi, the occasional free breakfast, a kitchen, and people to socialize with—with all the benefits of a hotel—a private, secure room.

Budget Hotels

Cheap hotel rooms start at $30 USD for a two-star hotel with breakfast, private bathroom, wi-fi, and double bed. If you want something nicer, with a more comfortable bed, fancier breakfast, nicer décor, and more amenities, expect nice three-plus-star hotels to start at $45 USD per night. In fact, hotel rooms are often so cheap that unless I am looking to be really social, I stay in them over hostel private rooms due to the better prices and additional privacy.

Apartment Rentals

Apartment rentals are gaining a larger and larger foothold each year. You tend to find the biggest selection of apartment rentals in capital cities. Generally, prices for an apartment are comparable to those of a cheap hotel. In larger and more popular destinations, like Prague, Budapest, Krakow, or Tallinn, prices are between $40 USD and $60 USD for a whole apartment. You can find cheaper if you are willing to share a room in someone's house, with prices beginning at $25 USD.

Camping

Camping is also less common in Eastern Europe and exists only around a few major cities, like Tallinn, Prague, Krakow, and Budapest. Many campsites only open during the summer. You'll find an especially short camping season in countries up north, where winter comes early. Camping costs around $8 USD, though can be as high as $12–15 USD if you need to rent a tent. If you have your own tent, you can find campsites for around $6 USD. In many cases, hostels will let you camp if you have your own tent, for a price a little less than a dorm room.

Hospitality Exchange

Couchsurfing is very popular in Eastern Europe, as many use it as a way to practice English. I used it in Ukraine and was the hit of a party simply because everyone wanted to try to speak English with me. Couchsurfing opportunities in Eastern Europe are limited in the countryside, but in the larger cities, you'll have no problem finding people who are willing to host travelers. In this region, hosts tend to be younger and are often students.

Servas and Hospitality Club don't have as many users here as they do in Western Europe, and I would stick more to Couchsurfing than those two.

Accommodations are already cheap in Eastern Europe, and you don't need to do much to make them cheaper. You are already paying very little money for accommodations, especially if you are staying at a hostel.

All accommodations can be booked at the booking sites mentioned in Chapter 11 or listed in Appendix A. Additionally, local tourist offices can help you secure accommodations.

WWOOF

WWOOFing in Central and Eastern Europe is relatively small, with most countries having only a few dozen opportunities. It's best to inquire about openings far in advance.

FOOD

Food is much cheaper in Eastern Europe than in the west. Even if you are eating out for all your meals, you can still get by on as little as $10 USD per day.

If you decide to buy your groceries, you'll average about $40 USD per week. This will get you everything you need for large dinners, hearty meals, pasta, and some sandwiches. While I was in Romania, I spent $35 USD for a week's supply of groceries that consisted of pasta, chicken, ground beef, and sandwiches. In Bulgaria, it cost me $35 USD for the week. In Bratislava, Slovakia, I spent $40 USD. Food prices tend to be higher in central Europe than in the eastern part of the continent.

There are cheap outdoor food stalls around this whole area, though they are especially abundant in Bulgaria, Poland, and Hungary. These street stalls typically sell fast meals like pizza, sandwiches, kebabs, or sausages. They typically cost between $1.50 USD and $4 USD. Just as in Western Europe, these meals present a quick and cheap way to eat. In Bulgaria, I practically lived off this little kebab and salad place near my hostel.

Moving up the food chain (pun intended), you'll find a lot of inexpensive eateries. One thing I really love about this part of the world is that unlike Western Europe, where getting a crepe in Paris or a plate of pasta in Italy is still expensive, the local food here is supercheap. You can expect a meal at a small corner shop to be between $4 USD and $6 USD. For example, eating at local restaurants like Puzata Khata (a delicious chain in Kiev) in Ukraine, a typical meal costs less than $4 USD. In Hungary, I would eat at the big markets, gorging on hearty local dishes for less than $5 USD. To find these places, you just need to ask the manager of your hotel/hostel, as he or she will know the local spots. I found the place in Ukraine this way.

If you are looking for something nicer, there's a wide selection of international food available in this region. A nice sit-down restaurant with a drink and a main meal will cost $15 USD and up.

Specific to Bulgaria, stay in Hostel Mostel (hostelmostel.com), which has three locations in the country: Sofia, Plovdiv, and Velinko Tarnovo. Not only do they offer a free breakfast, but they also offer free pasta dinner every night. In Krakow, Poland, Greg and Tom's hostel (gregtomhostel.com/intro.html) also provides free breakfast and dinner. That's two free meals a day, which can really go a long way toward reducing your food costs. It is very rare that hostels offer free dinner.

Eating in this region of the world is very cheap. You have to really try to spend lots of money on food here to do so.

TRANSPORTATION

Transportation is inexpensive in this region of the world if you are going to travel within cities, but there is a lot of variance when traveling between countries. Public transportation, buses, trams, and trains in the cities cost $1 USD to $2 USD.

Trains

Trains aren't as popular here because they are slow, old, and expensive. Eastern Europe gets the old trains Western Europe gets rid of when they upgrade to high-speed rail. When I went from Bratislava to Krakow, I had to change trains twice in Czech Republic and it took me twelve hours. The direct bus from Bratislava to Krakow is only seven hours. Intercountry trains usually cost between $50 USD and $100 USD when the ticket is booked last-minute. Short train rides of two to three hours within countries cost about $30 USD. As a general rule, each hour of travel is around $13 USD, rounding up to the highest hour— for example, a two-hour-and-thirty-minute train ride will cost between $26 USD and $39 USD.

As in Western Europe, Eurail passes can help save money, but you'll find that not all the countries are covered. Countries that are covered in the Eurail pass are Czech Republic, Croatia, Hungary, Poland, Romania, Bulgaria, Macedonia, Serbia, Slovakia, and Slovenia. However, unlike Western Europe, which is covered in one giant pass, Eastern Europe is split among various passes. In the Eastern Europe pass, the only countries that are covered are Poland, Czech Republic, Slovakia, Austria, and Hungary. There is also a separate Balkans pass that includes Bulgaria, Greece, Macedonia, Serbia, Montenegro, Romania, and Turkey.

The rail pass rules discussed in the Western Europe section apply to Eastern Europe too.

You'll find individual ticket prices are 50 percent off if you book at least a week in advance. In many countries, when booking tickets, get someone to write the specifics down in the local language, as English isn't always that well spoken. In Ukraine, I had to ask my hostel receptionist to write the date and time I needed, because of the lack of English proficiency in the country.

Since train travel isn't very convenient in this part of Europe, I tend to prefer buses throughout this region, as they are cheaper and often faster due to more direct routes.

Buses

Buses are a much better option for international travel here because they are cheaper and many of the trains don't go direct between cities due to old and different-sized train tracks. For example, from Romania to Ukraine, you need to switch trains because the countries have different tracks, but the bus just goes direct. To go from Bratislava to Krakow, you need to go via Czech Republic on the train, but again the bus is direct. Typical bus fares for this region are $10 USD to $20 USD for a short journey of a couple of hours.

In Eastern Europe, the major international bus company is also Ecolines (ecolines.net), which primarily serves central Europe, the Baltics, and other Eastern European countries, except the Balkans. (In the Balkans, national bus lines serve neighboring countries.) All countries have their own national bus service, which tends to serve their region. For example, buses in Bulgaria will go to Romania, Greece, Macedonia, and Turkey, but you can't get one of the local bus operators to go from Bulgaria to Estonia, which is where Ecolines comes in. (Eurolines also services a number of places in this region.)

Ecolines gives a discount on fares to students, those under twenty-six, and holders of an ISIC teachers or youth card. This discount usually amounts to 10 percent off the ticket price.

In the Baltic region, there is a backpacker bus called Scanbalt (scanbaltexperience.com) that runs from Tallinn down to Riga. It costs $25 USD and is double the price of the public bus, which costs $14 USD. I personally wouldn't take this bus unless you really want to take a bus with just travelers or just want something super-convenient, like a bus from hostel to hostel.

Flying

Airfare in this region is similarly priced to that of Western Europe. Ryanair, easyJet, and Transavia all serve this region of the world. In addition to these carriers, you will also find that Wizz Air, Carpatair, and Air Baltic all have a big network of routes. Relative to the cost of buses and trains, flying is less of a good deal than in Western Europe, since flights tend to be more expensive than local transportation. Flights are generally $100–150 USD if you don't find a deal (you can refer to Part One for how to find deals). No bus or train in the region is that expensive.

Hitchhiking

Hitchhiking is also a popular method of travel in this region. When I was in Bulgaria, we hitchhiked one day to a neighboring town. It took us a while to find someone to pick us up (we were a group of three), but eventually someone came. Central Europe, the Baltics,

Romania, and Bulgaria tend to be safer countries to hitchhike in, but use your common sense when hitchhiking with strangers. You can always say no if you feel the situation is unsafe, especially if you are traveling alone.

ACTIVITIES AND ATTRACTIONS

In Eastern Europe, you'll find that activities cost much less than in other parts of the world. Prices are a little less uniform than in Western Europe in part because in the east, all countries are on different currencies. However, the variation is about $1–2 USD, and generally museums, churches, and attractions in this region cost $5–8 USD.

There are a lot of good day trips to old monasteries, castles, lakes, and parks in Eastern Europe. Most day trips cost $25–35 USD. For example, a day trip to the famous Rila Monastery in Bulgaria is around $25 USD. A visit to Auschwitz in Poland is often just $30 USD. The exception to this rule is a visit to the Chernobyl site in Ukraine, which is upward of $170 USD. A good tour company for Chernobyl is SoloEast (tourkiev.com/chernobyltour).

Using your ISIC, YHA, or youth card will get you a discount on public attractions like churches and museums. These passes are widely accepted throughout this region of the world and usually offer a 50 percent discount off the standard adult price for museums. They won't get you a discount on day tours and trips organized by tour operators though.

Free tours, while not as common as they are in Western Europe, do exist, but instead of being run by big companies, they tend to be run a lot more by small, local, and often student organizations. Popular walking tours occur in most of the major cities. Appendix A has a list of the free tours in Eastern Europe. (Note: These tours also offer the majority of the pub crawls popular with travelers in the cities too.)

More and more free tours sprout up every summer, so if you are going to a destination not mentioned in the appendix, ask the staff at your hotel/hostel or visit the tourism board. Keep in mind that sometimes people don't know about these tours and the only way to find them is via Google. I found a free tour in Bucharest that way, as it was fairly new at the time.

Just like in the west, many Eastern European cities offer tourism cards. In more expensive cities like Prague, Budapest, or Krakow, these cards offer a good bargain because there are a lot of free attractions, tours, and public transportation. But this isn't always the case. In Tallinn, Estonia, a beautiful city in the Baltics, they have a Tallinn city card that costs $30 USD for a twenty-four-hour card, $42 USD for a forty-eight-hour card, and $56 USD for a seventy-two-hour card. They market the card as a way to save money, but honestly, if you look at the attractions offered and compare their prices, you aren't really saving anything. You are paying for five different Tallinn history museums and three guard towers and many other duplicates. If you factor in that most of the museums cost $3 USD to $5 USD to see, and the impossibility of seeing everything involved, you lose money. It's impossible to see ten museums in one day. Plus, since the city is so small, getting free public transportation isn't that much of a bonus— you can walk anywhere in fifteen minutes. I didn't buy this card, as I realized I would spend more for the card than the cost would be of what I wanted to see.

Be extra careful about making sure the tourist card savings are more than their cost in this region. Like everything else in Eastern Europe, attractions are quite cheap already.

Scandinavia
Denmark, Finland, Sweden, Norway

The Scandinavian countries are the most expensive in Europe. Everything here costs a lot of money. Everything. While this region is one of my favorite places to visit, it is by no way a good budget destination. It takes a lot more work here to save money, and even then you are still spending a lot. Most travelers speed through here because of its high costs, but if you have the time and money, stay here longer, as it is one of the most beautiful regions in the world.

ACCOMMODATIONS

Hostels

Hostels in this region are very sterile. Most hostels in the world have big common rooms, bars, and kitchens, and they try to organize activities. In this region, hostels have kitchens and other basic amenities, but they lack charm. Sure, I've stayed at some that were very fun (City Backpackers in Stockholm is very good), but overall, they lack the charm and charisma you find elsewhere in Europe.

Hostel prices range from $25 USD to $50 USD for a dorm room (the most expensive country in the region, Norway, costs the most). Private double rooms with a shared bathroom cost $80–100 USD per night. In short, even these aren't a real "budget" deal. They are just the cheapest option.

Furthermore, hostels in this region don't offer free breakfast the way hostels do in the rest of Europe, though all the ones I've stayed at have a large kitchen to compensate. In Sweden, you will also need to have your own sheets, as they aren't provided free by hostels. They usually cost $3 USD per night.

Budget Hotels

Budget hotels are widespread throughout the region, and their prices are on par with a hostel's private room. You get a little more for your money—a private bathroom, breakfast, and a TV. Rooms generally start at $70 USD on the cheaper end and go up from there.

Apartment Rentals

Apartment rentals cost $70–100 USD for a private apartment. If you are just looking for a single room in someone's apartment, you can find rooms for as little as $40 USD. I think this is a better option than hotels (and even some hostels) if you are looking to have your own room or accommodation near the city center. You'll pay less than for a hostel or hotel, most hosts provide breakfast, there is a kitchen to cook your own food, and you get more privacy. If you are in a group, the costs of splitting an apartment are much cheaper than the price of a dorm bed. I don't use apartment rental websites often, but in Scandinavia, I think they offer the best value in the region.

Camping

Camping is the cheapest option in the region. Because of the long winter, campsites are generally open only from April to October. Camping is usually free in Scandinavia due to open public land laws. You are allowed to camp at designated campsites and on public lands. Make sure you visit the country's tourist board, as laws change all the time.

You can also stay at camping sites costing from $8 USD to $14 USD per night. To stay at any campsite in the region, you will need the Camping Card Scandinavia. The card is free, but you need a validity sticker for the current year, for $21 USD. You can buy the card online at camping.se or at the first campsite you get to in Scandinavia. This card is good for all campsites in Norway, Sweden, Denmark, and Finland.

Camping sites require you to have your own tent, as they don't rent them out. If you don't have your own tent, you can stay in a cottage fitted as a dormitory, where a bed is the same price as a hostel.

In expensive Scandinavia, camping is one of the cheapest ways to lower your accommodation costs. Given the public access laws, it's an option that should be used often, especially in Norway where everything costs you your kidney!

Hospitality Exchange

If you truly want to save the most money possible in Scandinavia and don't mind where you sleep, Couchsurfing is the only way to save big. Couchsurfing is very popular among locals, and you'll find a lot of hosts, even in small rural communities up near the Arctic. However, because Scandinavia is so expensive, travelers rely heavily on Couchsurfing (or other hospitality exchanges) to save money, and most hosts get inundated with requests. As a consequence, you will get a low response rate to your inquiries. People simply get booked up or overwhelmed. If you plan on couch-surfing through this part of the world, I would advise you to send out your requests far in advance of your actual arrival date.

I wish I had some better news, but sadly, sometimes you just need to face facts and admit that there aren't a lot of ways to save money, and in Scandinavia, there especially aren't a lot of ways to save money on accommodations.

All accommodations can be booked at the booking sites mentioned in Chapter 11 or listed in Appendix A. Additionally, local tourist offices can help you secure accommodation.

FOOD

In Norway, food will be the most expensive in the region, including groceries. I bought two days' worth of groceries for pasta and sandwiches and it cost me $36 USD. To keep costs down, avoid fresh vegetables and chicken fillets, which cost a lot of money here because they tend to be imported—a lesson I learned after my food-shopping experience. If you cut those out of your groceries, stick to pasta, breads, some meats, and a few cheap vegetables and cheese, you are looking to spend about $110 USD per week. If you really want discount chicken or beef, do what the locals do: buy them on their expiration date. Due to strict food laws, most meats "expire" well before they do in the United States and become half off. That's when the locals come and pick them up as they are still perfectly good to eat. Do the same!

Eating out is expensive, with even fast food averaging between $10 USD and $15 USD and sit-down meals at a decent restaurant nearly always $30 USD or more for just a main course. For a cheap, quick snack Norwegian-style, look no farther than the nearest outside vendor or convenience store, where you can eat a hot dog or sausage for around $8 USD. Fish-and-chip meals are around $20 USD.

In Sweden, you'll find the food to be cheaper. Grocery shopping here will cost $70 USD per week for the same type of food that I mentioned above. You can get cheap meals from outdoor street vendors starting at $8 USD, such as Thai food, sandwiches, and burgers. For something really cheap, you can get hot dogs and sausages starting at $3 USD. Whole pizzas begin around $13 USD. Most sit-down restaurant meals begin at $20 USD for a main dish.

In Denmark, if you are going to eat out in a restaurant, be prepared to pay around $15 USD for a cheap meal with a main course and a drink. If you are looking for something fancier, meals including a drink start at $25 USD. You can find some lunchtime buffet specials for $10 USD, which allow you to eat out without breaking the bank. You can find cheap hot dog vendors lining the streets of the bigger cities selling dogs for $5 USD. Groceries will cost around $80 USD per week. When I come to Denmark, a country not really known for food, I tend to eat out for lunch and cook my own meals for dinner. That way I can average about $15 USD per day for food.

Since Finland is on the euro and not their own currency like the other countries in the region, food is cheapest here. Grocery shopping will cost you $60 USD per week for a fairly robust shopping list of vegetables, meats, pasta, snacks, and the like. You'll be able to feed yourself well for a week with that budget.

Inexpensive food, mostly pizza, kebab, and sandwich shops, will cost $6–10 USD for a tiny lunch special. Sit-down restaurant meals will cost $15 USD for a small meal and drink. During the lunch hour, many restaurants offer a lunchtime buffet costing about $12 USD, and Stockmann supermarkets also have a wide variety of premade cheap meals for around $7 USD. Helsinki has a lot of nice restaurants, and meals at high-end establishments begin at $35 USD.

Tap water is very safe to drink throughout this region. A bottle of water is generally $3. Save money and reuse your water bottle. You aren't going to get sick from drinking the tap water.

Buying your own food in Scandinavia is a must if you want to save money. Locals in this region of the world eat in far more than they eat out simply because of costs. All my friends in the region would never dream of eating out as often as we do in the United States. They simply couldn't afford to do so. During the summer months, farmer's markets offer a plethora of berries and fresh fruit that can be good and cheap snacks. If you do have to eat out, quick meals such as pizza, kebabs, fast food, or burgers, as well as outdoor sausage vendors, will be your cheapest food. This region of the world isn't a culinary dream either, so you aren't really missing out by not dining out or by sticking to the cheap eats.

TRANSPORTATION

Local transportation is relatively inexpensive in Scandinavia. Local trains and buses in the cities are around $5 USD per ride. All the major cities in this region of Europe offer weekly metro passes that are cheaper than purchasing single-ride tickets. If you are in a place for a while, consider buying them.

Trains

In Sweden, the majority of intercity trains cost $40–75 USD. They will cost $100–150 USD if it is a long overnight sleep train, like the fourteen-hour trip from Stockholm to Lulea up north. The farther north you go, the longer your train travel is and the more money it costs. If you want cheap train tickets, you need to purchase them at least one month before your departure date. Students and those under twenty-six are eligible for discounted train tickets.

Trains around Norway cost about $70 USD, depending on the distance and when you buy your ticket. Booking your train at least a week in advance (a "minipris" ticket) will get you a 50 percent discount. For example, from Oslo, the capital, to Bergen, on the west coast, the train costs $70–142 USD. It's $142 if you book the day of, but $70 USD if you book in advance. I always book in advance here because the substantial savings are worth the lack of flexibility in my schedule.

Train travel across Denmark (Jutland to Copenhagen) costs around $62 USD if you book the day of. Shorter distances of two hours or less are around $30 USD. Denmark is a really small country, so travel doesn't take that long. The closer you get to the travel date, the higher the cost. The train from the airport to Copenhagen center is $7 USD.

The Danish rail system offers cheap tickets called "Orange tickets" via their website (dsb.dk/om-billetter-og-kort/indland/billetter/dsb-orange). They are only available via the website, and you have to print out the ticket before you board the train. These tickets are a third of the cost of what you can buy at the railway station.

In Finland, train tickets cost between $60 USD and $80 USD regardless of the distance you travel. Booking in advance will get you a 25 percent discount off the day-of price. Groups of three or more can also get discounts of 15 percent off the ticket price.

Intercountry travel isn't that much more expensive than traveling around each country. A train from Stockholm to Oslo is about $57 USD, Stockholm to Copenhagen is around $75 USD. Copenhagen to Oslo varies between $60 USD and $120 USD.

Rail passes are offered for all the countries in the region, and I think they offer one of the best ways to save money here if you're traveling long distances. The global pass discussed in the Western Europe section covers all the countries in this region also. Additionally, there is a regional pass (eurail.com/eurail-passes/regional-pass/scandinavia) that begins at $322 USD for four days of travel. (You get 15 percent off when booking two or more tickets.)

If you are going vast distances or hopping between the countries in the region, then the passes work out. After all, each train ride with the pass is about an $80 USD value, and fares are often that high or higher on long-distance train journeys.

Buses

Buses are cheaper but slower than train travel. An extensive range of buses connects cities and even most national parks throughout the region. Buses booked a month or more in advance can be found for as cheap as $10 USD. However, those tickets are limited in number, and typically buses cost $35–50 USD.

In Finland, student discounts are available if you show a valid ISIC card. There is also a BusPass travel pass, which offers unlimited travel for $200 USD for seven days and $330 USD for fourteen days.

Regional and national bus companies include:

GoByBus: gobybus.se

Swebus: swebus.se

Abildskou: abildskou.dk

Nor-Way: nor-way.no

Nettbuss: nettbuss.no

Matkahuolto: matkahuolto.fi/en

Flying

There are four large airlines based out of Scandinavia:

SAS (flysas.com): A Star Alliance member, it operates the largest flight network in the region.

Finnair (finnair.com): A Oneworld member based out of Helsinki, this airline operates a small number of flights to major destinations in the region via their hub in Helsinki.

Norwegian Airlines (norwegian.no): Norwegian budget airline with extensive flights throughout the region.

Cimber Sterling (cimber.dk): A budget airline based out of Denmark that has flights around Denmark and to big cities in the region.

Booking months in advance can get you fares as low as $50 USD for flights around this region of Europe. Prices are generally more expensive here than elsewhere. You won't find very good flight deals, and unless you are really short on time (and long on money), buses and trains offer better value. The farther north you go, toward the Arctic, the more expensive and infrequent flights tend to be. In Denmark, flights to some of the smaller islands cost as much as $200 USD for a forty-five-minute flight.

The budget airlines discussed in previous chapters also have flights in and out of the region to other parts of Europe.

Museums in this region of the world typically cost $10 USD. Prices are pretty uniform throughout the region in that respect. There are a number of full-day activities to do in this region, and most involve going out and exploring the beautiful countryside. Most day trips cost $50 USD or more.

The best way to save money on attractions in Scandinavia is to buy the city tourism cards. Every big city or tourist destination offers one. Not only will they provide free public transportation, but they will save you a bundle on tourist sites, since most are very expensive here. For example, in Oslo, I saved $30 USD with the pass plus got free public transportation. In Helsinki, I saved $20 USD on attractions, plus I got discounts on some buffets and free city transportation.

Additionally, these cards offer discounts on many of the day trips offered from the cities, such as boat tours or hikes. City tourism cards can be bought at the local tourist office and often in the airport.

Using your ISIC, YIIA, or IYC card will also get you a discount between 20 and 50 percent on public attractions, museums, and tours.

How Much Money Do You Need?

Europe isn't the cheapest place to travel on $50 USD a day. Even Arthur Frommer, famed for his book *Europe on 5 Dollars a Day*, has upped his daily budget to $85 USD, but I don't think you need that much.

If you stick to the budget accommodations, food, and tours listed here and ignore all my tips on saving money, you'll need about $75 USD per day in Western Europe, $45 USD in Eastern Europe, and about $100 USD in Scandinavia. Those numbers reflect a traveler who stays in hostels, doesn't cook meals, eats mostly cheap food, drinks, and visits a lot of attractions. This is your typical backpacker budget. You aren't going to have a fancy time, but you aren't going to want for anything either.

However, by getting tourist cards and rail passes, avoiding flights, occasionally couch-surfing, and cooking some meals, you can travel a lot cheaper. In Western Europe, you can spend between $50 USD and $60 USD per day. In Eastern Europe, which is already cheap, by implementing my tips, you can travel on around $35 USD per day. In Scandinavia, there are so few ways to save that the cheapest you can do is around $70 USD per day.

On the ultra cheap, if you were to use Couchsurfing every day (or even camped), cooked all your meals, didn't drink, and saw a minimum of sights, you could do Western Europe on $35 USD per day, Eastern Europe on $20 USD, and Scandinavia on $50 USD. That would require you to take a train or a bus or hitchhike everywhere, skip most museums, and limit how often you go out.

By mixing destinations across Europe, you can keep your budget really low. Scandinavia cost me a lot of money, but by heading to Eastern Europe after I went there and spending less than $35 USD per day, I was able to lower my daily spending average to something more reasonable. While I may have spent $65 USD per day in Amsterdam, heading to Greece, where everything is much cheaper, I spent only $40 USD per day, thus bringing my daily average down again. Mix, match, save.

Europe can be a very expensive destination, and because of that, it requires more work to save money in. But it can be done. And it's how I'm able to afford trips to Europe every summer. By being conscious of when and where I'm spending my money, I've never had to turn down a wine tour in Italy or a night out on the town in Paris.

16

Australia

GROWING up, I had always viewed Australia as a cheap destination, but once I traveled there, I found it to be more expensive than Europe. Could you do Australia on $50 USD? Yes. Is it likely? Probably not. You can come close if you limit many of your activities. But Australia is made for people who want to get outside, and all those wonderful activities like camping in the outback, sailing the Whitsunday Islands, and diving the Great Barrier Reef eat into people's budgets very quickly. Moreover, Australia's strong economy and the large amount of mining money flowing through the country only contribute to the high cost of living there. Even Australians complain about costs!

But despite the costs, Australia remains one of the best places for travelers in the world. The country has a robust transportation system, a lot of hostels, lots of available jobs for travelers, and plenty of ways to see the country on a budget. It's an easy country to travel around. Add in friendly, helpful people eager to show visitors their country and a diverse and beautiful landscape, and you'll see why everyone who comes here leaves wanting more.

ACCOMMODATIONS

Hostels

Hostels in Australia are typically really nice. They are usually in very modern buildings, and many have pools, bars that serve food, extensive kitchens, comfortable beds, Internet, BBQ pits, common rooms, and a tour desk. However, most hostels in Australia do not serve breakfast.

Hostels cost $20–30 USD per night for a dorm room. Private rooms with a double bed with a shared bathroom range between $65 USD and $100 USD per night.

Hostels in the major cities on the east coast (that is, the popular backpacker trail) tend to be more expensive than out west due to higher demand.

It's slightly more expensive in Sydney and Melbourne and less expensive in Brisbane and Cairns. The majority of Perth's hostels fall into the $20–30 USD range.

As mentioned in Part One, Australian hostels accept a wide variety of discount cards, such as ISIC, VIP, and the Nomad MAD card. You can get a 10 percent savings off the price of a hostel.

While hostels in Australia are very expensive by any measure, they offer a wonderful community atmosphere, and many go out of their way to host events and dinners so travelers can meet each other. Australia has a real travel culture (almost every Australian goes backpacking at some point!), and they really bring that to the hostels they run. Although the costs are high, hostels are worth the price for travelers looking to meet other people or break out of their shell.

Budget Hotels

Budget hotels usually cost around $80 USD for a double room, private bathroom, TV, and breakfast. Budget hotels are nice and comfortable, but in Australia, I think you get more value from a hostel private room because of all the added amenities you end up paying for at a hotel. I generally avoid these budget hotels unless traveling with friends or a girlfriend. If you don't like hostels, I would use the rental apartments discussed next because they are a bit cheaper and you get all the privacy you want and the nice amenities of a home at a much better price.

Apartment Rentals

You can find apartment rentals in Australia. Apartment rentals have really taken off in Australia over the last two years, and you can find a lot of options, especially on the east coast. Airbnb lists over 5,500 listings in the greater Sydney area alone! Shared apartments typically start at $60 USD per night for a single room and $80 USD for an apartment. I would use these services over renting a hotel because they are usually cheaper, and you also have access to a kitchen, allowing you to cook and keep your food costs down. In Australia, the best apartment-finding website is Airbnb (airbnb.com).

Camping

Camping is the most popular way to save money in Australia, as it is a country with many car parks and campgrounds. Australians love the countryside, and you're never more than a couple of hours from a camp. Campsites cost between $10 USD and $20 USD per night for a spot that can be for either a car or a tent. At a minimum, they have toilet facilities and electricity. On the upper end, they can have pools, kitchen facilities, wi-fi, and cabins for rent.

Laurence Norah (findingtheuniverse.com) spent a year camping around Australia and never once had a problem locating an affordable place. As he states, "Campsites are easy to find, everywhere you go. They range from expensive to free. The closer you are to cities or popular destinations, such as most of the east coast, the harder it gets to find cheap sites. Good options are national parks, where there may be a nominal fee, or rest stops, which are free and legal to camp in, unless indicated otherwise."

Camps Australia (campsaustraliawide.com) produces a book that lists all the free and nearly free campsites around Australia (3,700-plus at last count). The book costs $89 USD. It's comprehensive and a good resource, but if you don't want to pay that price, hostel and hotel booking sites list campgrounds, just not as many as are included in the book.

Hospitality Exchanges

Hospitality exchanges are another cheap option, which is used in abundance here. I used Couchsurfing while I was in Broome, Australia, a small town on Australia's west coast. I had a great experience, and since the Australian election was occurring at the time, I learned a lot about Australian politics. You will find hosts wherever you go in Australia, and I've never had a problem finding a host here. In addition to Couchsurfing, Global Freeloaders is very big in Australia and your next best bet if Couchsurfing doesn't work out.

Servas and Hospitality Club also have a large number of

members in Australia. With so many members of all websites in this country, you will rarely have trouble finding a host, even last minute.

House-sitting is a fast and growing option in this country. There are plenty of available options, especially on the east coast. According to traveler Nora Dunn, "Because Australia is geographically so far from most of the rest of the world, many Australians choose to take extended leaves of absence from work and go away for up to months at a time. This means they like to have somebody to keep an eye on things at home, which gives house-sitters a chance to sample a slice of local Aussie life." One Australia-specific site is aussie housesitters.com.au.

WWOOF

Australia is one of the most popular destinations in the world for WWOOFing, as it has a large agricultural and cattle industry that relies heavily on the influx of young people who come to Australia to work and travel. It's very easy to find a job even if you don't have any farm or agriculture experience. The work isn't great—you'll be picking fruit most of the time—but you'll get free room and board. Jobs are so abundant in Australia that you are pretty much guaranteed to find a job. You'll get room and board covered, and in a country where those two cost so much, this is wonderful for your budget!

You'll need a working holiday visa to do this work (they keep everything legal), and Americans under thirty are eligible to get this type of visa in the United States before they come. You can get more information on working holiday visas from the Australian Immigration Board (immi.gov.au/visitors/working-holiday), and see Chapter 11 for more information on WWOOFing.

All accommodations can be booked at the booking sites mentioned in Chapter 11 or listed in Appendix A. Additionally, local tourist offices can help you secure accommodations.

FOOD

Australia is a very up-and-coming foodie place. I fondly remember eating at a restaurant in Sydney that had no menu—whatever was freshest at the market that day was cooked. However, the food in Australia isn't cheap—most meals cost $25 USD or more. Originally, I thought I was doing something wrong spending so much, but as a plethora of Australian friends told me, "We just get screwed here."

If you cook your meals, expect to pay $70–80 USD per week. For that price, your groceries will include pasta, vegetables, chicken, and some other basic foodstuffs. Kangaroo meat, which is their version of the cow, is very cheap, lean, and delicious, and can be a good alternative to more expensive steaks. Because food costs so much, campsites, hostels, apartments, and even some budget hotels have kitchen facilities for you to use. As Laurence from FindingtheUniverse.com told me, "Eating out with any regularity will massively cat into your budget. If you're camping, you should be equipped for cooking for yourself. Otherwise, hostels always have a kitchen where you can put together decent food yourself at a fraction of the cost of eating out. Stock up on the cheap food brands at the large supermarkets."

An average restaurant meal in Australia will run you $15–20 USD for no-frills eating. This includes pub food, fish-and-chip shops, Chinese restaurants, and quick lunch shops. If you are looking to eat out and on a budget, these restaurants are your best choice. A meal at a nice restaurant is around $35 USD for a starter and an entrée, without any alcohol. If you are staying in hostels, most offer meals each night for $6 USD and under. They call these "Special Backpacker meals," and the food is typically pasta, fish and chips, or burgers. It's not very healthy, but it is very cheap.

There are plenty of small sandwich shops where the price is $8–10 USD. Moreover, quick grab-and-go sushi restaurants abound throughout the country. You can get a few rolls that will provide a satisfying lunch for $10–12 USD. And you can eat these rolls even if you don't like fish—many are vegetarian.

There are unfortunately few ways to save money on food in this country. If you do want to eat out, you are going to spend a lot of money. Hostels do not offer free breakfast here either, so you will be spending money on three meals a day. You need to cook some if not a majority of your meals if you hope to avoid spending a lot of money on food. Treat yourself once in a while but stick to the BBQ—it's not Australia without putting some "shrimp on the barbie," right?

TRANSPORTATION

Locally, you'll find that medium to large towns have bus systems that cost around $2 USD. In the largest cities in Australia, you will also find a commuter rail and tram system that extends into the nearby suburbs. These train rides cost $2–3 USD. Prepaid day and weekly passes are available that reduce the rate of the daily fare.

In Melbourne, there is a free bus called the "Melbourne City Tourist Shuttle" that has a set thirteen-stop route around the city, stopping at all the main attractions. Sydney and Perth have free local bus service around their downtown (CBD) area but not to all the tourist sites.

Trains

Australia has a small train system that mainly covers the east coast. The rail system is split up among various carriers:

Countrylink: Covers the east coast, primarily Queensland and New South Wales via their coach network and Sunlander trail

The Ghan: Running from Adelaide to Darwin in the middle of the country

The Indian Pacific: Running from Sydney in the east to Perth on the west coast

The Overlander: Melbourne to Adelaide

The Rail Australia Alliance (railaustralia.com.au) has extensive information about train times and regional rail networks.

There are a handful of smaller train lines that connect one or two cities, but the four above are the only regional networks. One problem with the Australian rail network is that trains are infrequent (sometimes only one per week) and regional lines are not connected for seamless train travel to different parts of the country. Because of this, and the high cost of tickets, I would skip taking the train as your means of transportation.

If you are interested in taking the train, take the scenic multiday train journeys on the Ghan and the Indian Pacific route. These multi-day sleep routes offer an amazing experience and a unique way to see the countryside. Nora Dunn from theprofessionalhobo.com remarks, "My favorite way of seeing Australia is by train. Epic train rides like the Ghan and the Indian Pacific track across the vast outback and provide a land's-eye view of this great continent. And although it's not as cheap as a bus, it's not as expensive as you might think for what you get." And she is right because you can get some amazing discounts on those tickets!

Typically, the Ghan costs $1,450 USD for an adult ticket on a sleeper train, though those holding a YHA, ISIC, or VIP/MAD card get a discount to $1,000. The Indian Pacific costs $1,400 for an adult ticket and $1,050 for a youth ticket. This fare just includes the price of the train and your accommodation (seat or bed, depending on what you order). The basic fares do not include meals, though they are available to purchase on the train. Higher service tickets (gold or platinum) do include food.

The train rides last for a couple of days (days vary depending on the exact route you take). That shoots your daily average *way* higher than $50 USD.

Luckily, Rail Australia offers eight discount rail passes good for either three or six months that can be up to 60 percent off the cost of a single ticket. For example, you can get the Aus Reef and Outback pass (passes.railaustralia.com.au/pass/aus-reef-and-outback) for six months for about $900 USD, which gives you access to the Ghan, Indian Pacific, and any other train network. You essentially get all the trains for the price of one, and you can move in any direction as often as you like. These passes make both epic train journeys—two of the most famous in the world—incredibly affordable and attainable for travelers on a budget plus you get access to all the other trains too. Win-win! You can find out more about the eight rail passes offered at passes.railaustralia.com.au.

Buses

The easiest way to see Australia is via Greyhound Australia (greyhound.com.au). Greyhound offers two passes for travelers:

A kilometer-(distance-)based pass, with which you have up to twelve months to use your pool of kilometers with an option to top up as you go. You can choose from five hundred to twenty-five thousand km. Prices begin at $107 USD and go all the way up to $2,500 USD for the largest pass.

Don't use this pass. Paying per kilometer is a bad deal. The cheap one, for 500 km, is typically $107 USD for the suggested distance between Brisbane and Hervey Bay. Booking the ticket individually, I found it for $40 USD on Greyhound's website. The pass is a rip-off.

Instead, use the Mini Traveler passes. These passes provide travel between two popular destinations in one direction and give you ninety days to finish your route. Greyhound offers a number of set routes, so unlike with the kilometer-based pass, you can't choose your start and stop destinations—you must start and end in the cities listed on your pass.

I like this pass because you get more value for your money. On the popular Sydney to Cairns bus route, a normal bus ticket is about $400 USD for a direct one-way trip. However, the pass for the same route is typically $350 and lets you hop off and on as much as you would like. Not only is the pass cheaper, but it allows you to see other destinations on the way. Furthermore, you don't have to buy individual tickets along the way, which could add up if cheap tickets are not available.

There are also backpacker buses in Australia, like the Oz Experience (ozexperience.com). These buses cater to backpackers and young travelers. They tend to pick up and drop off in front of hostels (similar to Busabout, which was discussed in Chapter 15) and are not used by the locals. Prices begin at $500 USD and go up from there. The price really depends on the number of days you are traveling, your included activities, and the route you are taking. While these bus companies are typically more expensive than Greyhound, they often have sales to entice travelers to use their services over the normal Greyhound bus—but frankly, I don't think these services are worth it. You'll meet just as many travelers on the regular Greyhound as you would on these special backpacker buses, and unless they are offering a 30–50 percent sale, I don't see much value in using these companies.

If you get the VIP card, Nomad Mad card, or ISIC card mentioned in Part One, you will be able to get a discount of 10–15 percent off the price of your tickets from all the bus companies mentioned in this section.

Flying

With such a large country, the quickest way to get around is to fly. However, there is very limited air competition in Australia, so while flying is the quickest, it is also the most expensive form of transportation. In fact, Australians regularly complain that they can fly to Asia cheaper than they can fly across the country. Australia has four major airlines:

Qantas: qantas.com

Jetstar (a subsidiary of Qantas): jetstar.com

V Australia: virginaustralia.com/au/en

Tiger Airways: tigerairways.com

There are some very small regional airlines in Western Australia that fly routes between Perth and a few outback destinations but are mainly used by mining companies to shuttle employees around. With only four airlines, you rarely get rock-bottom fares like you do in Europe. There are occasional sales for routes along the east coast that bring fares in line with buses, and you can find these fares by using the flight tips mentioned in Part One. However, for the most part, flights, especially going across country, are prohibitively expensive and should be avoided.

Camper Vans

The most popular and cheapest way to travel around Australia is to drive yourself. Camper van and car rentals do two things: They lower your transportation costs because van rentals are really cheap and driving yourself is cheaper than taking the bus or flying. (A camper van can be bought as cheap as $500 USD for a used van or as much as $2,000 USD for a new one.) And they also double as a bedroom, so you can save on accommodation by sleeping in the van instead of a hostel. As mentioned before, campsites dot the country and are generally 50 percent less expensive than a hostel dorm bed. And because you can sleep in these vehicles and split the costs, a lot of travelers—young and old—use this method to get around Australia. It's the most economical way to explore the country.

If you decide not to buy a van, you can also rent one. The major companies for camper van rentals are:

Spaceships: spaceshipsrentals.com.au

Wicked Campers: wickedcampers.com.au

Traveller's Autobarn: travellers-autobarn.com.au

Rentals start as low as $35 USD per day and discount cards mentioned in Chapter 8 can get you between 5 and 10 percent off the listed price.

If you don't want to rent or buy new, but would instead like to buy a used vehicle or are just looking for travelers to share the journey with, web classifieds like Gumtree (gumtree.com.au) or hostel message boards can allow you to find travelers looking for rides or those wanting to get rid of their car. Taking a few travelers on to share the cost of the van and gas can cut your transportation/accommodation expenses to less than $20 USD per day! And when the journey is over, and you don't want to be stuck with a car, you can just sell it to a new group of travelers. It's a way for you to recover some of your up-front costs.

ATTRACTIONS AND ACTIVITIES

When talking about what to do in Australia, you're really talking about what you're going to do outdoors. Australians love to get outdoors, and with such a beautiful and diverse countryside, you will too. Like everything else in this country, tours are expensive and there are few ways to lower the costs. While I never regret the money

I spend seeing the country or diving the Great Barrier Reef, I've severely underestimated this part of my budget.

Most outdoor activities in Australia take up a whole day, though larger trips into the outback generally last at least one night.

Multiday activities are expensive, generally costing $300–400 USD. Day trips will cost $100–170 USD. For example, a one-day trip to the Great Barrier Reef can cost $170 USD, while two nights sailing the Whitsunday Islands can cost upward of $400. A three-day trip to Uluru from Alice Springs is around $355. (These prices reflect the average among companies aimed at budget travelers. Luxury and more all-inclusive tours cost more.)

Buying tours together can also help save you money. In Australia, it's cheaper to go to a hostel tour desk or places like Tribal Tours (tribaltravel.com.au) and book your activities in one package. You can expect to get around 10 percent off the tours.

The VIP and Nomad Mad cards discussed in Part One provide discounts on tours of up to 30 percent. These cards are essential if you're traveling in Australia, because tours there simply cost so much these days. They are double what I paid during my original trip to Australia in 2007.

Australia is a young country, and because of that, it lacks a lot of the sort of historical sites that you see in Europe and other parts of the world. Most of the activities you do will be ones that focus on nature as opposed to visiting ruins or exploring castles. There are few museums outside the large cities. Most of the museums are history or art museums, and admission fees are around $15 USD.

There is no single tourist card for Australia. Iventure (iventure card.com) offers a tourist card for Sydney, Melbourne, Queensland, and Tasmania. Two-day passes begin at $155 USD and cover all the museums and major attractions in each area. They only save you money though if you do at least half of the attractions and excursions included in the pass, which will mean that you'll be extremely busy during your visit.

How Much Money Do You Need?

On a very tight budget, I think a traveler could get by in Australia on $50 USD per day, but it would be really tough. It would entail couchsurfing and cooking just about every day, limiting your nights out, and spending most of your money on transportation and a few activities. While not impossible, it could be done if you were very frugal.

For example, if you did Melbourne to Cairns, which is the popular east coast route that most travelers take, your approximate costs for one month would be $810 USD for hostels (average price of $27 USD per night), $700 USD for food (mixing cooking and eating out), $1,000 USD for tours, and $500 USD for your Greyhound bus ticket. That works out to $100 USD per day. If you couch-surfed for ten nights and bought all your own food (at a cost of $80 USD per week or $440 USD for one month), you could lower your budget to $82 USD per day. But I think you can do it on less.

Realistically, I think if you were to budget $65 USD per day, you would be able to travel around the country without compromising too much luxury. You'd still have plenty of money for the tours and activities and to eat a few good meals. In order to hit that figure, you would need to stay in hostels, couch-surf, cook a number of your meals, car share, drink little, use discount cards, and only do two major activities.

Additionally, using a camper van for accommodation and getting around on your own, you could lower your daily average even further. As Laurence says, "I set myself a living budget of around $55 USD a day, which is absolutely achievable if you manage your money properly." If you are driving in a camper van, camping, cooking food, and limiting your activities, this budget is very realistic. After all, instead of paying for an expensive tour through the outback, you can just do it yourself in your car!

Australia isn't a cheap country, but like any place, if done smartly and skillfully using the budget tips mentioned in this section, it doesn't need to be overbearingly expensive. While a trip there won't be as cheap as a trip to Costa Rica or Thailand, you can still find ways to save money and reduce your costs.

New Zealand

NEW Zealand is another country that can destroy your budget. Day-to-day life here isn't expensive—the problem is that New Zealand has so many outstanding outdoor activities that it just sucks your money out of your wallet. This country is known for its natural landscape, and adventure activities here, like caving, skydiving, bungee jumping, fishing, and glacier trekking, can really add up. But while those costs can accumulate and travelers need to pick and choose their battles, New Zealand's jaw-dropping beauty makes any visit there worth it. Anyone who has ever seen *Lord of the Rings* knows just how beautiful this country is with its mountain ranges, green forests, meadows, caves, and inviting lakes that shimmer under clear blue skies. New Zealand is a country that may not always be friendly to your wallet but will always be friendly to your eyes.

ACCOMMODATIONS

Hostels

Hostels in New Zealand are very nice and feature a lot of amenities, such as common rooms, comfortable beds, bars, tour booking desks, work placement help, and Internet stations. One thing they don't have though is free breakfast.

Hostels in New Zealand cost around $22 USD per night for a six-bed dorm. There are three big hostel chains in the country: Base (stayatbase.com/hostels/new-zealand-hostels.aspx), YHA (yha .co.nz), and Nomads (nomadshostels.com), and their prices are similar. They have locations in all the major tourist destinations throughout the country.

Each hostel chain offers discounts through the Nomad Mad card, the YHA card, and Base, which offers a ten-stay "Base Jumping" package that gives you a $4 USD discount off each night.

There is also a network of independent hostels that have organized to form BBH (bbh.co.nz). These are typically $1–2 USD a night cheaper than the chains, unless they're in a popular destination like Queenstown or Taupo, where those prices are then equal. If you get the BBH card discussed in Part One, you can save a further $1–2 USD off the price.

Private rooms in hostels start around $66 USD per night for a double bed and en suite room.

B&Bs and Budget Hotels

B&Bs are very common in New Zealand, especially in the small outdoor towns. You'll get those picturesque homes with antique-looking rooms, big comfy beds, and a home-cooked meal for breakfast. Prices for a double room are $80–120 USD. While quaint, this accommodation option is not very affordable. If I really wanted my own room, I would choose a hostel private room because they are cheaper. A good website to find B&Bs is at bnb.co.nz.

Budget hotels are similarly priced to these bed-and-breakfasts but lack the charm of B&Bs. That being said, I still think hotels, guesthouses, and bed-and-breakfasts in New Zealand are all overpriced. There are so many cheaper options that I avoid these.

Apartment Rentals

Apartment rental prices range from $30 USD to $60 USD per night for a private room in a home. Large apartments for groups tend to cost $70–100 USD per night. In New Zealand, there aren't a lot of options here. You don't find many hosts if you aren't in one of the large cities, as this style of travel hasn't really caught on. If you are spending a lot of time in small towns and in the country, this option won't work very well.

Camping

Camping is the best budget option in New Zealand. Because it is such an outdoor-friendly country, you will find a lot of campgrounds, as well as car and camper van parks. Kiwis (locals) love to be outdoors, and like the Australians, they provide a lot of ways for you to do that too.

Campsites cost between $15 USD and $20 USD per night. You can rent cabins with a bed for two people for around $33 USD. The price includes use of all park communal facilities, such as kitchen, showers/toilets, and laundry. All people staying in the parks have access to the public facilities. Many of these sites have deluxe apartments that fit two to eight people, with their own shower, cooking, and laundry facilities. Prices begin at $60 USD.

The NZ Department of Conservation runs public camping facilities throughout the country, which include the amenities listed above. Prices begin at $6 USD per person (doc.govt.nz).

There is a collection of independent campsite owners who run Kiwi Holiday Parks and offer a membership ($25 USD) that will give you 10 percent off your stay. You can get more information at kiwi holidayparks.com/vipcards.php.

Hospitality Exchanges

Hospitality exchanges, especially Couchsurfing, are widespread here, and with so many people signed up for the service, you'll have no problem finding a host, even in off-the-beaten-path destinations. Global Freeloaders, the Australian-based website, is also popular here. Servas and Hospitality Club also have good networks in this area of the world.

House-sitting is very popular in New Zealand, and you will find a lot of hosts looking for sitters, especially in vacation areas such as the Bay of Islands, Queenstown, and the Coromandel. You can refer back to Chapter 11 for information on house-sitting.

WWOOF

WWOOFing opportunities are abundant in this country. Because a lot of the economy in New Zealand is land-based, with sheep farms, fruit farms, and wineries dotting the country (in fact, there are ten times more sheep in New Zealand than people), you find a high demand for willing farmworkers. You can find work using the methods discussed in Chapter 11 as well as by simply asking around. With so many travelers using this option in New Zealand, you can always find someone to point you toward a farm, and because of the transient nature of the workers, there is always at least one farm looking for workers.

All accommodations can be booked at the booking sites mentioned in Chapter 11 or listed in Appendix A. Additionally, local tourist offices can help you secure accommodations.

FOOD

There's a lot of mouthwatering food here and some world-class wine. While you can splurge here and there, eating out in New Zealand is always expensive. After all, at about $16 USD for a small meal, you'll bust your budget quicker than Homer Simpson in a donut store!

Grocery shopping will cost typically $60 USD per week. You'll be able to get the basics: pasta, meats, vegetables, and breads. I often found myself cooking a lot while there. I don't find the restaurants in New Zealand to be as good of a value as in the United States, so by cooking most of your food, you aren't missing out on a host of cultural dishes. There's no typical New Zealand food.

Cheap and inexpensive meals such as sandwiches, pizza, and grab-and-go eateries abound in this country and cost around $8 USD for a sandwich and a drink. Kebabs and noodle shops are usually $10–12 USD, as are fish-and-chip shops. As in Australia, sushi is very popular and there are a lot of fast-food sushi joints that serve premade rolls in the $5–8 USD range. When I got tired of cooking, all these shops kept me fed on a budget.

New Zealand cafés offer delicious gourmet food. I remember a beautiful summer salad with nuts, apples, and blue cheese I ate in Auckland. Or that wonderful lamb steak I had in Queenstown while sitting outside sipping a nice glass of white wine. New Zealanders take a lot of pride in their food. It's very artisanal but sadly very expensive. An average meal will cost around $25 USD for a starter and main course. If you are just looking for a starter, you can expect to pay $10–12 USD.

Besides grocery shopping, if you are looking to eat out in New Zealand, do so during lunchtime. Cafés and restaurants have lunch menus until about 3 p.m. that cost as little as $15 USD, which is still expensive compared to grocery shopping, but about half the price of dinner.

I like to mix eating out during lunch with cooking my own food for dinner. That way I enjoy some of New Zealand's delicious cafés while still saving money.

TRANSPORTATION

The best way to get around cities in New Zealand is via their extensive bus network (cities don't have subway systems in New Zealand). Local buses cost about $1 USD per trip for a trip around the city center.

Trains
New Zealand has a small train network that goes from Auckland down to Wellington in the North Island and down the coast from Picton to Christchurch in the South Island. Though scenic, it's ridiculously expensive. Prices for the Auckland-to-Christchurch route, which include the ferry between the north and south islands, are more than $190 USD. However, a flight can be as low as $38 USD.

Kiwirail (kiwirail.co.nz) offers a fourteen-day pass for $400 USD, but at $28 USD per train ride, you would have to travel every day just to have the price work out close to the bus price.

Unless you are a train enthusiast, this is not a good budget travel option. Skip the train, take the bus, or fly.

Buses

New Zealand has two main bus companies: Intercity Line and Naked Bus (no one is actually naked on the bus). Fares are typically between $15 USD and $25 USD on either line, with the Naked Bus being on the cheaper end. With the Naked Bus, you can purchase fares for as little as 75 cents USD if you book at least three months in advance. Tickets at this price level are first come, first served and available in limited numbers. Sometimes you get lucky and find one last-minute.

Intercity offers bus passes (intercity.co.nz/passes). The two of best value are the Flexipass and the Flexitrip pass. The Flexipass is an hour-based pass for from fifteen to sixty hours. Prices begin at $80 USD. Your pass is good for a set number of hours, and hours are calculated based on the hours per trip, in other words the time it takes to get from point A to point B. This is an awful deal. For example, a regular fare from Auckland to Wellington is $25 USD and takes eleven hours. So that $25 fare is three times less than the cost of the Flexipass!

A better pass is the Flexitrip pass, which starts at $117 USD for five trips. Five trips at the regular price of $25 USD would be $125 USD, so the pass represents a mild savings. It's not a substantial savings, but it's better than the other pass and saving money is still saving money. Either way, these passes aren't great. The nonrefundable fares are so cheap that there's no real incentive to get a pass.

The Naked Bus (nakedbus.com/nz/bus) has passes starting at $75 USD for three trips and going up to $450 USD for unlimited trips in a year. The more trips you get, the cheaper the pass is, and frankly, this is a wonderful money-saving deal. Any pass with ten trips or more brings the price to $19 USD or less. If you are going to do extensive bus travel, I would consider getting a pass, as the single-point fares on Naked Bus and the Intercity are rarely that low. Most passes are valid for one year.

A popular method of transportation among younger travelers is backpacker buses, such as Stray Travel (straytravel.com), Magic Bus (magicbus.co.nz), and the Kiwi Experience (kiwiexperience.com). Like the Oz Experience in Australia, these buses are a substitute for the local bus and are strictly used by tourists. Unlike in Australia, these buses actually provide a much better value for your money. You'll get included in your passes meals, activities, day trips, and discounts on attractions. Prices vary greatly depending on the pass you get. Prices are a lot higher during peak tourism season in December through February. The most basic passes start at $250 USD.

I am a huge fan of backpacker buses here. If you have the time and want to meet a lot of other travelers, I think they are better than the public bus. There are a lot of communal activities and events that get people socializing, and you can always get off if you don't like the crowd you are with, or stay on if you do, and travel at your own pace. Years later, I'm still good friends with the people I met on my Kiwi Experience bus. While the general age range for travelers on these buses is from eighteen to thirty, I found many older travelers on them too.

Camper Vans

As in Australia, a lot of travelers rent cars and vans in New Zealand because it's easy to get around and there are a lot of campsites along the way. I find it to be an even more economical way to travel than in Australia because the country is smaller and the weak New Zealand dollar makes it even cheaper to rent the cars and sleep in campsites. And as mentioned in the accommodations section, many hostels allow you to camp on their grounds too. The biggest car rental companies are:

Spaceships: spaceshipsrentals.co.nz

Hippie Campers: hippiecamper.com

Wicked Campers: wickedcampers.com.au

Backpacker Campervans: backpackercampervans.co.nz

Using the companies above, you can rent cars for as little as $25 USD per day. You can find tons of travelers selling their old cars too.

By getting other travelers to come with you and using these vans for accommodation, you can drastically reduce your housing and transportation costs. Sites like Gumtree NZ (auckland.gumtree .co.nz) and hostel message boards host inquiries from travelers finished with their trip and looking to make some of their money back by selling their vehicle. This is a good way to get a car cheaply. Within hours of arriving at my hostel in Auckland, I was offered about three cars by people looking to sell.

Flying

Flying around New Zealand is expensive, despite the short distances flown. New Zealand only has two countrywide carriers: Air New Zealand (airnewzealand.co.nz) and Jetstar (jetstar.com/nz/en/home). Since there is no competition, fares stay high. However, on heavy traffic routes, like from Auckland to Christchurch or from Christchurch to Queenstown, you can find very cheap fares. The two airlines really fight it out for customers, and between big cities you can find fares as low as $50 USD.

While I think New Zealand is best seen from the ground, if you are short on time, flying would be just as cost-effective as taking a bus from one end of an island to the other or the bus and ferry between islands. I flew from Wellington to Christchurch during the holidays, and it was only $40 USD. It was a much quicker and more economical route than the bus and ferry. But on the other end of the spectrum I flew from much smaller Nelson to Auckland and the ticket cost me $200 USD. Time but not money was saved.

You can refer to Part One for tips on how to find cheap flights.

Hitchhiking

Hitchhiking is also very popular in New Zealand and a relatively safe method of travel. As with hitchhiking anywhere in the world, you need to use common sense when getting into a stranger's car, especially if you are a solo female traveler. Not everyone will feel comfortable doing this, but if you are thumbing it by the side of the road, you'll find plenty of people will pull over and give you a lift.

ACTIVITIES AND ATTRACTIONS

Activities in New Zealand will really drive your costs up. This country revolves around outdoor activities, and its tourism industry markets this place as one of the top adventure travel destinations in the world. Since the activities here are so popular and in such demand, most tend to cost between $100 USD and $300 USD. For example, the Waitomo Glowworm Caves and a Maori cultural show are both around $80 USD, and bungee jumping is typically $150 USD. Skydiving costs about $300 USD.

Even though New Zealand is a young country, there are still a few museums and historical attractions worth seeing here. The main museum in the whole country is Te Papa in Wellington, the capital. It's free. However, most other history or art museums in the country cost around $5 USD for an entrance fee.

Occasionally, you'll find special offers from the companies that offer activity tours (see Appendix A for a list of companies), and you can sometimes get discounts through travel agencies or hostels. You may also find activity discounts if you buy a lot of tours at once.

The BBH, ISIC, VIP, and Mad cards discussed in Part One all offer some discounts for selected providers of up to 10 percent. If you are using any of the backpacker buses, they also have partnerships with tour operators for similar discounts.

Because of the high cost of tours here, you really need to pick and choose your battles. And if you start doing multiple bungee jumps or skydives, all hope is lost. I suggest choosing before you come here the five major outdoor activities you want to do and then just sticking to them.

New Zealand has a much more centralized tourist industry than Australia, but unlike many destinations in the world, they have not caught on to the tourist card trend. At the time of this writing, there's no national or city pass that gets you discounts on attractions or tours.

How Much Money Do You Need?

Without taking any money-saving measures, you'll find that New Zealand will cost you around $70 USD per day. That budget would include staying in hostels, eating cheap food and cooking your meals, transportation, and two or three big activities.

But there's no need to spend that much money while in NZ. Outside of all the activities, such as skydiving and bungee jumping, you aren't going to be spending a lot of money per day. By following the methods I talk about, you can reduce your expenses to $50 USD. Your biggest expenses will be accommodations and activities. There are a lot of free sights, parks, and hiking in New Zealand. Cooking your food and staying in a hostel will cost less than $30 USD per day. Once you begin to follow the tips on food and accommodations laid out in this chapter, that number can drop even more!

I've known people who have gotten by on around $30 USD per day in New Zealand simply by cooking every meal, working for their accommodations, and only spending money on activities, transportation, and alcohol. Realistically, most people probably won't go to that extreme.

If you are an adrenaline junkie, expect to double your daily $50 USD goal because, as you saw, the activities aren't cheap. But you can make up those costs by utilizing the budget tips discussed in this chapter. Like I said before, it's about knowing where you want to spend your money.

New Zealand is a country designed to suck your money away. You don't want to be indoors here—you want to be out exploring, eating at boutique restaurants, and drinking wine. And that destroys your budget. Budgeting here takes a lot of work because there are so many opportunities to spend money, but it's not impossible to do New Zealand on $50 USD per day if you pick and choose your battles properly.

Southeast Asia

Thailand, Singapore, Laos, Vietnam, Cambodia, Malaysia, Indonesia

S OUTHEAST Asia is so affordable that the typical travel trail is way less than $50 USD per day. I'm always shocked when people tell me they've spent more than that in this region. Yes, if you stay at big-name hotels, fly a lot, eat the same food as back home, and shop, you can spend a lot of money. But this is a region where the average yearly salary in some countries is less than $1,000 USD. In Thailand, one of the most developed countries in the region, the average annual salary is $3,700 USD. Live like a local, save lots of money.

As in Europe, costs in Southeast Asia aren't monolithic. Singapore, a highly developed shipping and financial center, is vastly more expensive than rural countries like Cambodia or Laos. Rural Thailand is a fraction of the cost of popular tourist and resort islands like Ko Samui. There are huge swings in prices in Thailand in part because there are vast disparities in wealth throughout the region. That said, the relatively inexpensive nature of the majority of the region (outside the major cities and developed tourist centers) makes it a lot more uniform in prices than other regions of the world. I can get a meal for a dollar anywhere in the region.

ACCOMMODATIONS

Guesthouses and Hostels

In Southeast Asia, you can get basic single rooms with a fan and shared bathrooms for as little as $1 USD per night or stay in luxury five-star beach resorts for thousands of dollars per night in Bali. Thailand, Malaysia, and Singapore are the most expensive countries, with Laos, Vietnam, Indonesia, and Cambodia being the cheapest.

Simple guesthouses throughout Southeast Asia generally cost $10 USD per night for a basic room, fan (sometimes air-conditioning), and hot water. If you want something nicer that includes a more comfortable bed and a TV, expect to pay $15–20 USD per night. If you want something cheaper and more basic, you can often find rooms for as little as $4 USD per night, especially in rural areas. You won't get five-star luxury here—the beds are probably uncomfortable, the water pressure low, and the rooms small, but if you are on a budget, they'll provide a good night's sleep in a clean environment. Unlike other regions of the world, there are no large brands or chains in Southeast Asia. Most guesthouses are small, family-run establishments.

Additionally, hostels as described throughout the book don't really exist in Southeast Asia, though that is slowly changing, and hostels are becoming more and more popular for the flashpacker crowd. In more expensive cities in Asia, you can find traditional hostels—dorm rooms, communal kitchen, shared bathrooms, tour desk, communal space. This is especially true in Singapore, where accommodations are expensive. Generally, hostels in Southeast Asia cost more than guesthouses and cater to travelers wanting nicer digs and a more Western accommodation experience.

Over the last few years, dormitories have become more prolific in the region. When I first traveled around this area in 2006, there were hardly any hostels, and ones with dormitory rooms were even rarer. Accommodations were so inexpensive there was never a need for them. Now dormitories are increasingly common in destinations popular with backpackers and are often the cheapest option out there. As accommodation prices have risen in the region, dormitory beds have come in to serve travelers on an ultra-tight budget. Dorm rooms cost between $3 USD and $5 USD per night. In Singapore, where accommodations are higher in price, you can expect to pay around $15 USD per night for a dorm room. Dorm rooms are generally found in the big cities and popular tourist locations where backpackers frequent.

Budget Hotels

Locally owned hotels begin at $30 USD per night throughout the region. These hotels tend to be small, with rooms that contain a double bed, TV, A/C, hot water, and private bathroom. In Singapore, a cheap double room can be around $45 USD with a shared bathroom and about $60 USD for a private bathroom. In cheaper countries, like Cambodia and Laos, you can find rooms beginning at $20 USD per night. If you're OK to stay at a hotel without air-conditioning, you'll pay $5–10 USD less. It should be noted that in this region of the world guesthouses and hostels do not provide breakfast, so you will need to buy your own.

TripAdvisor (tripadvisor.com) is an invaluable resource for this part of the world because many of the small guesthouses and hotels are not online. TripAdvisor is a website that allows people to leave reviews of the hotel they have stayed in. Because anyone can put a listing on the site for free, you'll find many hotels listed there that don't turn up in a Google search. These places don't have a website, nor do they pay the commission fees charged by larger booking sites like Hotels.com. But since TripAdvisor is free, you'll find that it becomes a good directory of properties in the region, where you can at least get phone numbers to call and make bookings.

When booking hotels in Southeast Asia, use the website Agoda (agoda.com). Agoda focuses on accommodations in Asia and has the most robust listings for guesthouses and hotels in this region. They regularly have sales and will list prices cheaper than those found on worldwide sites like Hotels.com or Booking.com.

Hospitality Exchanges

If you are looking to save money off already cheap accommodations, dorm rooms and Couchsurfing are the best methods for this region. Couchsurfing is widely used in large cities and major tourist destinations.

While most hosts are Westerners living in the region, hospitality networks are growing in popularity and more and more local hosts can be found with each passing day. While I believe accommodation in the region is cheap enough as it is, using hospitality networks is a wonderful way to have someone help you navigate the overwhelming nature of Southeast Asia, especially the variety of foods as that can be intimidating for many first-time visitors.

FOOD

Food is very inexpensive in Southeast Asia. If you are spending a lot of money on food, you are simply eating too many Western meals. Even with a balance of Western meals and local dishes, I rarely spend more than $10 USD per day on food unless I decide to feed my sushi addiction.

In Southeast Asia, street food is the most popular form of eating. "Street food" refers to little outdoor food stalls that line the streets of Asia, where residents eat snacks, have dinner, and buy prepared meals. I love nothing more than heading to the local market, sitting down, and grabbing a delicious plate of fried rice, pad Thai, noodle soup, or stir-fried noodles. Walking through the markets grabbing skewers of BBQ meats, fresh fruit shakes, and spring rolls makes Southeast Asia one of the funnest and most delicious regions of the world.

Many travelers are worried that street food isn't safe, but I assure you it is. If it made people sick, people wouldn't eat at these stalls in such large numbers. Your risk of food sickness is no greater than in a restaurant, and probably even less. After all, food at the stalls is cooked fresh in front of you and used every night. It doesn't sit around. And there are no cabinets for rats or bugs to get into. I eat street food wherever I can and prefer street stalls to sit-down restaurants.

On average, these meals cost no more than $1.50 USD. You find these stalls throughout Southeast Asia, lining major streets and at the markets. In Thailand, you even find markets dedicated to street food. There's the famous Thong Lor food market in Bangkok and the big night market at Chiang Mai Gate in the northern city of Chiang Mai. It seems that on the corner of every street in Vietnam is a *pho* (noodle soup) seller. In Singapore, you'll find street food (or "hawker stands" as they are called there) to be around $3 for a meal. Singapore also has cheap Chinese and Indian food in Chinatown and Little India respectively, where you can get meals from $5 USD.

Even if you go into small local restaurants, the price does not increase that much. What is $1.50 USD at a street stall is only $3–5 USD at a local restaurant. If you went into a restaurant in Thailand, you'd pay around $4 USD for a pad Thai that would have cost $1 USD on the street. In Cambodia, street food, which isn't as abundant as I would like it to be, is around $1 USD, while restaurants charge around $3 USD for a local dish like Amok (coconut milk dish) or Luc Lac (pepper gravy beef).

Western meals, including burgers, bad pizza, and sandwiches, cost around $5 USD for cheaply made food. This is going to be the most expensive part of your food budget in this region. If you want something that actually tastes like it does back home, you're looking at spending at least $10 USD for your meal. In the mood for a really nice bowl of pasta? About $8 USD. Want a deliciously made steak? At least $20 USD. In short, even though the food is cheaper than back home, it is expensive by local standards, and eating a lot of Western food will diminish your ability to save in this region.

There is a lot of high-end food in Southeast Asia, especially in very touristy and expat-filled places like Singapore, Bangkok, Kuala Lumpur, and Bali. I've had some of the best sushi of my life in Thailand and amazing Italian food in Bali. Some of the best BBQ ribs I've had were in a small beach town in Cambodia. But while the food is delicious, the price is only a little cheaper than what you would pay back home, and in some cases, it's even more. Splurge and try these tasty meals, but do so sparingly.

If you want to save money on food in Southeast Asia, simply buy local dishes (did you really come here to eat a shitty hamburger?) and you won't spend more than $6–8 USD a day.

As Stuart McDonald from travelfish.org, the best reference website on Asia, puts it, "Budget hotels and guesthouses in Thailand will often charge $3–5 USD for an American Breakfast at their café or restaurant. You'll get a steaming bowl of noodles and a good local coffee for a third of that on the street."

TRANSPORTATION

It is very cheap and easy to travel around Southeast Asia. Hub cities like Bangkok specialize in getting tourists to their next destination, even if it's two countries away. There is a whole industry in Asia meant to keep you, the tourist, happy and on the move.

Local public transportation costs from a few pennies to a few dollars. In Bangkok, the public bus costs 10 cents USD while the metro train system costs $1 USD per ride. In Singapore, the local train system starts at $1 USD. In Vietnam and Laos, a bus ride will cost you the same. No matter where you are in the region, you'll find yourself spending very little on local city transportation.

Taxis (metered taxis) and tuk tuks (small shared taxis with no meter, where you have to haggle) are normally double to triple what the local transportation is, and you often have to haggle over the price. They start really high and you work toward something you are willing to pay. Eventually you come to a compromise, which is usually about half the price they started with.

In Singapore and Indonesia, taxi drivers do put on the meter. In Bangkok, you can get taxi drivers to use the meter, but if you're hailing one in a tourist area, he might try to avoid using it. In Vietnam, the meter is usually rigged, but if you can get a reputable company like Mai Linh, you won't have any problems. This does not apply to tuk tuks, where you always need to haggle on a price.

Trains

Trains are also very cheap in this part of the world, but most train lines don't travel between countries. There is a train that runs from Singapore to Bangkok, though you have to switch trains twice in Malaysia (once in the capital, Kuala Lumpur, and once more at the border town of Butterworth). That's the closest thing they have to a regional train. That train costs $75 USD and takes a day and a half of travel. It's a beautiful scenic journey through the countryside, but if you are pressed for time, the three-hour flight from Singapore to Bangkok costs the same.

You can buy train tickets at the station or online at KTM (Malaysian Railways; ktmb.com.my) if you are going north to Bangkok. If you are going south to Singapore, you can use thailandtrainticket.com or simply book at the train station.

To book Malaysian trains by phone or email, email callcenter@ktmb.com.my or call them on + 60 3 2267 1200 if calling from outside Malaysia or 03 2267 1200 from within Malaysia.

But generally, I never prebook trains. I find it easier just to go to the train station and book the ticket there, as the online websites are very confusing and the price is the same online as it is in person.

Generally, in Southeast Asia, train prices are determined by distance and class, so the farther you go, the more you pay. Night trains with sleeper cars are more expensive than day trains. The night train to Chiang Mai, Thailand, from Bangkok takes twelve hours and costs $15 USD. However, that same train during the day is $7 USD. In Vietnam, trains run up and down the coast and cost $78 USD from Hanoi to Ho Chi Minh City. In Indonesia, trains go through the island of Java. The trains aren't glamorous, but the seats are comfortable and there's a dining car. Ticket prices start at $26 USD. There are no regular trains in Cambodia and only one train line in Laos—from the Thai border to the capital of Vientiane.

Train tickets in other countries are also best bought at the train station. At the time of this writing, there is no English version of Vietnamese or Indonesian train websites.

Buses

Buses are the best way to move around from country to country in Southeast Asia. Bus costs vary between $5 USD and $8 USD for a five- to six-hour journey. Overnight buses cost $10–15 USD, depending on distance. Buses go everywhere you want to go, and since there is no train system in the region, they are the main form of transportation for locals and tourists alike.

Buses are operated by a plethora of small operators. There is no version of Greyhound. You simply go with the operator who services the route you want or with the company the tourist agency/guesthouse sets you up with. All I do is show up at the station and book my ticket. You don't need to book in advance online.

There are many tourist-only buses in Southeast Asia. While they are very convenient, they are usually about 25 percent more expensive than the local buses. These buses will pick you up at your accommodation and drop you off at your accommodation in your next destination. Usually when you book buses from tourist agencies or guesthouses, they book you on these tourist buses.

And as Stuart, owner of the Asia travel website Travelfish.org, warns, "Saving money by taking local transportation can often be a false economy as it can take a lot longer than something more tourist-focused. It may be worth spending the extra $2 if it means you are on the beach four hours earlier."

While local buses are much cheaper, they aren't often direct. They always stay full, so they will pick up people along the way, drop people off, and then pick up new people. As Stuart says, this often means slower travel. As someone who has done this before, I can tell you it can become painful after a while when all you want is to get out of this cramped bus and reach your destination.

Ferries

Ferry prices vary greatly throughout the region and depend on the popularity of the island you are going to. For example, in Thailand, a country famous for its islands, a ferry ticket is $15 USD from the mainland. In Cambodia, round-trip tickets cost $10 USD from Sihanoukville on the mainland to the popular Monkey Island.

As with buses, there are no recommended lines. There is just the company that services the route you want, or the guesthouse that runs a boat from the mainland to your island paradise. The only exception is in Indonesia, where Perama Tours (peramatour.com) tends to be the best and main operator for tourists looking to get around Bali and Lombok.

Flying

If you want to fly, there are four budget airlines in this region:

Air Asia: airasia.com

Nok Air: nokair.com

Tiger Airways: tigerairways.com

Jetstar: jetstar.com

They often run fare deals as little as $10. Generally speaking though, fares are closer to $30 USD per one-way trip if booked in advance. Last-minute fares can cost more than $100 USD. On all of these airlines, you'll need to pay a bag fee as well as a "convenience fee" (really a not so convenient fee!) for using a credit card.

Air Asia is the biggest and most popular airline in the region. I like flying them a lot. You don't get much with them, but their planes are comfortable, and with such cheap fares, there's really nothing to complain about!

Generally, getting around Asia won't cost you much money, especially if you stick to the local buses and avoid the tourist transit system (private coaches that take tourists from one destination to another).

ACTIVITIES AND ATTRACTIONS

Activities and attractions see a wide range of prices in this region, depending on how touristy a destination you are in. Most Buddhist temples throughout the area are free to enter, though some of the more famous and larger ones, like Wat Phnom in Phnom Penh, Cambodia; Wat Pho in Bangkok; the Temple of Literature in Hanoi; and Vat Xieng Toung in Luang Prabang, Laos, cost $3–5 USD.

Large temple complexes such as the ultra-famous world heritage sites of Angkor Wat ($20–60 USD) in Cambodia, Borobudar ($15 USD) in Indonesia, or Sukkothai in Thailand ($6 USD) do cost a lot more money than smaller temples. These are the ruins of ancient cities and require a full day or, in the case of Angkor, multiple days to see.

Scuba diving in the region costs $300–400 USD to get your three-day open water PADI certificate, which will allow you to dive anywhere in the world. On the island of Ko Tao in Thailand, the course is $300 USD and includes free accommodation for the duration of the course, which lasts three or four days. This is the cheapest place in the world to get your certification because there are more than fifty dive shops on the island and competition is very fierce. If you want to learn to dive, learn here. Most single dives in the region cost $50 USD.

The region is also filled with other day activities that cost an average of $20 USD for a one-day tour. If you are going jungle trekking, seeing elephants, climbing mountains, or doing overnight trips, prices can go as high as $50 USD.

Throughout much of the region, there is no single tour operator that is amazing. In Appendix A, I list a few companies I enjoy, but most of the operators are nameless companies and offer mostly the same services.

Travel agents are the mainstay of travel in this region. You stop inside, tell them where you want to go, and they book your bus or train or ferry for you. Want to do a tour somewhere? You book that there too. Unlike in the developed world, there isn't a lot of online booking and do-it-yourself travel here, so you rely on these companies a lot. Most are simply nameless mom-and-pop establishments, one just as good as any other. But three are worth mentioning:

East West Travel (Phnom Penh, Cambodia): eastwest-travel.com

NS Travel (Bangkok, Thailand): nstravel.com

Bali Discovery (Bali, Indonesia): balidiscovery.com

Guesthouses can also help you book tours or transportation. The bad news in this region is that there are no discount cards or special passes for tours. The price is the price. If a tour costs $10 USD, you're paying $10 USD. Tour companies here aren't really large, formal organizations. Typically there is one company, and all the tour agents around town sell that tour. You'll find a bus full of people on the same tour who all booked at different places. So if you are in a large group of people booking together, you can usually haggle down a price from the tourist agency.

Singapore is the only place you can get a city discount card. It's not run by the city but by an outside organization called iVenture (seesingaporepass.iventurecard.com) and is widely accepted at all the tourist attractions. The two-day pass costs about $75 USD and covers all the major attractions in Singapore (which, being a small city-state, is not a lot). You'll get free access to the zoo, the night safari, and the aquarium along with others. The pass will save you about $18 USD.

How Much Money Do You Need?

Between the cheap local accommodations, street food, local buses, and even the tourist buses, your travel costs should average out at about $25 USD per day. If you get nice accommodations or indulge in the partying that is so widespread in this region, expect to spend $30–35 USD per day and up. I've done Southeast Asia on as little as $15 USD a day staying in cheap guesthouses, eating street food, and skipping alcohol. You can travel Southeast Asia with very little money and have it last a very long time.

If you start heading to very touristy places or some of the more expensive islands in Thailand, your daily average will go up a lot and you'll start to get close to $40 USD per day. Flying also shoots up your costs if you aren't getting a deal. But outside those exceptions, travel in Asia is incredibly cheap, so if you are spending a lot of money, you're doing something wrong.

Central America

Costa Rica, Panama, Belize, Guatemala, Honduras, El Salvador, Nicaragua

CENTRAL America is an incredible bargain and one not often visited enough by North Americans. The flights there are cheap, and getting around is cheap—it's the perfect travel alternative to more expensive regions of the world. I've been to this region many times, and it remains one of my favorites in the world. I love the relaxed lifestyle, the beautiful beaches and azure-blue water, the warm weather, the jungle treks, the friendly locals, and the flavorful food.

ACCOMMODATIONS

Hostels

Hostels are abundant in this region of the world. A night in a hostel ranges from just $4 USD to $10 USD for a dormitory room. In Costa Rica or Panama, you will pay on the higher end of that range. A private bed will cost you $15–20 USD for a double bed and a private bathroom.

Hostels in Central America tend to be basic, offering few of the amenities you find in the developed world. Not many have kitchens or common rooms. There are some that are really nice and modern that have pools and large kitchens (the Naked Tiger Hostel in Nicaragua and Costa Rica Backpackers in San José are two that come to mind), but for the most part, your hostels in Central America will be spartan establishments that offer you a cheap place to stay and meet other travelers but that aren't going to blow you away with their comfort.

Guesthouses

Family-owned guesthouses or hotels will be the most affordable accommodation besides hostels. This accommodation type costs about $25 per night for a private room with an en suite bathroom, and most of these hotels come with breakfast. In cheaper countries in the region, like El Salvador, a private room can cost $15 USD per night, while in a more expensive destination, like Panama City, you can expect to pay on the higher end, at $30 per night.

This is my favorite form of accommodation in Central America and one that is good for people on any length of holiday looking for a comfortable, quaint, and affordable place to stay. These small hotels and B&Bs have beautiful rooms and large breakfasts, and are safe and clean. Plus, your money stays within the community and family instead of being sent back to some corporate headquarters. If you're traveling as a family, you should stay at one of these places because for around $75 USD per night, you can have accommodations for a family of four. Marina Villatoro of travelexperta.com says, "My family and I only stay in the mom-and-pop, boutique-style hotels and B&Bs. They are usually the most unique, with the best service and family-owned as well. This allows my kids to meet other kids, usually from the country we are staying in. Overall, these have been our best experiences so far!"

As in Southeast Asia, most of these guesthouses aren't located on large booking sites like Hotels.com or Booking.com. The website TripAdvisor (tripadvisor.com) offers the most comprehensive list of family-owned and small hotels in Central America. I remember going to Puerto Viejo, Costa Rica, and finding only seven places to stay on Hotels.com but finding more than seventy on TripAdvisor. You get a lot more options on TripAdvisor, and it's my go-to site for accommodations in Central America.

If the hotel is listed with one of TripAdvisor's booking partners, you can book online, but if it isn't, there is usually a phone number or web address to contact.

Apartment Rentals

Apartment rentals aren't that common in this region of the world. A search for places revealed only a couple hundred in all of Panama, which is the most developed country for this in the region. While you can find apartments in most of the major cities, the selection is very small and the price higher than what you find for small local hotels using TripAdvisor. I recommend skipping this option, as it's not very economical.

Camping

Camping can be done easily at hostels and in national parks. Most hostels have space where you can pitch a tent or string up a hammock for $1–3 USD per night. National parks require camping fees that vary from country to country. Many places will let you string up your own hammock if they don't have any there. The same goes for tents. Some hostels will provide a tent, but if you have one with you, most any hostel outside of the big cities (there's not a lot of room in buildings in San Salvador or San José!) will let you pitch your own tent.

Everything is pretty easygoing in Central America, and if you want to string up a hammock or pitch a tent on some empty beach, you aren't really going to encounter much resistance. I've seen many travelers do it and I've never heard stories of problems.

Hospitality Exchange

While Couchsurfing.com is gaining popularity and you'll be able to find hosts in major cities, it's not that widespread and your pool of available hosts is often very limited. It's something you can try, but you should not count on it the way you can in other parts of the world. Servas and Hospitality Club also have good networks in this area of the world and are often a better choice here in terms of availability.

All accommodations can be booked at the booking sites mentioned in Chapter 11 or listed in Appendix A. Additionally, local tourist offices can help you secure accommodations.

FOOD

The cheapest places to eat are the roadside restaurants that dot this region. These restaurants tend to be small family establishments without a large menu, and they tend to sell whatever the main type of local dish is in the area. Eating at local restaurants, you can expect to pay around $4 USD for a two-course meal that consists of chicken, rice, and beans.

Dani and Jessica of globetrottergirls.com spent a lot of time in this region of the world and say of their experience eating: "For the most part, we would recommend eating street food, but stands in Central America offer up a lot of fried foods. They're great for quick snacks, but we'd also recommend eating in places like *comedores* in Guatemala or *sodas* in Costa Rica. Basically, these are local restaurants serving up local dishes that almost always include meat, rice, lots of fresh vegetables, and a fruit drink. You can eat that for lunch and dinner easily every day."

If you want really cheap food, you can find empanadas (fried pastries usually filled with meat, cheese, or potatoes) for 50 cents USD. Not only are they cheap, but they are tasty—they were a staple on my trip throughout Costa Rica. As Dani and Jessica continue to say, "In El Salvador, *pupusas* (similar to empanadas) are a cheap and delicious meal to subsist on for budget travelers. Essentially they are stuffed corn tortillas with either meat or beans and cheese, and then you load piles of a sort of pickled cabbage salad on top. Each one costs 40 cents and you easily fill up on three."

Additionally, premade plates of food (usually chicken or beef, rice, and tortillas) are often sold on local buses during stops on longer trips, for about $2 USD.

If you want to cook your own food, you can head down to the local market and pick up enough fruit, vegetables, meats, and dairy for around $15 USD per week. Many of the larger hostels and guesthouses have kitchens for you to use, but it's not something I would always count on. Be sure to double-check with your hostel/hotel before you book if you want to cook your own meals.

If you are looking to sit down at a restaurant that is slightly better than the local *sodas*, you can expect to pay at least 25 percent more money for that food. A typical meal in a restaurant with table service costs $6–10 USD for a main dish and a drink. A very nice meal in a tourist area will cost $12 USD and up. As Marina Villatoro from travelexperta.com says, "Every single country has their own delicious and super-cheap eateries. You can literally be fully fed with a fresh juice, salad, and a hearty meal and sometimes dessert for less than $8 per person."

Moving beyond the budget restaurant selection, you can still find very nice and inexpensive meals for around $15 USD and up. I once spent $45 USD for a meal in Panama City. It was delicious, gourmet, and filling, but it was also more money than I'd spent on food in the previous week.

If you are looking for Western food, you are going to pay a lot more. That burger, pasta, or pizza will cost about three times as much as the local dishes. If you are craving a burger or pizza, expect to pay around $10 USD for a meal with drink. As Dani and Jess from globetrottergirls.com both state, "In Central America you can get your hands on anything you want from home—Swiss chocolate, German beer, French cheese, Italian wine—but you'll have to pay for it." As in Southeast Asia, the local cuisine here is so delicious and filling that it's not worth spending the money on a bad and expensive version of what you can get back home.

Central American food vendors and markets will save you all the money you need on eating. Stick to them and you'll rarely spend more than $10 USD per day on food.

TRANSPORTATION

In the cities, city public buses are the cheapest and most convenient way to get around. Fares are less than a dollar everywhere within the city limits.

Trains

Trains are not a method of travel in Central America. Though there are some freight trains that move cargo in the region, you won't find an extensive passenger train network in any country (Belize doesn't even have a train line of any kind). If there are trains, they usually run from the capital to one other major city and are generally commuter trains. Trains to farther destinations are spotty and infrequent. For example, in Costa Rica there is a tourist train called the Tico Train Tour (email: americatravel@ice.co.cr) from San José to Caldera, near the tourist center of Limón, that only runs once per week on the weekends.

Buses

Countrywide and intercountry buses are the most widespread and easiest way to travel the region. You can catch most buses for $10 USD. Longer bus rides and overnight trips are generally around $30 USD. This is the most common way for people to travel—locals and tourists alike. Buses here (often called "chicken buses" due to the abundance of chickens and rice transported on them) stop everywhere, letting people on and off. They are slow, and very few are direct. They squeeze as many people on as possible, especially in Guatemala, Honduras, and El Salvador. You can even take these to the border, hop off, and jump on another after you cross the border, to save money.

Riding on these buses is an experience. You're cramped, you feel a bit lost, everyone is looking at you like "Who's the gringo who didn't take the tourist bus?" and if you're tall, the seats are going to feel quite small. But that's what makes these buses so fun. You meet a lot of interesting people on them and can get a really good sense of how the locals travel.

"We found taking local public transportation to be one of the highlights of our experience and ridiculously inexpensive by comparison. Bus drivers and their money-collecting helpers were always so helpful getting us on and off at the places we needed to change buses. There are buses going everywhere—and with a bit of asking around and planning, you'll get there no problem—and you'll be joined by indigenous locals in their colorful clothes, cowboys, slick young rapper types, entire families seated in just one or two seats, plus chickens, sacks of rice, and a whimsical sense of overall controlled chaos," says Dani.

Buses can simply be booked at the station or flagged down from the side of the road. In Central America, there's no system. There's no main operator. You don't book online. (And anyone selling bus tickets online is simply a private tour operator charging you three times the real price!) You just show up and get a ticket. Tourist offices and the registration desk at your hostel/hotel can give you more up-to-date information about bus times and pickup locations during your visit.

There has also been a growth in private tourist buses in this region over the last few years. These tourist buses are quicker and more direct than the local buses. They won't stop twenty times to pick people up on the way until they are full like the local buses, but they are generally double to triple the cost of the local bus. I took tourist buses a few times in Costa Rica because they were more direct and cut down my travel time. You pay more, and the bus will only be filled with other tourists, but sometimes you just need to move a little quicker.

These can be booked from your hostel or hotel (again, no online bookings). Booking the bus in Central America may seem complicated, but it's actually simple: All you do is show up and buy a ticket. There is always a bus and, normally, always a spot. It's only a pain because, since you can't prebook anything online, it can be hard to plan your trip.

Hitchhiking

Hitchhiking is a very popular method of getting around here. This region, though serviced heavily by bus, relies a lot on hitchhiking. The buses can be late or sporadic and sometimes extremely full. Many people simply can't afford the bus, and you'll find hitchhiking widespread and relatively safe. It is not uncommon to see single women, families, children, and old grandmothers on the side of the road looking for a ride. I've done this in Belize, Costa Rica, and Panama. Though hitchhiking is common in many parts of the region, use caution when entering someone's car, especially if you are a female traveler. I wouldn't hitchhike in El Salvador or Honduras because, in my opinion, the countries aren't as safe. Use your judgment, and if something feels off, wait for the next car.

Flying

There is a limited regional air network in this region. It's mostly led by COPA airlines, which is based out of Panama. There is also the airline TACA, which flies to many destinations here via their hubs in San José and San Salvador. But they too don't offer many direct flights between destinations; you have to travel via their hubs. For example, from Guatemala City to Belize City, you have to connect via San Salvador; you can't fly direct.

If you do want to fly between countries, there are generally small airlines that service each individual country. Outside of the capital cities and any international airports, the airports tend to be very small, and generally you get small propeller planes that fly into them.

I never fly around the region unless I am in a rush. Flights are overly expensive. A flight from Guatemala City to Belize City is typically as much as $230 USD, whereas the bus is only about $35 USD. This type of vast price difference is typical of the region. The bus rides may be longer, but if you are trying to see this region on a budget, you should not fly.

ACTIVITIES AND ATTRACTIONS

There isn't a huge selection of museums in Central America, and you'll find a lot of them only have their signs in Spanish. While in Panama, I went to the Panama Canal Museum (a very popular tourist attraction) only to find the signs in Spanish. Museums that do exist in this region tend to be small and focused on their colonial and indigenous (Mayan) history. Local museums cost about $5 USD.

Activities cost more money the farther south you go. Activities cost the most in Costa Rica and Panama, while activities are cheaper in countries like El Salvador and Nicaragua.

Entrance to the national parks is typically inexpensive, as are trips to see the Mayan ruin sites. Both are usually around $15 USD.

The entrance fee to Tikal in Guatemala is $20 USD. The Copán ruins can get expensive if you factor in entrance fee (around $9 USD), entrance to the tunnels ($11 USD), and a guided tour (typically $25 USD). Diving is likely to be your most expensive activity in the region, costing between $50 USD and $70 USD for a two-tank dive. An advanced open water course is generally around $260 for accommodations and the course (similar to the deal you find in Southeast Asia).

It isn't easy to save money on popular activities here. Tourism boards don't offer tourism cards like you see in developed countries, though sometimes local museums will sell combination passes that might save a dollar or two. In general, however, the listed price is the listed price.

You can get discounts on museums in the region with the student or youth discount cards discussed in Part One. These are generally 50 percent off the adult price.

How Much Money Do You Need?

Central America is very affordable. Outside of Panama, Belize, and Costa Rica, you can do this region for around $30 USD per day without any effort on budgeting. Costa Rica, Belize, and Panama are more expensive and require between $35 USD and $40 USD per day. As long as you stick to cheap accommodations, local food, and local transportation, you'll be hard-pressed to spend more than that as a daily average. Even if you decide to splurge every so often on a nice meal or hotel, it's hard to average out more than $50 USD per day unless you are splurging all the time.

On a really tight budget, you could do most of the region on $20

USD per day and do Panama and Costa Rica on $30–35 USD per day. You'll have to hitchhike a few times, eat only local cuisines and at markets, stay in dormitories, and maybe camp a few times. You also won't be able to drink that much alcohol.

Central America is a fabulous budget destination. The dollar goes very far here, and accommodations, food, and transportation are all cheap. It's also usually easy to get cheap flights to the region from the United States, so you'll save money on your airfare too. It's the perfect place to spend a lot of time on a limited budget.

20

South America

Argentina, Chile, Brazil, Peru, Ecuador, Bolivia, Colombia, Paraguay, Uruguay

S OUTH America is another area of the world where your money will go very far. Though costs vary dramatically and prices have risen over the last few years, you can still find a lot of value here. More expensive destinations, like Rio de Janeiro, Buenos Aires, Santiago, and Patagonia, will eat into your budget, as will big trips like the Galápagos Islands, Easter Island, and Machu Picchu. However, countries such as Ecuador, Peru, and Bolivia are very affordable and will offset the costs of the other destinations. There is a lot of variety in South America. With the region covering such a large landmass, make sure you devote considerable time to exploring it.

ACCOMMODATIONS

Hostels

Hostels in this region provide a host of amenities—free breakfast, Internet access, bars, game rooms, tour organization, and large kitchens. Most are independently owned and not part of the YHA hostel chain discussed previously in the book.

Hostels are abundant, but prices range greatly throughout the region. Most hostel dorm rooms cost between $6 USD and $10 USD per night. In more developed regions of Chile, Brazil, and Colombia and cities like Buenos Aires or Rio de Janeiro, you can expect to pay upward of $20 USD for a dormitory room. Private rooms with a shared bath are generally double the price of dorm rooms, though in Rio they are closer to triple the price of a dorm room.

Guesthouses

Small, family-owned budget hotels are also widely abundant and a cheap accommodation option if hostels don't interest you. For a double room with a private bathroom, breakfast, TV, and air-conditioning, you can expect to pay around $20–40 USD per night. More expensive places, like Rio and Patagonia, cost upward of $50 USD per night. As in Central America, the best family-owned hotels are found on TripAdvisor, for the same reasons discussed in that chapter. And just as in Central America, these guesthouses provide the right mix of comfort and affordability. If you are on a super-tight budget of a lot less than $50 USD per day, you're better off staying at a hostel. But if you want more comfort and have a bit more money to spend, I recommend these hotels over the larger international chains because they offer better value for your money.

South America is much more developed than Central America, and you'll find large international hotels here. These include larger four- to five-star hotels and big international brands like Hilton, Intercontinental, and Marriott. Hotels here begin at $50 USD per night and go up to $200 USD. These hotels are nice and you can often find deals on Hotels.com, but they are markedly more expensive than the family-operated hotels. I try to avoid these large chains because they are expensive, and unlike the small mom-and-pop shops, they send money out of the country, back to corporate headquarters, whereas with the small places more money stays within the local community. If you are traveling as a group, you can split the cost of these rooms to make them more affordable.

Apartment Rentals

The apartment rental trend has yet to hit South America the way it has elsewhere in the world. You will find very few available options once you leave the capital cities. In all of Ecuador, there are only about 230 hosts at the time of this writing and more than 50 percent of those on Airbnb are in the capital, Quito. Prices for rooms are comparable to those of a budget hotel, typically ranging from $10 USD to $30 USD for your own room in someone's home. Very rarely do you find whole apartments for rent outside of the larger cities.

An alternative to the apartment rental sites is Craigslist (craigslist.org). This site has more listed apartments and homestays due to the fact that unlike the rental sites, Craigslist does not take a commission. You don't get the verification offered by the other sites, but you can find more deals. As Marcello Arrambide of wanderingtrader.com says, "I found two exceptional apartments on Craigslist, one in Buenos Aires and the other in Chile, from owners at affordable prices. I couldn't find an apartment for that cheap anywhere else. There are many expats in cities like Medellin, Buenos Aires, and even Rio that advertise on Craigslist. It would definitely deserve a look for the larger tourist destinations." Rooms cost the same as on apartment rental sites like Airbnb and Roomorama. Be sure to watch out for scams though—don't send money before you see the apartment, make sure you see a lease, and don't go to the first session with a large pile of cash!

Additionally, homestays are a popular option in South America. A homestay is when a traveler stays with a local family for an extended period of time to learn about their culture. Homestays are done for a week at minimum. In South America they cost between $100 USD and $140 USD per week and include three meals a day. You'll stay in an extra bedroom of a local host family. You can find homestay listings on Craigslist or on Home Stay Web (homestayweb.com), a website specific to South America. Homestays are extremely popular with travelers who like to spend more time in a place.

Hospitality Exchange

If you can't commit to such a long period of time but still want to get to know locals, Couchsurfing is very popular throughout this region, and you'll find an abundance of hosts just about anywhere you go. Unlike in Central America, you can even find hosts in smaller, out-of-the-way destinations. It's a really good site to use in South America.

Servas and Hospitality Club also have good networks in this area of the world.

All accommodations can be booked at the booking sites mentioned in Chapter 11 or listed in Appendix A. Additionally, local tourist offices can help you secure accommodations.

FOOD

It's hard to spend a lot of money on food in South America if you stick to the local markets and street stalls. I remember when I was in Ecuador and found sandwiches for a dollar and a delicious ceviche dish for 50 cents. Even in a local diner, a large meal with chicken, rice, and a drink cost me $3 USD. Eating at local food stalls will cost you about $1 USD per meal for a hearty plate of meat and rice. You'll find these vendors in the local markets or just sitting on the side of the street selling tiny, easily made dishes like empanadas or BBQ skewers. In more expensive countries, like Chile, costs will be closer to $2 USD. In inflation-plagued Argentina, you won't find cheap street food; sometimes food prices increase in that country as much as 30 percent per month.

Small, locally owned restaurants throughout the region cost around $4 USD for a local meal that includes a couple of courses and a drink. Even in Puna, Peru, home to touristy and popular Lake Titicaca, you can get a complete three-course meal for $2 USD. Nicer meals at a casual restaurant with attractive décor will cost around $10 USD. In Argentina, again due to inflation, meal prices for even a cheap restaurant will begin at around $10 USD and move up from there.

As David Lee (gobackpacking.com) says about Colombia: "The easiest way to save money on food in Colombia is to eat like a local. In the cities, walk a few blocks away from any tourist-oriented restaurant and you'll find smaller places filled with Colombians taking advantage of set lunches. These daily deals, which can cost as little as $3–4 USD, include soup, a main course (typically meat or fish, plus rice and potatoes), and drink."

Throughout the region, local eateries are easy on the wallet. Look for signs that say "Menus ejecutivos." These are the best budget option for eating out and usually only available for lunch. They will include a starter, main course, and dessert and usually a drink. They are simple meals, but they are simply wonderful on the wallet.

Western food is going to cost the most, especially if you want something that actually tastes like it does back home. Most restaurants can't do a good burger to save their life. However, if you're just looking for anything, most Western dishes will cost about $7 USD for a burger, sandwich, or pizza, with higher-quality meals costing $10–15 USD. If you are looking for a really nice sit-down meal with good steak and wine, expect to pay $25 USD and up. Prices in Argentina, Uruguay, and Brazil will cost about 25 percent more.

Grocery shopping is very cheap, costing $15–20 USD per week. In more expensive Argentina, where inflation is very bad, groceries cost about $30 USD per week. Colombia and Chile are also more expensive, and you will most likely spend $40 USD a week in both countries. I personally don't do a lot of grocery shopping while in South America. It's cheaper than eating locally, but anything I am going to make—pasta, burgers—can be easier to just go buy already made. You can eat well on $10 USD anyway. If you do choose to cook, the local markets will provide a large array of beans, rice, vegetables, meats, and fruits for you. Fresh food will be very cheap, but anything that needs to be imported will only cost slightly less than it would at home.

Outside of Argentina, Chile, or Colombia, South America is a place where cooking your own food doesn't make sense as the food is already so cheap. You'll spend more money cooking your own food than purchasing it already made. Simply put—eat at the vendors, enjoy the local cuisine and culinary style, and save some money.

TRANSPORTATION

Local buses are the most effective way to get around in South America. Most cities, even large ones, lack extensive commuter rail systems. The buses are typically old tour or school buses from the United States. Buses cost around 50 cents USD inside a city. Taxis are available everywhere and cost $2–5 USD per trip within a city's limits. Larger metropolitan and capital cities have subway systems that cost around $1 USD per ride.

Trains

Trains in this region are virtually nonexistent. There are no inter-country trains here, just a few intra-country lines. You'll find a few small lines in Ecuador, Argentina, Brazil, Peru, and Chile, but generally these are scenic tourist trains. Most long-haul transportation in this region revolves around buses and airplanes.

Trains in Argentina are experiencing something of a revival, since the government intends to reestablish long-distance passenger trains between all major cities.

There is already rail service between the country's three largest cities: Buenos Aires, Córdoba, and Rosario.

The trip to Mar del Plata is fast (six hours), very popular with Argentinians, and half the price of taking the bus if you ride the low-cost *Tren Diario* that runs daily. Pricing and schedule information for this route can be found at southamericaliving.com/trains-from-buenos-aires-to-mar-del-plata-argentina.

Unfortunately, there is no central place online to look up national Argentina train times. This website (in Spanish) can give you times for trains leaving out of Buenos Aires: ferrobaires.gba.gov.ar/index.html.

The most popular train service right now is the Train to the Clouds (*El Tren a las Nubes*, trenalasnubes.com.ar). This is a scenic tourist train that runs from Salta in northern Argentina and takes about a day to go round-trip. It costs $185 USD. Operation is seasonal. Be sure to check if the train is running ahead of time.

In Chile, passenger trains (efe.cl) only operate in a few places. The state railway runs a train from Santiago to Temuco once a day. There is also train service between Santiago and Chillán. It's fast and mostly reliable. Trains connect Arica in Chile with Tacna in Peru and La Paz in Bolivia. However, trains are about 20 percent more expensive than buses, and with very limited departures. I generally would avoid train travel in Chile in favor of the bus.

There are a few train services in Bolivia, operated by two train companies, eastern (ferroviariaoriental.com) and western (fca.com.bo). The western network is more tourist-oriented. There is also a working branch line to Calama in Chile, but this only runs rarely, perhaps once a week. The main line in the west runs from Oruro to Tupiza almost daily.

Molly McHugh of southamericaliving.com writes: "If at all possible, take the train out of Tupiza instead of the bus. There is service to Uyuni, Oruro Atoche, and the border town Villazon, only slightly more expensive than taking a bus. All cars have comfortable seats, heating, TV showing movies, and a dining car to boot. To get to La Paz you can ride to Oruro then take a three-hour bus. There is no first-class bus service out of Tupiza and the roads are unpaved and bumpy; a guaranteed very unpleasant bus journey!"

In the east of Bolivia, the rail hub is Santa Cruz, and trains go east to the Brazilian border and south to Argentina. There is a normal train, an express train, and an expensive and fast railcar that costs $20 USD per person.

In Brazil, train service is very poor. There is currently no train service at all between Rio de Janeiro and São Paulo. Service is mostly limited to the tourist-oriented steam train that offers transportation between two important Brazilian tourist towns, São João del Rei and Tiradentes. There is also train service between Vitória and Belo Horizonte. Fares for both lines begin at $20 USD. However, due to the Olympics and the World Cup coming in 2016, Brazil is building their train system and even considering building a high-speed rail line. Because of this, rail service might expand and change greatly in the future.

Trains in Peru (perurail.com/en) go from Cusco to the tourist towns of Machu Picchu and Puno. They are tourist trains and not meant for local travel. Tickets begin at $100 USD.

Countries not listed here do not have train service.

At the time of this writing, long-distance train travel should be avoided in the region. There are few tracks, limited departures, and poor rail conditions, making train travel much slower and far more expensive than buses. While countries are trying to improve train travel, currently it will be cheaper and easier for you to get around by bus.

Buses

Bus transportation is the cheapest option in South America. There's no real train network in the region and flights are expensive, so the majority of people take the bus. There are a lot of tourist buses in South America, but even on those, you are going to be traveling with a good number of locals, as buses are the mainstay here. Simply put, long- and short-distance buses are the best way to get around unless you are really pinched for time (in which case, flying is your only other option).

As Michael Hodson of goseewrite.com says, "Traveling by bus is the most convenient way to get around South America. Your day-to-day transport there is going to be in buses and minivans."

Buses generally cost between $8 USD and $80 USD per trip. Domestic bus travel costs around $10 USD, while international or fancier buses cost $80 USD. For example, a twelve-hour bus ride in Argentina might cost $50–60 USD, while in Bolivia the same journey might be $20 USD. Generally, Ecuador, Peru, Bolivia, and Paraguay are cheaper and you can get fares for as little as $1 USD per hour of travel. In the larger countries of Chile, Argentina, Colombia, and Brazil, which use full-service, double-decker sleeper buses, expect to pay on the higher end. These prices refer to second-class travel—nice coaches, amenities, and first-class seats will be more expensive.

Argentina boasts an outstanding short- and long-distance bus network. The more expensive buses generally offer high-quality service, and for distances longer than 200 km, it is common to have food served on board as well as wi-fi and alcohol. There is generally a good amount of legroom, and many buses have seats that recline horizontally into beds (*camas*), making the experience a lot like traveling business class on a plane. The best category, with completely reclining seats, is normally called *cama suite*, but other names, such as *tutto leto*, *executive*, or *salón real* are also in use. Somewhat cheaper seats only recline partially (*semi-camas*) or not at all (*servicio común*).

Information about buses and timetables can be found on the website of Omnilíneas (omnilineas.com).

In Brazil, long-distance buses are a convenient, economical, and sometimes (usually if you buy the most expensive ticket) rather comfortable way to travel between regions. You should check distance and time while traveling within Brazil; going from Rio de Janeiro to the south region could take more than twenty-four hours, so it may be worth going by plane if you can afford it.

There is no one bus company that serves all of Brazil, so you need to identify the company that connects your two cities in particular by calling the bus station of one city. ANTT, the national authority for land transportation, has a search engine for buses (appweb.antt.gov .br/transp/secao_duas_localidades.asp), but it is only in Portuguese. Big cities, like São Paulo and Rio, have more than one bus station, each covering certain areas of the city. Be sure to check in advance for which bus station you are going to.

Bus prices are quite expensive in Colombia, although long-distance trips rarely cost more than $55 USD one way. Long-distance bus travel tends to be very slow because main highways are two-lane roads with lots of truck traffic. Fares are sometimes as high as $100 USD. Budget airlines are often cheaper than buses in Colombia, so make sure to check the airline websites listed below for fare information. The websites for the bus companies are:

expresobrasilia.com

copetran.com.co

berlinasdelfonce.com

rapidoochoa.com

bolivariano.com.co

expresopalmira.com.co

coomotor.com.co

In Peru, *colectivo* buses (those that pick up people as they go) are the cheapest option, following the rule of $1 USD per hour of travel. For some routes in Peru, such as from Lima to Mancora or Cusco, there are more expensive buses run by private companies that have first- and second-class service. Light meals and snacks are provided, and there may be private security guards on board due to bandits. These buses cost upward of $30 USD.

One thing to remember is that in many of these countries, you will be traveling long distances and through winding mountains, so bus journeys are very long. Some bus rides can be eighteen hours or more. The roads in South America are not well kept, the distances are long, and the terrain is difficult, so it is often better to get a plane ride if you are short on time.

Hitchhiking

Hitchhiking is *not* recommended anywhere in South America. I don't do it and I know few people who do. It's simply not safe, due to kidnappings, robberies, and theft. It's especially unsafe if you are a single female. Additionally, drunk driving is a big problem in many parts of South America. It's just too dangerous to hitchhike, in my opinion, and you do so at your own risk.

Flying

Flying around this region is expensive when compared to the cost of living, but given the vast distances here, it can often be a good option for travelers with limited time. After all, bus rides can be eighteen-plus hours here. Sometimes it is worth it to spend the extra money on a flight to avoid traveling for two days. The major airlines in South America are:

TACA: taca.com (now partnered with Avianca, avianca.com)

LAN: lan.com

TAM: tam.com.br

GOL: voegol.com

Copa: copaair.com

Aerolíneas Argentinas: aerolineas.com.ar/home.asp

Aerogal: aerogal.com.ec/?lang=en

In Colombia, there are often flight sales that make flying cheaper than buses, and the long-distance routes in Argentina (think Buenos Aires to the tip in Patagonia) are also a good deal because flights can save you lots of time. However, minus any last-minute sales, I wouldn't fly in South America unless I was really short on time. Local buses are simply too cheap to pass up.

For ways to find a cheap ticket, refer back to Chapter 13 in Part One.

ACTIVITIES AND ATTRACTIONS

Activities vary, costing as much as hundreds or thousands of dollars. Simple day tours cost around $40 or $50 USD. Museums and city attractions cost around $5 USD. There are a number of good art and historical museums throughout the region. I love the historical museums that give insight into the fabulous Inca civilization and the Spanish occupation of the region.

Activities are very expensive in this region simply because most people who visit on short holidays come for the Machu Picchu, jungle tours, and Galápagos Island adventures. These tours can cost up into the thousands of dollars, for the simple fact that people are willing to pay that much for them. Whereas in other parts of the world you can find specific backpacker/budget traveler tours, in South America, while there are some lower-end tours, there is nothing specifically geared to budget travelers. For example, a weeklong Galápagos tour costs about $2,400 USD, a three-day Amazon tour is $200 USD, and the weeklong Machu Picchu trek starts at $500 USD.

If you try to get to places by your own transportation, you'll save the most money, especially on attractions, like wine tours, the salt flats, or national parks, that can be easily driven to from nearby cities such as Punta Arenas. For epic adventures like Antarctica, Galápagos, Amazon River tours, and, of course, the Inca Trail, you will get the best prices if you book far in advance or shop around to the smaller companies. Additionally, arriving without a plan and getting a spot on a last-minute tour will cut prices down by 50 percent, but you run the risk of having to wait awhile until a spot opens up on an unfilled tour.

David Lee of gobackpacking.com did this when he booked his

tour to Machu Picchu: "Wait until you get to Cusco to book your trip to Machu Picchu. There are tons of budget tour shops around the Plaza de Armas, and the competition keeps prices low. If you want to do a trek, skip the Inca Trail, which normally costs about $500, and instead go on either the five-day Salkantay trek or the easier four-day Inca Jungle trek. Both are all-inclusive, and cost about $180, including admission to Machu Picchu."

Jeff Jung of Careerbreaksecrets.com had a similar experience: "You need to be flexible with your timing, but booking local is usually recommended. In Ecuador, because I was flexible on my time, I was able to book a Galápagos and Amazon jungle tour for less than a typical Galápagos tour. This was off-season too. I had the same luck with Easter Island in Chile. I happened to go into a local travel agent when they were having a sale on packages to the island."

Being flexible, waiting until the last minute, and visiting a local travel agent will allow those amazing dream tours you see advertised in the States to become far more affordable and realistic.

The discount cards discussed in Part One can get you 50 percent off museums and national parks. Student discounts also apply throughout the region.

How Much Money Do You Need?

South America is a cheap area of the world to travel to, but costs are rising quickly as countries continue to develop. The region is still relatively inexpensive, but nations like Brazil, Chile, and Colombia are becoming increasingly expensive by the day. It's relatively easy to keep costs below $25 USD per day in the less developed countries and $45 per day in Chile, Argentina, and Brazil.

There's a big divide in the continent along prices. You'll be hard-pressed to eat for less than $20 USD per day in Argentina, while on the other hand you'll be hard-pressed to spend more than $20 USD per week on local food in Peru.

Moreover, you should budget a little more if you plan on doing a lot of activities. While the Galápagos Islands and Machu Picchu will spike your expenses, the low price of everything else can help you maintain a daily average, especially if your food is costing less than $10 USD per day,

Given the low cost of local food and accommodation, if you stay in a cheap hostel, eat set meals at local restaurants, shop around for affordable tours, and negotiate local transportation, you'll average $25–30 USD per day easily without any luxuries. If you choose to fly around more, or stay longer in Brazil or Argentina, you should plan on $45 USD as a daily average.

Travel in South America, like travel in Europe, is about balancing expensive countries versus inexpensive countries. If your whole trip is in Chile, Brazil, and Argentina, taking tours and drinking a lot, you'll spend more than $50 USD per day. But if you balance out these countries with the more inexpensive ones, you'll drop your average way below that. South America may not be the bargain that Central America is, but it's still a cheap region of the world for travelers.

21

China

CHINA has fascinated travelers ever since Marco Polo traversed the Silk Road. Now as China's prominence and economic might in the world grows, more and more people flock there seeking to explore and understand the country like the explorers of yore. This gigantic and diverse place can be challenging for many travelers—there's a strong language barrier, it's chaotic, confusing, and stressful—but those brave enough to travel in the region are richly rewarded with friendly people; delicious food; a country in constant flux; beautiful mountains, beaches, and valleys.

China remains a fascinating place where travelers can view cutting-edge, high-tech mega cities and small villages steeped in ancient traditions. While the days of China being a super-cheap destination are long gone, the country remains a budget destination with many opportunities for savings, especially in the countryside.

ACCOMMODATIONS

Hostels

Unlike most other parts of Asia, traditional dormitory-style hostels are quite popular throughout the country. A search on the booking site Hostelworld in 2014 revealed fifty-eight hostels for Beijing, twenty-three for Shanghai, and sixty for Hong Kong. And while that is not a lot for such populous cities, it's a lot more when compared to other parts of Asia, which still prefer traditional guesthouses. A bed in a dormitory costs between $4 USD and $8 USD, and private twin or double rooms in hostels cost around $16 USD. In Beijing and Shanghai, hostel dormitory beds can go as high as $14 USD per night. In Hong Kong, prices are even higher, with beds ranging between $10 USD and $16 USD.

Hostels in China are a great value for the money and include a lot of amenities. Guests typically get free drinking water, wi-fi, and heated blankets (those winters are cold!). Hostels also have large common rooms, and lockers. In short, they have everything a traveler could need and are similar to hostels in the West. In some hostels in remote locations, they may or may not have squat toilets in lieu of Western toilets so bring your own toilet paper!

Kristin Addis of Be My Travel Muse (bemytravelmuse.com) spent a lot of time hosteling in China and writes, "I was blown away by the great value provided by the hostels in China. They were inexpensive, clean, tended to be well-decorated with wonderful common rooms, had free and decent wi-fi, provided free clean drinking water for hot tea, often offered group meals at good prices, and tended to be easily available and in central locations. There was a good mix of foreigners and Chinese travelers in them too."

Budget Hotels

Budget hotels begin around $22 USD for a twin room. In these hotels, you'll find basic accommodations—private rooms, a bathroom, a heated blanket, air-conditioning and/or heat, a water kettle, and quite often a television set (but with only Chinese-speaking channels). These hotels are inexpensive and the best value option for travelers who want private accommodation.

One thing to keep in mind is that hotels advertising breakfast rarely serve a Western-style or continental breakfast. You should expect dumplings, steamed bread, various vegetables, rice, congee, and warm water.

In Hong Kong, hotel prices will be much higher than on mainland China. A single room in a hotel starts around $33 USD and goes as high as $70 USD per night. I don't find hotels very affordable there and prefer to stay in a private room in a hostel, where prices are lower.

Apartment Rentals

Because of the abundance of cheap accommodations throughout China and Hong Kong, you don't find many people listing rooms or apartments for these areas, and oftentimes when you do, they aren't offering a great deal. For example, a 2014 search on Airbnb, the largest of the apartment rental sites, had only 449 listings for Beijing. In contrast, New York City has over 15,000 listings. Hong Kong, which is a lot more Westernized than mainland China, had 1,140 listings. HomeAway has 670 listings in *all* of China. In short, relative to its population size, apartment rentals haven't caught on yet, and you'll face limited options.

Typically, you can find rooms in apartments from $27 USD per night. That will get you a bed and your own room in someone else's apartment. Keep in mind that in the really large cities, rooms can be very, very far from the city center and attractions. Luxury apartments cost around $100 USD per night.

I personally find hotels and hostels such great value in China that given the limited options you have, I would avoid using the rental websites. The exception is Hong Kong, where the abundance of listings and high hotel prices make rental apartment prices competitive.

Chris Bush Walker from Aussie on the Road (aussieontheroad .com) urges caution when using these websites: "Often, Airbnb is used by Chinese hotels or apartment managers to advertise their apartments. Don't expect a B&B-style service—it's usually just an apartment with little or no contact with the 'host.'"

Hospitality Exchange

Hospitality exchanges are really big in China; the Couchsurfing network has more than 250,000 members in the country. Though Chinese citizens are often reluctant to house foreigners, especially in rural areas, you won't have a problem in larger cities. Most hosts are international citizens living in the country.

FOOD

Chinese food isn't what we are used to in the West. There's no sesame chicken, crab rangoon, fortune cookies, or General Tso. We have a highly Westernized version of what Chinese food really is. In fact, Chinese people are quite perplexed by what we call "Chinese food." In China, food is less fried, contains more random parts of the animal (there's a good chance your chicken soup will have an entire chicken in it!), and is often a lot spicier. Be prepared for the difference. If you expect the same as you get in the West, you'll be very, very disappointed. Chinese food elicits a love it or hate it reaction from travelers.

But the food in China is its own kind of delicious. For breakfast, locals tend to eat either a noodle soup, a thin rice porridge, or steamed buns. Lunches and dinners consist of shared plates with everyone getting their own bowl of rice. (This is generally how food is eaten throughout Asia. The idea of the individual meals is not common in this region. Everyone shares a bunch of dishes and then splits the bill.)

And a great thing about all this delicious food? It's cheap! A meal from a street vendor usually goes for $1–2 USD. For this you might get noodles, rice, pork buns, or a soup. The street stalls in China are similar in style to those described in the section on Southeast Asia. A full meal in a sit-down restaurant will cost between $2 USD and $8 USD plus the fee for a bowl of rice and clean bowls (yes, these cost extra!), which is often around 50 cents. If you stick to the local food, you'll never go broke. You could spend less than $10 for an entire day's worth of food.

As Chris notes, "Like most of Asia, I've found the best local food has invariably been street food. There's no shortage of stalls selling shao kao (BBQ), jian bing, and all manner of other things. They're usually clustered around the entrances and exits of schools, so starving students can flood out during their infrequent breaks for a snack. The visual of a few thousand kids pouring out of a too small gate to swarm the stalls is something to see, that's for sure."

In western China, southwestern China, and the interior, food is much cheaper than in the big metropolises (Beijing, Shanghai, etc.), and you can eat for under $5 USD per day; about half the costs of the big cities.

Depending on where you are in China, the food can be very spicy. Kristin notes, "I'm a big fan of spicy food and found that in China, even Sichuanese food which is known for its spice, wasn't too overpowering for me. Usually chili is provided on the side so those who prefer spicier food can add it to soups and noodles. The owners of the restaurants or street stalls will also usually ask if you want it 'la de' which means 'spicy.'"

For Western food, you can expect to pay much higher prices for food that will be a disappointment compared to home, if you're outside of the more Westernized cities like Hong Kong. A Western-style sandwich can run about $6 USD, and a cup of coffee can be similarly priced as back home. But again, what's the point of coming overseas to eat bad versions of what you can get without traveling? While I'm guilty of sneaking Western food when I want the pleasures of home, the Western food in China, especially on the budget end, just won't be good. The exceptions are Shanghai and Hong Kong, where there is a huge international food scene. Here you will find excellent food from around the world. Once you get out of the major cities, Chinese food will pretty much be your only choice, except for an occasional McDonald's or KFC.

Quoting Kristin again: "It's generally best to stick to local foods anywhere in the world when trying to save money and eat well. I'd say stay away from Western foods or at least be prepared to pay more for something that will be different from what you're used to at home though it may masquerade as the same thing. If you're in China, eat Chinese food! It's a great way to better understand a culture. If you're unsure of what's written on the menu, look at the tables of those around you and indicate you'd like to eat what they're having."

Since food is so cheap, there's no need to self-cater or cook your own meals. You are better off eating the street food and at the restaurants. Moreover, most hostels don't have kitchen facilities for you to use even if you did go grocery shopping. Therefore, self-catering is not something I recommend.

TRANSPORTATION

China may be a huge country but it's easy and cheap to get from one place to the next (especially if you are prepared to travel third class). Train and bus are inexpensive, reliable, and run consistently.

Local transport within a city or area costs about 30 cents USD per subway ride or 15–30 cents USD per bus ride. Taxis charge around $1 USD to start and 30 cents USD per kilometer if they're willing to run their meter, which is sometimes a battle. Keep in mind that it is rare to find a taxi driver who knows enough English for you to explain where to go. Have your destination written out in Chinese whenever possible.

Apart from bikes, buses are the most common means of getting around in the cities. Service in the major cities is fairly extensive, buses go to most places and fares are inexpensive but expect buses to be always packed. Traffic is also really bad in big cities in China so don't be in a rush—you're not going anywhere quickly.

Major cities in China have underground metro systems. Wuhan has a limited light rail system in Haikou (at the time of writing, Wuhan is building a subway system), as does Tianjin. Chongqing benefits from a monorail. The price of a typical subway ticket is less than $1 USD, depending on distance; in Hong Kong it is between 60 cents USD and about $3 USD, also depending on the distance.

Trains

Although crowded, trains are the best way to travel in China as they are fast and comfortable. At any given time over 10 million people are traveling by rail.

Moreover, China has been upgrading their very old trains to modern ones similar to those in Europe or Japan. The new fleet is cleaner and has air-conditioning. The Z class express trains (such as the train between Beijing and Shanghai) are on par with European high-speed train standards and oftentimes have meal service and power outlets.

According to expat Joel Ward, who has lived in China for many years, "The high-speed rail system in China is comfortable, fast and efficient. For mid-range journeys within China, they're often faster than flying after you account for the much quicker processes of check-in and security (not to mention flight delays)."

Ticket prices are calculated according to distance traveled and, on some longer routes, by the class you are in. Third-class hard seats are the cheapest and therefore most packed as those tickets are the only ones most Chinese can afford (while the train may seem cheap to us, for many Chinese it's anything but). In this class, you'll get a ticket with an assigned seat number. If seats are sold out, you can opt for a standing ticket, which will at least get you on the train.

On a high-speed train, the ticket from Beijing to Shanghai is around $81 USD for second class, around $138 USD for first class, and around $267 USD for a VIP seat. For the longer, full-day train, a second-class seat is around $66 USD and a first-class seat is around $80 USD. On the popular Shanghai to Xi'an route, tickets for a hard sleeper are $49 USD, soft sleeper is between $77 USD and $122 USD.

On short express journeys (such as Beijing to Tianjin) some trains have soft-seat carriages. These trains have comfortable seats arranged two abreast. Soft seats cost about the same as a hard sleeper and carriages are often double-decker.

Sleeper cars are doorless compartments with bunks on three levels and come with sheets, pillows, and blankets. Lower bunks are less expensive than top bunks and lights and speakers go out at around 10 p.m. To get a ticket for this class, you will need to purchase a few days in advance. They are usually sold out by the departure day.

Joel issues a word of caution, though. "The top bunk is generally the furthest removed from the noise and activity on the ground, which is why it's more expensive. However, on some of the older trains the space between the top bunk and the roof is nearly nonexistent. Even when you're laying down, there's barely enough space to lift a book above your head to read."

The top level of service is a soft sleeper carriage. They consist of four very comfortable bunks in a closed compartment, with lace curtains, teacups, clean washrooms, carpets, and air-conditioning. They cost about double the price of hard sleeper bunks.

Some large stations have special ticket offices for foreigners; otherwise there is always someone around with basic English skills. It should also be noted that foreigners need to present their passport when buying tickets.

Touts swarm around train stations selling black-market tickets;

this can be a way of getting scarce tickets, but foreigners frequently get ripped off, so avoid doing this.

Long-Distance Buses

Long-distance bus service is extensive, and main roads are rapidly improving and the number of highways is increasing. Buses are generally cheaper than trains. For example, the nine-hour bus from Beijing to Anshan is $28 USD, while the train is between $34 USD and $143 USD. The two-hour bus from Beijing to Tianjin is $4–6 USD, while the high-speed train is around $9. The trip from Shanghai to Hangzhou is two and a half hours by bus and costs $11 USD, while the train is $14.

On the other hand, if you are traveling in slower trains and in the cheap hard seats, you will often find them to be a less expensive alternative to the bus, so be sure to check the prices of both before you book.

Flying

Although traveling around China in buses or trains is the best way to see the country's vast and lush countryside, given the country's vast size, sometimes it's more efficient to fly. If you don't have the time or inclination for a long overland trip (and getting around China does take a while), flying is your most efficient option. China has numerous airlines; major ones are the following:

Air China: airchina.com.cn

China Eastern Airlines: ce-air.com

China Southern Airlines: cs-air.com

China Southwest Airlines: cswa.com

Spring Airlines: china-sss.com

Additionally, nearly every province of China has regional carriers that operate primarily within the borders of the country, such as Hainan Airlines, Shanghai Airlines, and dozens of smaller regional carriers.

Chris from Aussie on the Road notes that you should be wary of one-time arrivals and departures: "I have literally only ever had one flight in China leave on time. It's led to more than one missed connecting flight. It seems like a mandatory part of travel here to wait for your flight to be delayed at least once or twice. I even made it all the way onto the plane one night only to wait ninety minutes in the sweltering cabin before they had us disembark and go back to the terminal to wait another two hours."

ATTRACTIONS AND ACTIVITIES

Sights and activities are inexpensive in China—even the popular attractions such as the Great Wall and Forbidden City are under $10 USD. While the Great Wall never kept out invaders, it's beautiful and is only $7 USD, the Forbidden City is $10 USD. (Also known as the Palace Museum, the Forbidden City is closed on Mondays.) Smaller temples, activities, and sights are much more reasonably priced and cost around $2 USD.

If you want to see giant pandas, the breeding facility in Chéngdū costs around $9 USD to get in. In the hometown of Confucius (Qufu), one of the most famous philosophers in Chinese history, you will find tickets for the Confucius Temple, Confucius's home, and the Confucius Mausoleum between $8 USD and $17 USD. Seeing the famous terracotta army will only set you back about $15 USD. No matter how you slice it, attractions in China are reasonably priced. The listed prices above give you a good range to plan your budget with.

While most attractions and temples are less than $10 USD, prices for hikes and outdoor activities tend to be around $30 USD. For example, a trip to the Jade Dragon Snow Mountain costs around $26 USD, a visit to the Jiuzhai Valley is a whopping $59 USD, and a three-day pass to the Wuyi Mountains in Fujian Province is $40 USD. You'll pay $37 USD to visit the Yellow Mountains in Anhui Province.

In Hong Kong, activities and attractions are much costlier than in mainland China. Most museums begin around $10 USD, and observation decks and activities are between $20 USD and $30 USD. If you are visiting Hong Kong, budget more money.

While Hong Kong has a city tourist pass, mainland China does not, and you won't find discount cards and offers like you can in other parts of the world. If you are a student, however, you can get great discounts to most of the national parks and UNESCO World Heritage sites, which can otherwise cost upward of $32 USD to visit.

The Hong Kong city pass is offered by iVentures and also covers Macau. The three-day pass is $87 USD, and the five-day pass is $115 USD. They come with many benefits and can be a good deal if you plan to visit a lot of the big attractions and amusement parks in Hong Kong and Macau.

HOW MUCH MONEY DO YOU NEED?

Thanks to rapid economic growth, China isn't the bargain basement destination it used to be but a visit here will hardly ever break the bank.

Staying in dormitories, traveling by bus or bicycle rather than by taxi, eating from street stalls or small restaurants, and resisting the urge to splurge means it is possible to live on less than $22 USD per day. Realistically, including food and drink, accommodations, and transportation, the cost would be closer to $27 USD per day. If you are traveling only to the major cities, I would increase that to $35 USD a day. If you want more comfort, including more Western food and nicer sleeper berths, I'd go closer to $40 USD a day.

22

India

THERE'S an expression often said among travelers: There is the world and then there is India. Traveling around India is different. It's almost mystical. India is big, chaotic, mystic, beautiful, difficult, rich, poor, developing, developed, and everything in between. From the beaches of Goa to the Taj Mahal, the crowded streets of Mumbai, and the deserts of Rajasthan, India offers a lot to intrepid travelers. Because of the vast distances, plethora of sites to visit, and slow travel time around the country, most visitors should spend at least a month or two here. Or, at the very least, break your trips up into smaller geographic sections. India is not a place for the rushed.

India has always been an inexpensive place to visit, but a 2014 decline in the Indian rupee has made this country an even better bargain than it was before. Throw in cheap flight deals (from anywhere), and you have the recipe for a very affordable destination. You can travel well here for very little money and increasing your budget just a few dollars can often lead to substantial increases in luxury.

ACCOMMODATIONS

Hostels

European-style hostels (think big dorms, common rooms, kitchens, organized activities) are not popular in India as small, family-run guesthouses are the preferred accommodation option. Accommodation is already so cheap, few people desire to stay in dorm rooms. New Delhi, a city with around 22 million people, had only twenty-three hostels in 2014 according to Hostelworld, and most have only private rooms, which really makes them hotels, not hostels. Clearly, hostels are not very widespread!

As Derek Baron of Wandering Earl (wanderingearl.com) and a tour guide in India states: "When it comes to budget accommodation in India, hostels are generally not the option of choice, even for the most budget conscious traveler. They are harder to find, usually not of good quality and they typically charge only slightly less than what it costs to have your own private room in a budget hotel. In 2.5 years of traveling around India on a budget, I stayed in a hostel once."

And while dorm beds can cost as little as $2 USD per night in very rural destinations, they usually range from $3 USD to $7 USD per night, making them just as expensive as a simple private room in a budget hotel. For example, International Youth Hostel Association (yhaindia.org) has beds in non-air-conditioned dorm rooms ranging between $5 USD and $10 USD per night, which is about the price of a nice budget hotel. Why share a room when you can get your own room for the same price?

In short, while hostels do exist, they aren't worth staying in, and there are better options you can choose from that are equally filled with travelers to make friends with.

Budget Hotels and Guesthouses

India is awash with affordable, family-run guesthouses and cheap budget hotels. These (and they are often interchangeable) are a traveler's best accommodation option in the country. You can get a single or double (the price is usually the same for both) room between $5 USD and $30 USD (that's on the very high end!), with rooms around $10–15 USD offering the best value for your money. These independent budget hotels provide you with the basics: a large, semi-comfy bed, some furniture, and a somewhat clean bathroom with Western toilet. They are basic but what more do you need when you're traveling on a budget!

Hotels over $20 USD a night will get you a more spacious room, twenty-four-hour hot water, a comfy mattress that won't kill your back, television, and some additional furniture.

It is fairly easy to find rooms last minute in India. This is especially true during monsoon season (late June through August) when many hotels have high vacancy rates and offer deep discounts. As mentioned before, hotels in Mumbai, Delhi, and Bangalore will usually be double or triple the price of elsewhere.

Mariellen Ward of Breathe Dream Go (breathedreamgo.com), an India-inspired blog, says she has found many clean, safe, and comfortable budget guesthouses in India. "I look for places that are family run, in a good location and that get good reviews online. Sometimes, I will spend extra to get a place with great atmosphere—such as a view of an ancient fort."

Apartment Rentals

Apartment rentals aren't that popular in India. For a country with over 1 billion people, Airbnb only has 9,000 listings. Wimdu listed only 133 properties, and HomeAway only 1,285. A shared room will run between $20 USD and $31 USD, with a chance you'll find one at $12 USD per night. Private rooms can cost as little as $15 USD per night, but are usually around $31–57 USD. An entire apartment to yourself will cost $51–82 USD, depending on the size.

While you get all the amenities of home, these apartments cost more than hotels and, unless you are traveling as a family or in a big group, are an option I would stay away from. You get better value for your money at the local guesthouses and hotels.

Camping

Camping is not very widespread in India and though there are a few places where you can camp, it's not something I would suggest doing, unless you are on an organized hiking/camping trip in the desert or mountain regions.

This is very important for female travelers. As Mariellen cautions, "It's important to stick to the popular tourist-friendly areas of India for female travelers, especially solo female travelers," and suggests females avoid camping in rural areas alone.

Hospitality Exchanges

Couchsurfing is the most popular network in the country. There are over 105,000 Couchsurfing hosts in India. Indians are generally really hospitable to foreigners and really like meeting and sharing their culture. It's quite easy to find hosts. The other hospitality exchanges mentioned in other sections of this book don't have large and extensive networks in India. There are some hosts but not as many. Hospitality Club, an older organization that has more families in it, has over 6,000 hosts, and Global Freeloaders has 3,342.

WWOOF

WWOOF India has been growing steadily. From just a few hosts at the start, it now has more than 150 hosts. If you are going to WWOOF, do your research and pay very special attention to the climate at the time you plan to go. During the heavy monsoon rains or when temperatures are over 40°C (104°F), it's not going to be a very comfortable experience.

FOOD

Indian food is delicious, spicy, flavorful, and incredibly diverse. I love Indian food, so much so I can never figure out what to get. Every time I walk into an Indian restaurant, I scratch my head in confusion from all the options. I always end up getting ten dishes and having leftovers that can last for days. From mouthwatering naan bread, to fire-inducing chili-enhanced curries, to the soothing flavor of a lassi, Indian food blows my mind and there's nothing like getting the food right from the source.

Keep in mind Indian cuisine varies quite a lot by region. North Indian food uses a variety of lentils, gravies, chilies, vegetables, and bread. They also use a lot of dairy in their food. Most Indian food in America is from northern India so this will be familiar to many travelers. By contrast, south Indian cuisine is much more rice based and often consists of large dosas (big rice pancakes with filling) and nuts as well as traditional curries.

Moreover, food in India is plentiful! You'll always find a place to eat. As Derek describes his experience, "You can barely walk two meters without facing another street stall or restaurant serving up some kind of snack or dish that you suddenly want to devour. Whether it be samosas, pakoras, lassis or momos, whether it be North Indian or South Indian cuisine . . . it is all so very tempting."

Restaurant meals cost between $1 USD and $6 USD for most main courses. At most restaurants in north India, you choose from a long list of dishes (like the ones I just listed) and then you order either rice or naan/chapati to go with it. For those who get easily overwhelmed like me (I can never decide what to get!), there is always a thali, which means "plate" and usually comes with two or three curries, a lentil dish, rice, bread, a few other accompaniments, and often a dessert, making it a great overall value.

Oftentimes a particular restaurant might be known for a specific dish, whether it be their thali or biryani (rice mixed with vegetables and spices), a particular curry, or their massive masala dosas, so it often pays to ask what the specialty is before ordering.

If you're traveling with a friend or another traveler you just met, sharing dishes is the way to go. Order a couple of curries, some rice, and bread and just split it all so that you get to taste even more. Sharing Indian food is by far the best method of trying a variety of dishes.

You'll generally find street stalls selling food on the cheaper end (even less than that) and sit-down restaurants in bigger cities on the higher end. Here is an example of food costs in 2014 (USD):

Samosas or pakoras from a street vendor: 20–50 cents

Sweet lassi from a stall: 35 cents

Plate of four Tibetan momos: 20 cents

Bananas (½ kilogram): 45 cents

Thali (meal consisting of vegetable dishes, dhal, rice, roti, and more): $1–3

Dish of mattar paneer (peas and cheese curry): 85 cents to $2

Dhal and rice: $1

Chicken tandoori (½ chicken): $2.50

Butter naan: 25–50 cents

Masala dosa: $1–2

Chai from a vendor: 10–20 cents

Egg sandwich from a street stall: 35 cents

Cup of tea: 10–20 cents from a stall; more than $1.40 in a top hotel

Beer (650-milliliter bottle): $1 in a shop; $4 in a top hotel (without taxes)

Pretty inexpensive, right? If you stick to Indian food, you are going to be able to eat for less than $10 a day.

From fast-food chains (McDonald's, Subway, and Domino's Pizza) to restaurants that cater to foreigners, Western food is mostly Italian dishes, with the occasional Mexican cuisine, salads, and sandwiches thrown in. Eating Western food is an expensive affair in India. Prices for a plate of pasta will cost $2–4 USD, a six-inch sandwich at Subway is between $2 USD and $3 USD, while a plate of enchiladas at a restaurant in the heart of Varanasi would cost around $3 USD. While that doesn't sound like a lot, when compared to the price of Indian food, it's a fortune! While Western food is abundant, the quality certainly varies, and at the budget end of the spectrum, you shouldn't expect anything extraordinary.

Moreover, it's important to keep in mind that the cow is sacred in India and thus burgers are very, very hard to come by. Don't expect to eat or find much red meat while in the country.

Derek offers good advice for those looking for something besides curries: "If you need a break from Indian food, I recommend finding a Nepali-owned restaurant, which can be found in most destinations that are popular with backpackers. These places cater to foreigners and usually offer a wide range of inexpensive, typically delicious salads, sandwiches, Italian, Israeli, Mexican, Nepali and other Western dishes, all prepared fresh, with all vegetables washed in purified water as well, so that you can enjoy a quality non-Indian meal."

Since food is so cheap, I don't recommend going food shopping and cooking for yourself. While there's nothing wrong with buying food from markets for snacks, if you try to cook meals you are going to end up spending more money than you would have if you just went out and bought food. But if you plan to cook, you should do so with filtered water and nothing from the tap—ever!

India is a great place for vegetarians as a large percentage of the Indian population is vegetarian. You won't have a problem finding food. Mariellen is a vegetarian and cannot eat gluten (wheat). She says, "In South India, rice is the basis for many dishes; whereas in North India, bread such as roti, chapapti or naan is used to eat with. It is very easy to be vegetarian in India (and sometimes the wisest choice as refrigeration and hygiene can be spotty), and also to eat gluten-free meals. For example, pakoras are usually made with besan flour, which is ground chickpea flour."

Lastly, let's talk about food safety. The phrase *Delhi belly* exists for a reason. Food sanitation isn't top notch and a lot of people get very, very sick in India. I know even experienced travelers incapacitated for weeks by this. In order to minimize your chances of getting sick, follow these rules:

- Don't drink the tap water. *Ever.* This includes ice cubes. (Seriously, don't!)

- Make sure your bottled water is sealed before you open it.

- Avoid street food that nobody else is eating; and don't eat anything that hasn't been cooked.

- Minimize the amount of meat you eat.

- Start taking probiotics two weeks before you travel to India. Take them every day before your trip and then every day throughout your trip as well. This significantly reduces any chance whatsoever of getting Delhi belly. (If probiotics are expensive in your home country, buy only enough for the two weeks before your trip as you can buy a week's worth at any pharmacy in India once you arrive for about $1 USD.)

Just like in Southeast Asia, common sense with street food goes a long way. Derek advises: "If a restaurant looks sketchy and has no Indian customers, it's a good idea to avoid it. But if a local hole-in-the-wall restaurant is full of local customers, you can try it out as well. Local people do not want to eat bad, non-fresh food either! So if it's a popular place with locals, it's popular for a reason—good, fresh food is being served and as a result it would be safe for you to eat there too."

Eat where others are eating to minimize your risks!

TRANSPORTATION

Let's get it out of the way now: transportation in India is slow. Departure and arrival times are often mere suggestions. You aren't going anywhere fast unless you fly! Any overland travel will take time. And even when trains and buses stick to their schedule, the great distance involved combined with the slow speeds means it still takes a while.

Trains

Around 14 million passengers travel by train in India every day and Indian Railways is one of the largest employers in the world, with a staggering 1.6 million workers.

Train journeys in India are more than the means to get from point A to point B —they are an adventure in themselves and an incredible way to meet and chat with locals.

"Train travel in India should not be viewed as a dreaded necessity. While it might not be the most comfortable or luxurious train system, you are bound to meet endless people on every journey, have some interesting conversations, see some beautiful countryside and in the end, have some of the most memorable experiences of your entire trip," says Derek.

Service on the trains can range from rough, crowded, and smelly to relaxing and comfortable.

For the cheapest travel, go third class. In third class, there are no assigned seats, it's unbelievably crowded, with people sleeping on the floor (and even on the luggage racks!), and there's poor ventilation. It's uncomfortable, rough, and tight, but tickets are dirt cheap—costing around $1 USD for most journeys, such as from Delhi to Varanasi or Goa to Kochi. If you're traveling on a tight budget, there's no better way to get around!

The next class up is the second-class sleeper, which comes with assigned seats, beds, and a lot less people. It is more private and comfortable and prices are around $6 USD for a typical twelve-hour journey.

At the top end is first class, which actually has three different subclasses. The 3A has six beds in each compartment, the 2A has four beds, and the 1A has only two beds. They all have more comfortable beds than other classes, and come with sheets, pillow, and blanket, air-conditioning, and outlets. A 3A bed would cost about $17 USD for an overnight journey while 1A would cost around $39 USD.

As a budget traveler, the second-class sleeper is the best class to travel in—it's affordable, comfortable, and a great way to meet locals.

For comprehensive timetables and routes, use the Indian Railways website (indianrail.gov.in) or the very user-friendly eRail site (erail.in).

In terms of travel for women, Mariellen never hesitates to travel by train in India by herself, even on long journeys. "I have never felt unsafe on a train," she says. "One time, I was booked into a second-class sleeper for an overnight journey, and I saw the compartment was filled with men. I asked to be moved and the conductor was very understanding. He put me in a 1st class compartment with a family. Generally, I recommend second class for female solo travelers."

Buses

Government-run buses are cheap, and their quality varies greatly as each individual state runs their own government bus operation. The quality of private buses can vary as well. Ultimately, it's a gamble since there are no uniform standards or level of care. In my view, trains are a much better transportation option unless you *have* to take a bus.

A normal government bus (bench seats, no air-conditioning, lots of stops, super crowded) from Delhi to Dharamsala, a journey of eleven hours, will cost around $8 USD, while a private bus (with semi-reclining seats, sometimes working air-conditioning, limited stops, and no more passengers than the number of seats) will be around $12 USD for the same journey.

Bus prices vary from state to state but are generally between $7 USD and $15 USD. For example, Bangalore to Hyderabad is around $8 USD, Bangalore to Chennai is about $5 USD, Delhi to Manali is $15 USD, and Bangalore to Mumbai is $13 USD.

On many long-distance buses, you can purchase a bed. The double beds are a great value; there is enough space for two people and their backpacks.

One thing to keep in mind is that bus travel can be accident prone. In the mountains, the roads are perilous and buses are driven a bit recklessly and accidents are always a risk. Try to avoid night buses unless there is no alternative.

Flying

The number of budget airlines in India seems to be growing all the time, and as a result, the fares are often remarkably low. Since travel around the country can be long and tiring, flights can represent a quick and easy way to cut out a twenty-hour train journey. Most intra-country flights range between $50 USD and $120 USD, though deals often abound for much less than that. The following are the major airlines in the country:

Air Asia: airasia.com/my/en/home.page

Air India: airindia.com

GoAir: goair.in

IndiGo: goindigo.in

Jagson Airlines: jagsonairline.com

Jet Airways: jetairways.com

Spicejet: spicejet.com

ATTRACTIONS AND ACTIVITIES

Like many developing countries, India has a two-tier fee system where foreigners pay significantly more than locals. However, prices are never that expensive and rarely more than $10 USD, and that's usually just for big attractions. The Taj Mahal costs around $13 USD, Humayun's Tomb in Delhi is $4 USD, the Red Fort in Delhi costs about $12 USD, and Bundi Palace costs around $3 USD.

Prices vary wildly, depending on popularity but overall are incredibly affordable; as you can see even the popular and beautiful Taj Mahal is a bargain! One thing to note is that there may also be additional charges for photo and video cameras, and those fees can be pretty steep.

Derek says, "Before buying an entrance ticket to any attraction, be sure to ask what it includes. Oftentimes your ticket will include the entrance fee to other nearby attractions as well and sometimes, you'll have the option of purchasing a package that, for a little more money, allows you to visit several sites on that one ticket as well."

Unlike other destinations in the world, India does not have any discount cards or offers that travelers can use.

HOW MUCH MONEY DO YOU NEED?

For those on a really tight budget, you could survive in India for around $15 USD a day. This would include staying at cheap (and dirty) guesthouses, eating local food at cheap restaurants and street stalls, and traveling in third-class trains or on local buses. You can further reduce your costs by Couchsurfing or sticking to ultra-cheap street food and avoiding the major cities. But on that bare-bones budget, you wouldn't be able to do a lot of activities, drink, or eat at a nice restaurant.

On a more comfortable and realistic budget of $25 USD per day, you'll be able to travel significantly better—better food, better lodging, second-class sleeper, and more activities. There will be room for the occasional beer and even first-class sleeper trains every now and then.

In the larger cities of Mumbai, New Delhi, and Bangalore as well as beach destinations like Goa, you can expect to spend around $40 USD per day as costs are higher—more people, more tourists, and city life is just generally more expensive. In the countryside, you'll pay about 50 percent less.

If you are a female traveling alone, says Mariellen, you may find that you have to pay more to ensure your safety and comfort. "Go with your gut instinct. If a guesthouse looks sketchy, avoid it and spend more to get a better place if you have to. If you feel uneasy in the 3rd class train, upgrade to 2nd class. It is always worth the extra money."

Overall, India is not expensive and anything above $35 USD per day would allow you *substantial* comfort and flexibility in traveling throughout the country.

Safety Tips for Women in India

BY CANDACE ROSE RARDON

Before traveling to India for the first time, I was all too aware of the various threats facing Indian women and foreign visitors alike: staring, groping, stalking, and most seriously, rape. With such threats forever hanging over a female traveler's head, I couldn't help wondering if India would be worth the worry and the hassle.

Having now spent nine months in the country, let me assure you it is worth it. Although I did encounter men who stared at me inappropriately, there were countless others who in no way treated me as a sexual object—farmers and pharmacists, shopkeepers and teachers, men whose warmth, kindness, and compassion moved me in unexpected ways.

It is impossible to stereotype a nation of 1 billion people, and bad experiences there will naturally be impossible to avoid. The challenge lies in refusing to accept such occurrences as the status quo, while still choosing to focus on the positive. This might sound trite or naive, but it's a choice that India demands of you.

Travel in India will require heightened attention and common sense. Here are ten tips to help ward off unwanted situations but also to keep you open to positive experiences:

1. Do Your Homework

As you would for any destination, spend time learning about India and its customs before arriving. Go in with your eyes wide open, having taken the necessary steps to be educated and prepared, and understand that what awaits you there may be vastly different from what you're used to.

In my own experience, the most important preparation for India was mental. Between worrying about what shots to get, what would happen when I got sick for the first time, and whether or not I would be safe, India required a huge mental adjustment—this wouldn't be another beach holiday or European city break.

2. Dress Appropriately

This goes without saying, but deserves repeating: India is a conservative country, so be respectful of that by covering your shoulders and legs and watching your cleavage.

Consider wearing Indian attire such as a *kurta* (long, loose tunic) or a *shalwar kameez* suit, which can easily be picked up once you arrive at local markets or from stores like Fabindia. This is by no means a guarantee of your safety and may not change the way men act toward you, but there's no need to draw unnecessary attention to yourself.

The only possible exception to this is Goa, whose well-known beaches have become increasingly Westernized. But be aware that although it is more acceptable to wear a bikini here, you might still attract unwanted advances.

3. Discern When Doctoring the Truth May Help You

I'm never a fan of not telling the truth on the road. I believe that, when appropriate, it's as important to share our own customs and ways of life with other cultures as it is to learn about theirs. This mutual exchange is one of the many things I love about travel, so I don't make it a practice of wearing a fake wedding ring or pretending that I have a husband who works in Delhi.

But while eating dinner alone in Mumbai one night, an Indian man sitting at another table asked if he could join me. Our conversation was interesting and I was glad for the chance to chat, but afterward he asked if we could go somewhere else for a drink or meet again the next night. I didn't feel comfortable doing so on my own, and told him that I already had plans with friends. Use discernment and get a sense of whether or not such a white lie may help protect you.

4. On Train Journeys, Book an Upper Berth

Everyone has their memorable tale from the Indian rails—the couple who helped them get off at the right station, the family who insisted on sharing their dahl and chapatis, the college student who said to wake him if there was any trouble. Nowhere else in the world is the journey as fun as the destination as it is in India.

But it's also important to take certain precautions. When booking your journey, request an upper berth. This will not only be a place to keep your bags secure during the day, but will also give you a sense of privacy and keep you out of the fray at night as you sleep.

And while the idea of more space and cooler air in second-class air-conditioning may be appealing, consider traveling in the sleeper class instead. The constant hustle and bustle of vendors and passengers will make it more difficult for unwelcome encounters to happen.

5. Don't Arrive at a New Destination at Night

Try to avoid late-night arrivals or departures. This is as much an issue of safety as it is for financial reasons—cunning touts will be out, hoping to take advantage of those who appear lost or without a plan. Book at least your first night's accommodation in advance so that you're confident on where you're headed when you leave the airport or train station.

Also avoid traveling on foot at night, as well as by public transportation (especially if the bus or train carriage is empty); opt for prepaid taxis or auto-rickshaws instead.

6. Be Assertive

In a country whose classic head bobble can mean yes, no, maybe, not now, or we'll see, it makes sense that it's difficult to firmly tell someone no in India. But as a woman on your own, this is necessary at times, just as it's occasionally necessary to ignore unwanted or uncomfortable conversations.

When you are traveling alone as a woman, especially in a country like India, it is your responsibility to protect yourself—so don't hesitate to do so, be it with a strong word or silent response.

Nowhere did I feel the need to be assertive more than when in a market. To make it through a gauntlet of persistent and persuasive vendors, saying a polite "no thank you" will often have little effect. As rude as it felt as someone who is typically more soft-spoken, I would sometimes reply with just "no" in a sharp tone of voice or even with *nahi*, the Hindi word for "no."

7. Watch Your Body Language

The challenge I mentioned earlier—between staying on your guard and keeping an open heart—is perhaps most relevant to how you act toward men in India and the messages you may subconsciously send.

The important thing to remember is that an action or gesture that may come naturally to you, such as touching someone's arm while talking to them, might be misinterpreted in a conservative country like India. Be mindful of keeping your physical distance from men even while being open to them, especially on public transportation where personal space is at a premium.

8. Don't Do Anything You Wouldn't Do at Home

It's true that travel opens you up to new experiences and pushes you out of your comfort zone, but at the same time, be sensible and ask yourself if you would do something at home. Things like hitchhiking, going out alone at night, and accepting drinks from men you don't know are risky no matter where you are in the world.

9. Consider Traveling with a Group

The thought of visiting India for the first time is intimidating enough, so perhaps beginning your time there on a tour (through companies such as G Adventures or WanderTours) can help you get acclimated.

A huge part of traveling alone is learning to trust your own instincts when you don't have friends or family there to discuss your options with. Before you can trust those you meet on the road, you have to learn to trust yourself. Develop this sense of self-trust before venturing to India alone.

10. Know That Mass Photo-Taking Sessions Will Happen

This happens enough in India that I feel it's worth mentioning: If you suddenly find yourself at the center of a flurry of photo requests, especially at key historic sites, go with the flow—for as long as you feel comfortable.

It happened to me at the Taj Mahal, in front of the Gateway of India in Mumbai, and even on a beach in Puri, Orissa—I was asked to have my photo taken with at least a dozen different families or groups of young men. This may seem strange, but it's usually harmless.

Although India can be a difficult place to travel and there will be moments when being the center of attention is overwhelming, it is an experience I would redo again in a heartbeat. By using the tips above, you can mitigate the feeling of having eyes inappropriately on you and transform uncomfortable situations into positive ones.

Ultimately, there is no secret to staying safe in India. It is a continual process of being wise and keenly listening to your instincts—just as you would anywhere else in the world. Indians love to welcome foreigners into their country, so trust your gut in accepting their hospitality and learn from their kindness.

Candace Rose Rardon is a travel writer who writes at A Great Affair (agreataffair.com). Her work has appeared in the BBC and *National Geographic*.

Japan

FOR years, I put off visiting Japan because I was scared by rumors of the country's high prices. I've loved Japanese culture since the first time I ate sushi and knew any visit would involve gorging myself on sushi and ramen noodles, visits to lots of temples, and heavy train travel through the countryside. And the thought of how much that would cost made me constantly think, "I'll wait until I have more money."

But I decided to finally just go and found I was wrong about the country. Japan is not that expensive and on par with (and sometimes cheaper than) countries in Western Europe. I was shocked. Japan is simply not as expensive as the myth goes, and with a few travel ninja moves, you can turn this seemingly expensive destination into one any budget traveler could love.

ACCOMMODATIONS

Hostels

Hostels in Japan are normally found in the big cities and are really wonderful places to stay. They are run really well and outside of using a hospitality network, hostels are the only option for saving money on accommodations. Plus they include a kitchen (which can save you money eating out), common area to relax and socialize in, wi-fi, computers, bike hire, and laundry. Plus, sometimes they even have a Japanese onsen, or spa. A dormitory bed typically costs around $22 USD per night (sometimes as low as $15 USD or as high as $42 USD in Tokyo) while twin private rooms can be as cheap as $27 USD in the countryside or as high as $95 USD in the cities.

The staff at the hostel is also likely to speak very good English (which isn't common in Japan) and can be a lifesaver helping you get around the city. Even if you don't stay at a hostel in Japan, visit them for assistance. They will be your best chance at getting directions and help.

Additionally, hostels in Japan let you stay for free if you are willing to clean up for a few hours a day. This is a great way to stay for no cost, and for those with more time than money, it's the easiest way to visit some of Japan's expensive megacities on a shoestring budget.

Budget Hotels

There are a lot of cheap budget hotels and guesthouses in Japan for those who want a little more comfort. Ryokan are Japanese inns that provide an opportunity to experience traditional Japanese accommodations. They feature tatami mats, onsens, traditional futon beds, and sometimes include meals.

Ryokan prices vary greatly and can cost as little as $50 USD a night to upward of $200 USD. While they are not very budget friendly, they are unique and should be experienced at least once as they are totally worth the splurge!

For more modern-style hotels, expect to pay around $40 USD per night for a room that comes with a bed and shared shower. However, the price depends heavily on the location. Hotels in Osaka can cost as little as $20 USD for a single room while the cheapest hotel room you can find in Tokyo is often around $40 USD. Countryside hotels are also on the lower end.

Then there are the capsule hotels, which are exactly like they sound. You sleep in a little tiny pod. It's like being in a coffin or a space capsule in a sci-fi movie. You share bathrooms and common areas and your capsule has a light, outlet, and maybe a small television. They are frequently used by businessmen who work late and miss the last train home. They are a little weird to stay in, and if you aren't comfortable in tight spaces, they probably won't be for you. One night in them was all I could take, but it's definitely a unique experience and an inexpensive option for solo travelers. Capsule hotels begin around $27 USD per night.

Booking sites like Agoda and Booking.com have the best rates in Asia for large hotels and are my go-to search sites. Rakuten Travel (travel.rakuten.com) is a Japan-only website that features smaller and more traditional hotels not found on the large booking sites.

Apartment Rentals

There are better options than apartment rental sites, but if you want an apartment, you'll find very limited options outside the major cities. In Tokyo, as of 2014, Airbnb lists over 1,000 private rooms and

180 shared rooms, while the smaller site Roomorama shows 473 listings in greater Tokyo.

The lack of available options in such a large megacity is because Japanese culture is very private and most apartments are very small, so you can't really have houseguests. Most people just don't have a spare room. As such, if you are traveling as a group, apartment rentals can be a really good option because renting entire apartments is fairly easy but for solo or couple travelers, you'll be hard-pressed to find private rooms.

Solo travelers can rent one of the very limited beds for between $25 USD and $35 USD a night around the country. Entire apartments range from $100 USD and up per night.

Camping

Camping is allowed in Japan only in national parks. There are more than 3,000 campsites scattered all over the country, owned and managed by local municipalities. Metropolitan areas don't have campsites, so don't expect to camp anywhere other than in the woods. In the national parks, camping outside the designated areas is strictly prohibited.

Hospitality Exchanges

Hospitality exchanges are not as widespread in Japan as elsewhere in the world, but there is a small but active Couchsurfing community in the country (26,000 members in spring 2014). Couchsurfing simply is not a part of Japanese culture, and many people do not feel comfortable hosting strangers. Most of the hosts on the hospitality websites are younger. Many of the Couchsurfing profiles I saw were foreigners or Japanese who had been overseas.

There are not many hosts outside the big cities, so make sure you request rooms well ahead of time to increase your odds of success as the response rate is often very low.

WWOOF

WWOOF Japan (wwoofjapan.com) has hundreds of hosts all over the country. WWOOFing is very, very new to Japan so there are not that many options, but you'll find a variety of farms, health centers, and traditional homesteads looking for workers. To WWOOF in Japan, you will need a work visa.

FOOD

Since Japan imports most of their food, I was afraid of paying through the nose for even the most basic meal, but surprisingly, I found food to be inexpensive in Japan. True, I have a sushi addiction and that got pricey, but overall, I found that I was spending far less on food than I anticipated. As long as I didn't feed my sushi addiction, I found I could eat for less than $15 USD per day.

From the melt-in-your-mouth sushi to the silky miso soups, curry bowls, and thick ramen soup, I find Japanese food to be delicious and a flavorful delight. There's nothing better than sitting down in a traditional little hole in the wall with Japanese businessmen washing their meal down with a beer while everyone looks at the *gaijin* (foreigner) trying to navigate the menu before helping you out. I remember being in Kanazawa staring bewildered at a menu when the guy next to me helped me out. We struck up a conversation, and over sake, I learned his story as well as about life in Japan.

If you want to eat cheap, stick to the trifecta of curry, ramen, and donburi. I essentially lived off these three foods during my time in Japan. Curry bowls were as cheap as $3 USD per plate. Donburi, bowls of meat and rice, are between $4 USD and $5 USD. Ramen is never more than $7 USD. These are the best ways to eat cheap and filling meals while in Japan. You'll find places all over Japan, especially in train stations.

And that's an important part I want to bring up—if you want to eat cheap and well, head to a Japanese train station. These are not just train stations but huge complexes featuring shops, restaurants, and takeaways. Here you will always find a ramen, 7-Eleven, sushi train, supermarket, or whatever else your budget food needs require. They are incredibly popular with locals, who stop for a delicious and inexpensive meal on their way to and from work.

Most other traditional Japanese meals such as tempura, meat, and bento boxes cost between $12 USD and $15 USD for lunch, while dinners cost from $20 USD.

For Western food, you can expect to pay $4 USD for a small plate of pasta; other Western meal set menus (sandwich, burger, or pizza with drink) begin around $12 USD.

McDonald's Value Menu is about $6 USD. I found Western food to be lacking in deliciousness and stinging to my wallet. Unless you are eating on the high end or really need that burger, avoid eating Western food. (And you'll find nothing even remotely appetizing in the countryside!)

For those who love sushi (who doesn't?), sushi in Japan is delicious at all levels. While I had a few fancy sit-down meals, you can't beat the sushi trains for value. At $1–2 USD per plate, I could stuff my face for less than $15 USD most of the time. I usually just ate there. Traditional sushi sets still cost around $16 USD or more. If you want a nice restaurant with waitstaff and a formal dining setting, be prepared to pay $75 USD or more for a filling sushi dinner. The sushi isn't cheap, but if you have to splurge, it's worth it. The fish market in Tokyo also has cheap sushi served in the morning after the fish auction.

If you're just looking for a light meal, head to the convenience stores. They often have fresh fruit, prepared meals, and sandwiches for only a few dollars. Many locals stop by here for prepared meals on their way home from work. Popular convenience stores include 7-Eleven, Food Mart, Family Mart, SunRus, and Lawson.

Self-catering is the most effective way to eat on a budget in Japan. As noted above, convenience and other corner stores have a lot of preset meals for $1–3 USD that make for a cheap lunch option. Additionally, supermarkets also have many set meals at similar prices. I noticed this was a popular eating method for many Japanese people. Hostels have kitchens where you can cook and cut your food expenses to less than $8 USD per day, especially by shopping at the 100 Yen Stores (Dollar Stores).

One rumor about Japan that turned out to be true was that fresh fruits and vegetables were expensive. Outside of shopping for an apple or banana at the market, I generally avoided buying fresh fruits and vegetables.

It's very possible to eat cheap in Japan if you stick to the tiny restaurants around the country, buy prepared meals at convenience stores (which are still delicious), and self-cater many of your meals. This will also allow you to splurge on meals once in a while.

TRANSPORTATION

Most of the city metro tickets cost $1–2 USD for a single journey. (The price varies by distance and may often be higher.) Fares were usually around $2 USD to travel across Tokyo but less for shorter distances. In most major cities, you can buy a day pass, which gives you unlimited travel for twenty-four hours for between $8 USD and $10 USD.

Trains

Transportation is one of the most expensive aspects of travel in Japan and made up the bulk of my expenses. The bullet trains, while punctual, comfortable, and extremely fast, are not cheap. Individual tickets can cost hundreds of dollars.

But train travel is the best way to see the country, so in order to reduce your train costs get a Japan Rail pass. The pass is indispensable for travel in Japan. If you are planning on visiting more than two or three long-distance destinations in Japan, then it is highly advised to purchase a JR Rail Pass (jrpass.com), which gives you unlimited journeys on all JR Rails, JR Ferries, and JR Buses throughout the country.

These passes cost around $280 USD for seven days, $450 USD for fourteen days, and $575 USD for twenty-one days (all pass times are for consecutive travel). And while that may seem pricey, when you compare them to the price of individual tickets, a pass is a bargain.

For example, here are the costs of some popular routes without the pass:

Tokyo–Kyoto: $137 USD

Tokyo–Osaka: $142 USD

Tokyo–Hiroshima: $186 USD

Kyoto–Hiroshima: $112 USD

Osaka–Hiroshima: $109 USD

Just buying a seven-day pass and taking any three of these routes will save you money. As long as you are going to travel by train at least three times, a JR Rail Pass will always be your best option. Even if you won't use all the days on the pass, buy the pass if you plan on taking more than three trains—especially for the added flexibility.

Keep in mind the JR Rail Pass *must* be booked *before* your arrival in Japan.

When available, the Seishun 18 Ticket (jreast.co.jp/e) is the most economic deal in Japan, offering five days of unlimited train travel for just $115 USD. It's available three times per year during school holidays and can be bought at any rail station in Japan. You can visit Japan Guide (japan-guide.com/e/e2362.html) to see the latest school holidays.

Moreover, use the website HyperDia (hyperdia.com/en) to find train times and schedules in English. It's an invaluable resource.

Buses

Buses are a much cheaper alternative to the bullet train system in Japan. But while the cost is less, the trip will take considerably more time. For example, the two-hour bullet train ride from Tokyo to Osaka becomes a ten-hour bus ride.

Long-distance highway buses service many of the intercity routes covered by trains at significantly lower prices. Bus journeys around the country begin around $35 USD. There is a multitude of operators, including Star Express and Willer Express (willerexpress .com/en), Kansai Bus, and the bus company operated by the JR group (the people who run the trains).

A few overnight buses are women only, such as the Ladies Dream Osaka bus service between Tokyo and Osaka.

Willer Express offers a Japan Bus Pass (willerexpress.com/x/bus/ dynamic/3/en/html/pc/buspass). It is available to both Japanese and foreigners but must be purchased outside of Japan. The cost of a bus pass is $100 USD for three days or $150 USD for five days. Travel days are nonconsecutive, but passes must be used within two months.

If you have a lot of time on your hands, want to visit several major cities in a single trip, and do not mind the time spent on buses (including sleeping), then the Bus Pass is worth considering. The more trips you take, the more cost-effective the pass will be. You can potentially ride Willer Express buses for as little as $14 USD per trip. You'll never be able to ride the train that cheap!

Keep in mind that the bus pass restricts you to buses seating four in a row, can't be used during major holidays, and often have blackout dates (you need to check with the company for the exact dates). However, with all that in mind, if you have time in Japan and aren't in a rush, buses are the cheapest (but not the quickest) way to travel the country.

Taxis

Taxis, especially in Tokyo, are ridiculously expensive and should be avoided unless absolutely necessary. A twenty-minute journey home after a night out in Tokyo cost nearly $60 USD!

Flying

Flying between most cities is not necessary as the bullet trains are pretty fast and prices are comparable to flights. You get all the speed without the hassle of going through airport security! If you are hopping between the islands of Japan, you'll need to fly; here are the best airlines to get you there:

JAL Group (Japan Airlines): jal.com

ANA Group (Japan Airlines): ana.co.jp

Skymark Airlines: skymark.jp/en

Peach Aviation: flypeach.com

Jetstar Japan: jetstar.com

Air Do: airdo.jp

Vanilla Air: vanilla-air.com

Starflyer: starflyer.jp/en

Fuji Dream Airlines: fujidream.co.jp

ATTRACTIONS AND ACTIVITIES

Most of the attractions in Japan are very cheap. On average, I didn't spend more than $5 USD per museum or temple. Admission to famous temples costs between $1 USD and $7 USD (around $2 USD in Kamakura and around $4 USD in Kyoto and Nara). Most museums and castles charge $2–10 USD per person.

In Kyoto, there is a temple pass that gives you unlimited transportation and access to the temples for $12 USD. It's a good deal, considering you are probably going to see a lot of museums in Kyoto. Osaka and Tokyo had similar passes for their attractions.

Some tourist attractions distribute coupons and discount cards at local tourist information centers and hotels. Be sure to stop in and pick some up to save you money.

The Grutt Museum Pass (japanvisitor.com/japan-city-guides/grutt-pass-museums) provides free or discounted admission to over seventy-five attractions in the Tokyo area. The pass costs $20 USD, is sold from April through January, and is valid for two months. For those doing a lot of sightseeing in Tokyo, it's a must buy.

Free walking tours are just starting to take off, and at the time of this writing, there were three major ones to choose from in Tokyo:

Tokyo Free Guide: tokyofreeguide.com

Go Tokyo: gotokyo.org/en/tourists/guideservice/guideservice/index.html

Tokyo Free Walking Tour (TFWT): tfwt.sharepoint.com/Pages/default.aspx

HOW MUCH MONEY DO YOU NEED?

Japan has an image of being one of the most expensive countries in the world, and if you are staying in hotels, eating out, and traveling around a lot, it can be. You can easily spend over $200 USD per day by traveling that way. However, I don't think a trip to Japan needs to be that expensive.

Staying in a hostel, buying a rail pass, eating relatively cheap food, and visiting a few attractions will cost around $100 USD per day.

Instead, by using the tips given in this chapter, I think you can get by on $70–75 USD per day. This would mean more bus travel, a (very) limited amount of sushi, only cheap restaurants, and the occasional night Couchsurfing (or another method for free accommodation).

On a bare-bones budget, you can get by for $50 USD per day if you stick to Couchsurfing, cheap food, bus travel (trains would be far too expensive), and free attractions. I saw lots of travelers in Japan traveling on the cheap. They did it, and it's possible—as long as you don't have a sushi addiction to feed!

PUTTING IT ALL TOGETHER

THIS book has laid out a lot of numbers in front of you like pieces of a puzzle. Now it's time to put those pieces together. The promise of this book is that you can travel around the world for $50 USD per day, or $18,250 USD per year. Now, that number didn't just come to me out of thin air. I picked $50 USD per day because my own years of travel experience have taught me that that's exactly how much money you need for a world trip. That's a daily average. Some days you may spend more, some days you may spend a lot less. If your whole trip is just to Southeast Asia, you'll spend less than that in one year. But if you are going away for a shorter time period or spending two weeks in Norway, it will be harder to reach as low as $50 USD per day.

After years of traveling the world, I've realized that there are so many easy ways to save money that don't require a lot of work. So long as you get out of the "expensive hotel/dinners/flights" mentality, you'll find incredible value for your money throughout the world and ways to spend less money than you would living back home.

We get programmed to do our travel bookings on just a few large, popular websites, but as we have seen in the book, there are smaller sites that can help us book the same thing for less.

For this last chapter, I'd like to turn all the costs and expenses peppered throughout this book into a yearly budget. I want to show you how all these numbers and figures work together to make $18,250 USD.

First, let's discuss pre-trip expenses. As we saw in Part One, there aren't many pre-trip expenses. There are a few big things, but mostly your days will be spent organizing your life in preparation for your big journey. Your biggest pre-trip expenses will be:

Travel insurance: $1,000 USD

Flight: $2,700 USD

Backpack: $200 USD

Discount cards: $100 USD

Note: Flight costs can vary due to where you are going, time you are booking, and how many reward miles you use for free flights. If you don't use my tips on getting free flights, you'll end up spending a lot more.

So even before we go away, we are looking at spending around $4,000 USD. That's a lot of money, but it takes care of all our sunken costs, and the discount cards will end up saving us more on the road than they cost (as previously discussed). Plus, by averaging that amount out over a year, it's only $10 USD per day.

Next, let's talk about expenses on the road, because this is where you are going to spend most of your money. In this book, I included the most popular destinations people visit on a round-the-world trip.

For the purposes of adding it all together, I'm going to use the most common route people take around the world (in order) along with the time and money people typically spend in each region:

South America: $30 per day x 90 days = $2,700

Europe (assuming a mix of Western and Eastern Europe): $50 USD per day x 90 days = $4,500

Southeast Asia: $25 USD per day x 90 days = $2,250 USD

Australia: $55 USD per day x 60 days = $3,300

New Zealand: $50 USD per day x 30 days = $1,500 USD

TOTAL = $14,250

Adding this number to our pre-trip expenses gives us exactly $18,250 USD or $50 USD per day. If you replaced some of the destinations on this list with China ($30 per day) or India ($25 per day), you would be able to lower the cost of your trip.

We all have different travel styles and budgets. Where you go and what you do greatly factor into what your final needed amount is. As you can see above, you can spend *three* months in Southeast Asia for a lot less than you can spend in *two* months in Australia.

The above figures assume you listened to my advice about finding cheap flights and traveling on the cheap. But if there is one thing I've always learned from travel, it is that plans never go as expected, and your specific circumstances might cause you to go over or even under this budget. My numbers are a guideline, and my tips will help you reach those numbers. What you do with the information I give you is up to you, so the actual amount of money you spend will depend on how many of my tips you use and where you go.

Note that the average daily budgets above do not factor in such measures as staying in free accommodations all the time (hospitality exchanges), hitchhiking, eating only local meals, or even cooking all your meals, and the above numbers still allow you to come within the $50-a-day budget. Once you add in these other tricks, your costs can be lowered even more. I once went to London for 10 days and spent $700 USD (including my flight) simply by using miles for free flights and rooms, cooking my meals, sticking to lunch specials, and staying with a friend. Booking the "normal" way (that is through Expedia and Hotels.com), that trip would have cost $2,000 USD!

What these numbers really illustrate is that traveling the world can be as cost-effective as living at home, and that you shouldn't think travel is unaffordable. I was recently home in Boston, and while I was out at night, a girl overheard what I did for work and started asking me about how to get to Ireland cheaply. She and her boyfriend were planning a trip. I had a dream job, she said, but she could never afford to do what I do. When I told her how much I spent on traveling my entire life per year ($18,250), her first reaction was that it was a lot of money. But when I asked her to think about all her expenses last year and to add them all up, after thinking for a minute, she admitted that the total cost was a lot more than I spent traveling the world.

As I've shown throughout this book, there are a number of ways to save money when you arrive at your destination. It is possible to travel. The world is affordable. We don't have to be afraid that we don't have enough money to see it. Even if you can't find $18,000, all of these destinations can be seen on their own. If you only have a few weeks, you can find a cheap flight and visit somewhere close, using my tips to save money. You can skip expensive Europe and Australia and spend more time visiting developing and cheaper countries. My tips are universal.

I firmly believe that travel is not expensive. My own personal motto is "Travel cheaper, longer, and better." As I've traveled, I've come to realize that you can have a first-class travel experience on an economy-class budget as long as you are flexible and think outside the box. This book is my attempt to break down that perception and show that with a little knowledge and flexibility your dream trip around the world or honeymoon in Italy doesn't need to be a dream at all—it can be an affordable reality.

Whether or not you decide to go around the world, or spend $30, $50, or $70 per day, remember to look for value when you travel. Don't just go with the first pick. Traveling the world on the cheap is as much about finding value as it is about saving money.

And after reading this book, I hope you've realized that travel is within your grasp.

SEE YOU ON THE ROAD,
MATT

ACKNOWLEDGMENTS

Writing a book takes a lot of work, and there are a lot of people I want to thank for helping me put this together. First and foremost, I'd like to thank Maria Gagliano, for approaching me about turning my old online ebook into the book you just read. She saw the potential for this book to be even more than it already was, and I thank her immensely for her support. I'm still unsure how she stumbled across my website, but I'm glad she did. Without her, this book wouldn't be here. Plus, she spent time editing my verboseness into something concise and coherent! I'd also like to thank my editor, Jeanette Shaw.

Next, I'd like to thank my literary agent, Lindsay Edgecombe, for handling all the contract issues and my annoying questions about the process of writing a book and dealing with publishers. I knew nothing.

I'd really like to thank my friend and mentor Jason Cochran (found at Jason-Cochran.com). As a fellow travel writer who has done this before, his edits, guidance, and criticisms were instrumental in getting me to where I am today. Writing a blog is not like writing a guidebook, and he helped me through this process more than anyone else. He picked me apart, lifted me up, and provided invaluable notes. And, along the way, he made me a much better writer.

I'd also like to thank those who read my book, gave comments, feedback, and quotes: David Whitely, Audrey Scott and Dan Noll, Chris Guillebeau, David Lee, Brooke Schoeman, Matthew Khynn, Amanda Williams, Steve Kamb, Tim Leffel, Brook Silva Braga, Marina Villatoro, Dani Heinrich, Jessica Ainlay, Jeff Jung, Molly McHugh, Marcello Arrambide, Stuart McDonald, Dani and Craig James, Sean and Dawn Lynch, Benny Lewis, Brian Kelly, Bethany Salvon, Nora Dunn, Raymond Walsh, Lawrence Norah, Lee Abamonte, Michael Hodson, Sarah Muir, Kristin Addis, Mariellen Ward, Joel Ward, Derek Baron, and Chris Walker-Bush.

Finally, I'd like to thank all the travelers I've met since I left that day in 2006. You are an inspiration to me. Thank you for teaching me so much, the good times, the hangovers, the lifelong friendships, and the wonderful and exciting adventures. Every part of this book is based on experiences shared with you. Thank you.

TRAVEL COMPANIES

The following are lists of all the travel companies, tour operators, and hostels I use and recommend. Most of these sites are in addition to the sites already mentioned in the book. Restaurants and bars are not included here.

INTERNATIONAL RESOURCES

TOUR COMPANIES

Busabout: busabout.com
Context Travel: contexttravel.com
G Adventures: gadventures.com
Go-today: go-today.com
Intrepid Travel: intrepidtravel.com
Kiwi Experience: kiwiexperience.com
Oz Experience: ozexperience.com
STA Travel: statravel.com
Stray: straytravel.com

FLIGHT RESOURCES

Airfarewatchdog: airfarewatchdog.com
AirTreks: airtreks.com
Expedia: expedia.com
The Flight Deal: theflightdeal.com

Google Flights: google.com/flights
Hipmunk: hipmunk.com
Holiday Pirates: holidaypirates.com
Kayak: kayak.com
Momondo: momondo.com
Oneworld: oneworld.com
Orbitz: orbitz.com
Skyscanner: skyscanner.com
SkyTeam: skyteam.com
Star Alliance: staralliance.com/en
Travel Hacking Cartel: travelhacking.org
Travelocity: travelocity.com
Vayama: vayama.com

BACKPACK COMPANIES

Backcountry: backcountry.com
Campmor: campmor.com
Eastern Mountain Sports (EMS): ems.com
Mountain Equipment Co-operative (MEC): mec.ca
Recreational Equipment Inc. (REI): rei.com
Sierra Trading Post: sierratradingpost.com

DISCOUNT CARDS

Budget Backpacker Hostels New Zealand: bbh.co.nz
Hostelling International Card: hihostels.com
ISIC Student/Teacher/Youth Card: isic.org
Nomads MAD Card: nomadshostels.com
VIP Backpackers Card: vipbackpackers.com

ACCOMMODATION BOOKING SITES

9 flats: 9flats.com
Agoda: agoda.com
Airbnb: airbnb.com

BetterBidding: betterbidding.com
BidOnTravel: bidontravel.com
The Bidding Traveler: biddingtraveler.com
BeWelcome: bewelcome.org
Camp in My Garden: campinmygarden.com
The Caretaker Gazette: caretaker.org
Couchsurfing: couchsurfing.org
GlobalFreeloaders: globalfreeloaders.com
HomeAway: homeaway.com
Hospitality Club: hospitalityclub.org
HostelBookers: hostelbookers.com
Hostelworld: hostelworld.com
Hotels.com: hotels.com
Hotwire: hotwire.com
HouseCarers: housecarers.com
Lastminute: lastminute.com
LateRooms: laterooms.com
MindMyHouse: mindmyhouse.com
Priceline: priceline.com
Roomorama: roomorama.com
Servas International: servas.org
TravelPony: travelpony.com
TripAdvisor: tripadvisor.com
Warm Showers: warmshowers.org
Wimdu: wimdu.com

TRAVEL INSURANCE

Clements Insurance: clements.com
FrontierMEDEX Insurance: medexassist.com
IMG Insurance: imgglobal.com
InsureMyTrip: insuremytrip.com
MedjetAssist: medjetassist.com
World Nomads Travel Insurance: worldnomads.com

TRAVEL CREDIT CARD AND POINT-RELATED RESOURCES
BoardingArea: boardingarea.com
Flyertalk: flyertalk.com
The Points Guy: thepointsguy.com

MEAL SHARING SITES
COlunching: colunching.com
EatWith: eatwith.com
The Ghetto Gourmet: theghet.com
Meal Sharing: mealsharing.com

RIDE AND CAR SHARING
BlaBlaCar (Europe): blablacar.com
Carpooling (UK/Europe): carpooling.co.uk
Gumtree (UK/Australia/NZ): gumtree.com
Kangaride (Canada): kangaride.com
Liftshare (UK): liftshare.com/uk
Lyft (US): lyft.com
Sidecar (US): side.cr
Uber (US): uber.com

MISCELLANEOUS
Cruise Sheet: cruisesheet.com
Grassroots Volunteering: grassrootsvolunteering.org
Lonely Planet Guidebooks: lonelyplanet.com
The Man in Seat 61 (trains): seat61.com

DESTINATION-SPECIFIC RESOURCES

AUSTRALIA
Accommodations
Aussie House Sitters: aussiehousesitters.com.au
Base Magnetic Island Hostel: stayatbase.com/hostels/australia
-hostels/base-magnetic-island.aspx

Base Melbourne Hostel (Melbourne): stayatbase.com/hostels/
australia-hostels/base-backpackers-melbourne

Beaches of Broome (Broome): beachesofbroome.com.au

Calypso Inn (Cairns): calypsobackpackers.com.au

Camps Australia Wide: campsaustraliawide.com

Chillis Backpackers (Darwin): chillis.com.au

Nomad's Noosa Hostel (Noosa): nomadshostels.com/Noosa/
nomads-noosa-backpackers-hostel-noosa-australia

Surf n Sun Beachside Hostel (Surfer's Paradise): surfnsun
-goldcoast.com

Wake Up! Sydney Hostel (Sydney): wakeup.com.au

Witch's Hat Hostel (Perth): witchs-hat.com

Tour Operators

Adventure Tours Australia: adventuretours.com.au

OzSail Whitsunday Tours: ozsail.com.au

Darwin Walking Tour: darwinwalkingtours.com

Fraser Island Tours: fraserexplorertours.com.au

Kakadu Tour: ozbackpackertours.com/backpackertours/nt.htm

Tribal Tours: tribaltravel.com.au

Tusa Diving Great Barrier Reef: tusadive.com

Uncle Brian's Tours: unclebrian.com.au

Transportation

Greyhound Australia: greyhound.com.au

Oz Experience: ozexperience.com

Rail Australia: railaustralia.com.au

Spaceships: spaceshipsrentals.com.au

Traveler's Autobarn: travellers-autobarn.com.au

Wicked Campers: wickedcampers.com.au

NEW ZEALAND

Accommodations

Base: stayatbase.com

Kiwi Holiday Parks: kiwiholidayparks.com

New Zealand Bed and Breakfast Book: bnb.co.nz

New Zealand Department of Conservation Campsites:
doc.govt.nz

Nomads Queenstown: nomadshostels.com/hostels/new-zealand/
queenstown-nomads-backpackers

Rainbow Lodge (Taupo): rainbowlodge.co.nz

Tour Operators

AJ Hackett International: ajhackett.com

AwesomeNZ (dolphin tours): awesomenz.com/dolphin
-eco-experience

The Legendary Blackwater Rafting Company: waitomo.com/
black-water-rafting.aspx

Tamaki Maori Village: maoriculture.co.nz

Taupo Tandem Skydiving: tts.net.nz

Ziptrek Queenstown: ziptrek.com

Transportation

Hippie Camper Hire: hippiecamper.com

Intercity: intercity.co.nz

Kiwi Experience Bus: kiwiexperience.com

Kiwirail: kiwirail.co.nz

Magic Bus: magicbus.co.nz

Mighty Cars and Campers: backpackercampervans.co.nz

Naked Bus: nakedbus.co.nz

Spaceships: spaceshipsrentals.co.nz

Stray Travel Bus: straytravel.com

Wicked Campervans: wickedcampers.com.au

EUROPE

Accommodations

Balmers Herberge Interlaken: balmers.com

Camping Scandinavia: camping.se

City Backpackers (Stockholm): citybackpackers.org

Clown and Bard Hostel (Prague): clownandbard.com

The Flying Pig (Amsterdam): flyingpig.nl

Francesco's Hostel (Ios): francescos.net

Gallery Hostel Porto: gallery-hostel.com

Generator Hostels: generatorhostels.com

Goodnight Lisbon Hostel: goodnighthostel.com

Greg and Tom's Hostel (Krakow): gregtomhostel.com

Hostel Archi Rossi (Florence): hostelarchirossi.com

Hostel Blues (Slovakia): hostelblues.sk

Hostel Mostel (Bulgaria): hostelmostel.com

Kabul Hostel (Barcelona): kabul.es

Kismet Dao (Brasov): kismetdao.com

The Meeting Point (Amsterdam): hostel-meetingpoint.nl

Miss Sophie's (Prague): miss-sophies.com

Monk's Bunk (Tallinn): themonksbunk.com/social-hostel

Nest Hostels (Spain): nesthostelsvalencia.com

Pink Palace (Corfu): thepinkpalace.com

St. Christopher's: st-christophers.co.uk

Skanstull Hostel (Stockholm): skanstulls.se

Snuffel Hostel (Tallinn): snuffel.be

Tallinn Backpackers: tallinnbackpackers.com

Wombats: wombats-hostels.com

The Yellow (Rome): yellowhostel.com

European Free Walking Tours

Athens: athensfreewalkingtour.com

Belgrade: belgradewalkingtours.com

Braşov: guided-brasov.com

Bratislava: befreetours.com

Bucharest: guided-bucharest.com

Budapest: triptobudapest.hu

Krakow: freewalkingtour.com

Ljubljana: ljubljanafreetour.com

New Europe Walking Tours: neweuropetours.eu

Prague: newpraguetours.com: extravaganzafreetour.com

Sarajevo: sarajevowalkingtours.com

Tallinn: traveller.ee/tour/tallinn-free-tour

Tour Operators

1 Big Night Out: 1bignightout.com

Chernobyl Tours Kiev: stayinkiev.com/en/Chernobyl-Tour

Cracow City Tours Poland: cracowcitytours.pl

Divina Cucina Tuscany Food Tours: divinacucina.com

Fat Tire Bike Tours Berlin: fattirebiketours.com/berlin

Haggis Adventures Scotland: haggisadventures.com

Ultimate Party Pub Crawl: joinultimateparty.com

Walks of Italy: walksofitaly.com

Transportation

Busabout Backpacker Buses: busabout.com

Ecolines: ecolines.net

Eurail: eurail.com/home

Eurolines Buslines: eurolines.com

InterRail: interrail.eu

Megabus UK: uk.megabus.com

National Rail UK: nationalrail.co.uk

Rail Europe: raileurope.com

Scanbalt: scanbaltexperience.com

CENTRAL AMERICA

Accommodations

Costa Rica Backpackers (San Jose): costaricabackpackers.com

Hostal El Momento (Granada): hostelgranadanicaragua.com

Hostel Pangea (San Jose): hostelpangea.com

Luna's Castle (Panama City): lunascastlehostel.com

Lost and Found Panama (Bocas del Toro): lostandfoundlodge.com

Mondo Taitu (Bocas del Toro): mondotaitu.com

Naked Tiger Hostel (San Juan del Sur): facebook.com/ SanJuanDelSurHostel

PachaMama (San Juan del Sur): pachamama.com

Roatan Backpackers' Hostel (Roatan): roatanbackpackers.com

Rocking J's Hostels & Cabinas (Puerto Viejo): rockingjs.com

Tour Operators

Alton Dive Shop (Honduras): diveinutila.com/site

Raggamuffin Tours (Belize): raggamuffintours.com

SOUTH AMERICA

Accommodations

America del Sur Hostel Buenos Aires:
americahostel.com.ar

CabanaCopa: cabanacopa.com.br

La Casa Filipe: lacasadefelipe.com

Home Stay Web: homestayweb.com

Hostel Lao: laohostel.comLoki Hostel: lokihostel.com

Media Luna Hostel: medialunahostel.com

Pariwana Hostel Cusco: pariwana-hostel.com/pariwana-hostel
-cusco.php

Terra Extremus Hostel: terraextremus.com

Tucano House Backpackers: tucanohouse.com

Transportation

Berlinas: berlinasdelfonce.com

Bolivariano: bolivariano.com.co

Chile passenger trains: efe.cl

Coomotor: coomotor.com.co

Copetran: copetran.com.co

La Empresa Ferroviaria Andina: ferroviariaoriental.com
(eastern), fca.com.bo (western)

Expreso Brasilia: expresobrasilia.com

Ferrobaires: ferrobaires.gba.gov.ar/index.html

Omnilineas: omnilineas.com

Perurail: perurail.com/en

Rápido Ochoa: rapidoochoa.com

Train to the Clouds (El Tren a las Nubes): trenalasnubes.com.ar

SOUTHEAST ASIA
Accommodations

> **Beach Road Sihounkville:** beachroad-hotel.com
> **Dream Hotels (Bangkok):** dreambkk.com
> **The Green Kiwi (Singapore):** greenkiwi.com.sg
> **Julie Guest House (Chiang Mai):** julieguesthouse.com
> **Khao Sok Paradise Resort:** khaosok-hotels.com
> **Kodchasri Thani (Chiang Mai):** kodchasri.com
> **The Magic Sponge Guesthouse (Kampot):** magicspongekampot
> .com
> **Monkey Republic (Sihanoukville):** monkeyrepublic.info
> **Pooh's (Ko Lipe):** poohlipe.com
> **Sairee Hut Dive Resort (Koh Tao):** saireehutkohtao.com
> **Suk 11 Guesthouse (Bangkok):** suk11.com

General

> **Travelfish:** travelfish.org

Tour Operators

> **Bali Discovery Tours:** balidiscovery.com
> **Elephant Nature Park (Chiang Mai):** elephantnaturepark.org
> **East West Travel (Phnom Penh):** eastwest-travel.com
> **Gibbon Experience:** gibbonexperience.org
> **NS Travel & Tours (Bangkok):** nstravel.com
> **Perama Tour & Travel (Indonesia):** peramatour.com

JAPAN

> **Backpackers Hostel K's House:** kshouse.jp
> **Japan Rail Pass:** japanrailpass.net
> **J-Hoppers Hostels:** j-hoppers.com
> **Khaosan Tokyo Guesthouse:** khaosan-tokyo.com

CHINA

> **YHA China:** yhachina.com

SUGGESTED PACKING LIST

A lot of people ask me what they should pack when they travel. That's a hard question to answer because we all have our own clothing and style preferences. I subscribe to the general rule of packing light. You quickly learn when you travel that you don't need a lot of stuff. You can wear that shirt and those pants for a few days in a row. As the saying goes, "Take double as much money and half as much stuff." To help you with your packing, below is a list of what I carry with me:

CLOTHES

1 dress shirt for when I go out to a respectable place in the evening
1 pair of jeans because I like jeans. They may be heavy and not
    easily dried, but I wear them a lot. A good alternative can be
    khaki pants.
1 pair of shorts
1 bathing suit
6 T-shirts
1 long-sleeve T-shirt
1 pair of flip-flops
1 pair of sneakers
8 pairs of socks

1 pair of black socks
1 pair of dress shoes
1 umbrella
7 pairs of boxer shorts (I'm not a briefs guy!)
Umbrella

TOILETRIES

1 toothbrush
1 tube of toothpaste
1 razor
1 package of dental floss
1 small bottle of shampoo
1 small bar of soap
hair gel
deodorant

SMALL MEDICAL KIT

Band-Aids
Hydrocortisone cream
Antibacterial cream
Eyedrops
Earplugs
Doctor-prescribed antibiotics

This is just what's in my bag, but there's nothing else I've ever found that I needed. I've met a lot of travelers who take even less than me. If you are a girl, there are a few things not included on this list (feminine hygiene products, additional toiletries, etc.) that you may want to take. I've found that this list leaves me wanting for nothing when I am on the road. If something does come up (like if I stay somewhere where it is cold), I simply buy what I need on the road—light jackets and sweaters can be found anywhere.

VACCINATIONS

I've been sick many times on the road. Once in Costa Rica, I had bad sushi and ended up in a hospital for three days. I've gotten mild food poisoning in Thailand in which I've woken up in the middle of the night, clutched my stomach, run to the bathroom, and drunk Pepto-Bismol like it was going out of fashion. I had a flu in Romania that required me to find a pharmacy in the middle of the night in a tiny town where no one spoke English. Germs are everywhere, and as travelers we are often more susceptible to them. We expose our bodies and specifically our immune systems to germs we aren't used to. Staying healthy on the road is important because you don't want to end up like me and spend your time in a beautiful historic village in Europe in bed for the week.

I'm not going to give you specific medical advice here, but I do want to touch on a few things. You need to consult with your own doctor about what you should or should not do while traveling. I get asked a lot about which vaccinations you should or should not get or if you need malaria tablets everywhere. Before you go away, you should consult a medical expert as well as do research on the areas you are going and find out the latest information.

The U. S. Centers for Disease Control has a detailed section on medicine and travel at wwwnc.cdc.gov/travel/page/vaccinations.htm and a complete list of vaccinations at cdc.gov/vaccines/schedules/hcp/adult.html.

You can also consult the World Health Organization's website for additional information (who.int/ith/en), which features a free digital book for travelers.

If you don't have a doctor, many hospitals have travel clinics where you can visit a doctor and get any shots or vaccines that you need. You'll have to pay for this out of pocket if you don't have insurance, and it's usually not covered by U.S. health insurance plans. There are also a number of private travel clinics around the country where you can get the medical advice you need. Some of these clinics are even free. You can get a list of these clinics from the CDC website (wwwnc.cdc.gov/travel/page/travel-clinics.htm).

While you need to consult with a doctor, I would make sure you get a typhoid, tetanus, hepatitis, and, if you are traveling in Asia, a Japanese encephalitis shot. Those four shots are basic and will cover you for the most common of illnesses and problems that might occur on the road. You'll need to get any of these vaccinations months in advance, and some require a second, follow-up shot. You should see your doctor or visit a travel clinic at least six months prior to your trip.

One of the biggest concerns among potential travelers is the threat of malaria, especially in developing countries. When I first went away, I had the malaria drug Malarone with me for when I went to Southeast Asia. I was told there was malaria in some parts of the area and I'd need the medication. I took it for a while, until I realized that none of the Westerners who lived in Asia took it. I stopped taking it. I didn't get malaria. In my nonmedical opinion, while you can never fully get rid of the threat of malaria, if you are going to very touristy, popular, and developed destinations, your risk of catching it is minimal. What you decide to do should be based on your conversations with a medical professional and your feelings about taking medicine every day, but in all my years of travel, outside of Africa or the jungle in the Amazon, I've never known people to take malaria medication.

If you do decide to get shots and vaccines, you will get a small yellow book listing all your vaccinations. This is for your records as well as for health officials in other countries, in case they need to know (for example, at a border crossing or a doctor's office). Make sure you carry this book around with you.

WHAT ABOUT MEDICINE?

People always ask me—what do you do when you get sick while traveling? Well, I do the same thing I do when at home. I rest, take medicine, drink lots of fluids, see a doctor if I have to, and watch movies until I get better. We live in the twenty-first century. Globalization and technology have made medicine and treatment widely available throughout the world. In fact, one of the fastest-growing areas of the tourism industry is medical tourism, in which people travel to destinations around the world in search of affordable health care. Mexico is popular for dental work (many of their doctors are trained in the United States), Israel for in vitro fertilization, Argentina for plastic surgery, and Thailand for just about everything.

There is a common misconception that the United States is the only place you can get good health care. That is not true. Most countries in the world actually have a first-class health care system, even what we would consider "developing" countries. Think of all the Westerners who live in non-Western countries around the world—they aren't going to move and live in a country where they will get poor-quality medical care. After all, it would be too expensive to fly back home every time they got sick.

I spend a lot of time in Bangkok. It's like my second home, and while I'm there, I often get medical treatment. I spent $40 USD for a dermatologist appointment, and getting my eardrum looked at after my scuba diving accident, plus the follow-ups and medicine, cost me less than $200 USD. I've had dental work done for $20 USD. And these aren't at back-alley places. They are at internationally accredited hospitals and clinics, like Bumrungrad Hospital and Samitivej Hospital.

Just because you are overseas, don't assume you can't get any quality treatment. You can, and if you need something done, you can look up international accredited hospitals (jointcommissioninternational.org/JCI-Acc redited-Organizations).

Outside of some very rural areas of the world, you will be able to find all the basic supplies you need at a local pharmacy. I have never encountered a problem where I couldn't find cold medicine, ointments, or allergy medicine. It's important to remember that the whole world doesn't call every product by the same name. Oftentimes, travelers go in asking for Tylenol or Benadryl, find the pharmacy doesn't have it, and leave discouraged. Well, they do have it, but they just call it by a different name. We are used to calling medicines by their brand names and not their medical name. To ensure I get the medicine I need, I simply Google search to find the active medical ingredient in the product I'm looking for, give that name to the pharmacist, and get what I need. Same thing, different name. Here are some examples of popular drugs and their medical names:

Tylenol is often called acetaminophen or nurofen.
Pepto-Bismol is bismuth subsalicylate.
Neosporin is a simple antibacterial ointment.
Sudafed is pseudoephedrine.
Benadryl is diphenhydramine.

The point is that you'll find what you are looking for overseas, so don't feel the need to overload on medicine before you leave.

ABOUT THE AUTHOR

Matt Kepnes didn't take his first trip overseas until he was twenty-three. It was a trip to Costa Rica that got him hooked on traveling. But like most Americans, he only had two weeks of vacation per year and didn't know any of the genius ways to save money and travel longer. Then, in 2005 on a trip to Thailand, everything changed. He met five backpackers who showed him that he didn't have to be tied down to his job and that he didn't need to be rich to travel.

After that trip, he came home, quit his job, finished graduate school, and in July 2006, embarked on a yearlong trip around the world. He's still going today and showing how other people can do the same. He is deathly afraid of heights and, ironically, a really nervous flier. When he isn't traveling, he resides in New York City, where he likes to eat lots of sushi, catch up with friends, and enjoy the fact that movie theaters are open at 11 p.m.